OLD
BLUE'S
ROAD

OLD BLUE'S ROAD

A Historian's Motorcycle Journeys in the American West

JAMES WHITESIDE

UNIVERSITY PRESS OF COLORADO
Boulder

Published by University Press of Colorado
5589 Arapahoe Avenue, Suite 206C
Boulder, Colorado 80303

 The University Press of Colorado is a proud member of
the Association of American University Presses.

The University Press of Colorado is a cooperative publishing enterprise supported, in part,
by Adams State University, Colorado State University, Fort Lewis College, Metropolitan State
University of Denver, Regis University, University of Colorado, University of Northern Colorado,
Utah State University, and Western State Colorado University.

∞ This paper meets the requirements of the ANSI/NISO Z39.48-1992 (Permanence of Paper).

Library of Congress Cataloging-in-Publication Data

Whiteside, James, 1950–
  Old Blue's road : a historian's motorcycle journeys in the American West / by James Whiteside.
    pages cm
    ISBN 978-1-60732-326-6 (paperback) — ISBN 978-1-60732-327-3 (ebook)
  1. West (U.S.)—Description and travel. 2. Whiteside, James, 1950—Travel—West (U.S.)
  3. Historians—Travel—West (U.S.) 4. Motorcycling—West (U.S.) 5. Historians—United States—
  Biography. 6. West (U.S.)—History, Local. 7. West (U.S.)—Social Life and customs. 8. West
  (U.S.)—Social conditions. 9. Social change—West (U.S.) I. Title.
  F595.3.W49 2014
  978—dc23
                              2014007899

24   23   22   21   20   19   18   17   16   15   10   9   8   7   6   5   4   3   2   1

Cover photographs by author

MaryAnn and Blair
and
For Phineas

Contents

Acknowledgments

Any author who says "I wrote this book" is lying. Book writing is always a collaborative effort drawing on the knowledge and talents of authors, editors, friends, colleagues, family, and sometimes complete strangers. This project has benefited immeasurably from the support and input of my small gang of friends, colleagues, editors, family, and, yes, strangers and strange people. MaryAnn Whiteside, Rebecca Hunt, Philip Strain, Pamela W. Laird, Thomas J. Noel, Carl Pletsch, John Monnett, and Derek Everett read all or parts of the manuscript. They saved me from any number of boneheaded errors but bear no responsibility for those that remain. Pam Laird's tough love editorial criticism was especially helpful, if painful. Rebecca Hunt and Tom Noel, living storehouses of knowledge about and insight into the history of the American West, helped me navigate many of the twists and turns of this journey. Carl Pletsch, a really smart fellow who teaches and writes about modern German intellectual history, encouraged me to write in the voice he calls "first-person curious." The result may not be what he had in mind, but he did convince me that it is occasionally okay for the historian to put him/herself into the story. Derek Everett and John Monnett offered important corrections, suggestions, and encouragement.

W. James Smith set me on the path that led to Old Blue's Road, while proving that it is possible to be both a university administrator and a person of the highest integrity.

Darrin Pratt and the University Press of Colorado generously granted permission to use material from *Colorado: A Sports History* (2000). Darrin and Acquisitions Editor Jessica d'Arbonne were unflagging in their support and encouragement of a project that does not fit the standard mold of the scholarly monograph usually published by academic presses. I had the good fortune to work with copyeditor Cheryl Carnahan, a relentless taskmaster who transformed my manuscript into a book.

Nicholas Wharton created the maps of my journeys, and Dana Rae Echohawk allowed me to use her photographs of New Mexico's Shiprock and of Bear Butte in South Dakota. (All of the other photographs are mine.)

MaryAnn and Blair Whiteside generously granted me permission to neglect the duties of husband and father for long stretches of time while I rode around the West and then closeted myself in my study to write about my adventures. They are my most important collaborators.

Finally, my friend and riding partner, Phineas, has been a congenial and patient companion and sounding board during long days in the saddle, over thousands of miles in heat, cold, dust, thunderstorms, bug storms, cheap hotels, and bad restaurants, enduring too many stops at historical sites and markers, as well as the occasional snipe hunt.

I am grateful to you all.

OLD
BLUE'S
ROAD

Old Blue, the West, and Me

"This is nuts."

Sitting on my motorcycle just after sunrise on a cool, misty August morning, my travel bag stuffed with extra jeans, socks, T-shirts, tools, and maps and strapped to the bike's sissy bar, we—the bike and me—seemed set to take off on a trip across much of the northwestern United States and southern British Columbia. The turnaround point was to be Victoria, on Vancouver Island, where I was to meet my wife and daughter, my sister-in-law and her family, and various of their cousins, nieces, and nephews. I expected the trip to cover about 3,000 miles. I had been planning the trip for months, but now a voice from somewhere deep inside kept saying, "This is nuts. You are in your mid-fifties; you are going to get yourself killed out there; you have a wife and a teenage daughter; have you thought about them? Really?" As I sat there, Reasonable Jim seemed to be getting the upper hand over Irresponsible Jim, insisting that I roll the bike back into the garage, put the travel bag in the car, and head for the airport. But after a couple of minutes of to-be-or-not-to-be, I set good sense aside, fired up the bike's engine, and rolled away.

DOI: 10.5876/9781607323273.c000

The trip I began that August morning was the first of a series of motorcycling adventures around the western United States. The American West—its places and people, its past and present—is this book's main character. I have lived my entire life in the West and, as a historian, I have read and written and lectured about the region's history. But that was book learning. Experiencing the West from the saddle of a motorcycle helped me to see and experience how profoundly the past and the present rub up against each other.

When I was a kid, I dreamed of riding across the country on two wheels. In one version of the fantasy, the national press became entranced with my daring bicycle adventure and reported my daily progress. When I finally arrived in Washington, DC, the president met me at the White House gate and invited me to stay as his personal guest for as long as I wanted. My childhood fantasy treks always went eastward. After all, I was not stupid. I lived in Denver, and to the west lay the seemingly impenetrable Rockies. For some reason, it never occurred to me to head north or south.

One summer day, when I was about twelve or thirteen years old, I actually did it. I was pissed off at my parents in that incendiary way adolescent boys get pissed off at their parents. I would show them. I stole some cans of food from the kitchen cabinet, wrapped them in a blanket, somehow fastened the package to my bicycle, and took off. I headed toward Colfax Avenue, which led to US 36. That, I knew from family trips to Indiana, would take me all the way to Indianapolis. There I would get directions to Washington—and to the glory awaiting me.

About a half-mile into the journey, it occurred to me that I had forgotten to steal a can opener. "Oh well," I thought, "I'll just buy one on the road." I realized, though, that I had only about a buck thirty-nine in my pocket. I guessed that I could probably buy a can opener for about thirty-nine cents, leaving me a dollar for the rest of the trip. No problem. I would get jobs along the way. I knew how to run a power mower. I hated mowing grass. That was why I was pissed off at my parents.

Another quarter-mile along, I accepted the futility of my plan. I made a U-turn and headed back home. The grand, heroic journey had lasted about seven minutes and covered less than a mile. As I pedaled home, I glanced at the Rockies rising above the horizon.

The dream faded away after that. The agonies and pleasures of high school and college in the Vietnam War era left little room for such fantasies.

I finished college and, my hard-won political science degree in hand, cooked pizzas and hamburgers for a time. I met a terrific young woman. She was pretty and much smarter than me, but she married me anyway and then went to law school. I worked part-time and went to graduate school to study history. We moved in with her mother—a lovely lady and a fabulous cook— and I got comfortable and fat.

Eventually, after my wife finished law school, we bought a home—a century-old house in the Denver neighborhood where I grew up. The house needed a lot of repairs and upgrades, and I became skilled at making sawdust. I finished my doctoral studies and began teaching at various colleges and universities between Denver and Fort Collins. I was an academic "freeway flyer," one of the growing corps of underemployed, vagabond PhDs working for miserable pay and no benefits. Freeway flyers are popular with higher education administrators because they are cheap and disposable.

As I sharpened my teaching and driving skills, I was drawn back to the bicycle. I had to do something to fight the weight and high blood pressure caused by my mother-in-law's great cooking and a decade of sitting around libraries and archives. Once we (i.e., my wife) began earning some real money, I discovered expensive, custom-built bicycles. I loved teaching and was good at it, but riding became my passion. Even though I never again had a visible waistline, I grew stronger and felt great as my thighs bulged and my blood pressure dropped. At age fifty I could pedal more than 100 miles in a day without great fatigue. For several years I rode in "centuries," 100-mile tours organized by charities or sometimes as business ventures. The Santa Fe Century was my favorite. The route followed the old Turquoise Road out of Santa Fe into the Sandia Mountains, passed through decomposing mining towns in the general direction of Albuquerque, descended from Golden into the Estancia Valley, turned east and north through Stanley and Galisteo—where many western movies have been filmed—and back to Santa Fe. The tour took place in mid-May each year and was a physical and sensory delight, with mountains of red sandstone, piñon pine, sagebrush desert, endless blue skies, and Santa Fe's world-class dining all in one day. For a historian, simply being in Santa Fe was a satisfying experience.

The bicycling and making sawdust kept me more or less sane. I became a very good teacher, popular with my students and even respected among my colleagues. I wrote a couple of books and several articles and won some awards for them. I finally landed a tenure-track job at the University of Colorado at Denver (UCD) and seemed to be on a roll professionally. I liked UCD's students because they were, for the most part, paying their own way; they worked hard, were not involved in fraternities or sororities, and did not care about University of Colorado (CU) football. I took over the history department's graduate program and integrated the School of Education's social studies teacher licensing and graduate programs into it, making it one of the largest and most productive programs at the university.

Universities employ three basic types of personnel: the staff, who keep things running; the faculty, who do the work of scholarship and teaching; and the administrators, who invent ways to keep the staff and faculty from doing their jobs. At UCD, two of the latter species were the Vice-Chancellor for Featherbedding and the Vice-Chancellor for International Boondoggles. Because no good deed ever goes unpunished in the academic world, I found myself locked in bureaucratic battles with those two grand panjandrums. The struggles lasted only slightly longer than the Napoleonic Wars. I cannot honestly claim that I won the War of the Vice-Chancellors; rather, like the Russian general Mikhail Kutusov at Borodino, I simply declared victory and abandoned the battle. Eventually, both vice-chancellors left the university and, like Russia after Napoleon's retreat, I was still there. The problem was that I really no longer wanted to be there. I ached for something honest and unspoiled by pettiness, something new and exciting—something vice-chancellors and other noxious creatures could not spoil.

In early 2005, as the War of the Vice-Chancellors drew to its dismal end, I saw an ad for a Harley-Davidson V-Rod motorcycle. I had seen *Easy Rider* in college and still remembered most of the lyrics of "Born to Be Wild."[1] Beyond that, I had never given much thought to motorcycles. On that dreary January day, though, the Harley ad touched me in a place where, until then, only custom bicycles and expensive table saws had reached. I tried to ignore the call. Then I tried to push it away. I even bought an expensive table saw. Nothing helped.

Making matters worse, in March 2005 my friend and bicycling partner, Phineas, announced that he would not be available to ride the coming weekend. He was taking a motorcycle licensing course. A Texan by birth (and a survivor of that state's high school football insanity), a Tennessean by choice of graduate schools, and a Coloradan by employment, Phineas also happened to work at UCD. We had met about ten years earlier, not on campus but bicycling in Denver's Washington Park. Smart, funny, and diligently searching for his third or fourth ex-wife, Phineas was a congenial companion, both complementing and contrasting my talents and eccentricities.

By the end of March, Phineas was beginning each bicycle ride with tales about his morning motorcycle tours around town on his Harley. Especially satisfying for Phineas were the flirty looks and waves from pretty young women. Finally, in August, two months before my fifty-fifth birthday, I succumbed. I took the motorcycling course, got my license, and visited a Harley dealer. As soon as I sat on a V-Rod, I knew it was not right. To ride it, I would have to sit in a racing posture—too low for my stiff back and rounded midsection. Then I tried a Heritage Softail. It was big and deep red; with full, sculpted fenders. The bike fit me, and I fit it. I had ridden only the small Honda Nighthawk provided by the motorcycling school, and that only in the big high school parking lot where the course was taught. I confessed my inexperience to the salesman who cheerfully, and without condescension, arranged to deliver the bike. Later that afternoon the gleaming Harley, already—for no special reason—christened "Old Blue," was parked in my garage.

"What the hell have I done? That thing weighs 700 pounds and has more horsepower than some cars!" I stared at the bike for two days. I was scared of it and even more afraid that I might hurt it. Finally, I pulled on my shiny new boots, gloves, helmet, and leather jacket, pushed the bike out of the garage, and fired it up. Even with its stock, EPA-approved pipes, its engine had a deep, satisfying rumble. I rolled slowly out of the alley onto the street and rode around my immediate neighborhood, reaching speeds as high as 18 miles per hour, getting the feel of the bike's clutch, shifter, brakes, and steering. My turns varied from too tight to too wide. I was not too concerned, though, because in the final road test at motorcycle school the instructor told me I had "killed" myself only twice (four "fatal" errors were the standard for flunking the test). That first ride went on for 4 miles. When I parked the bike, I noticed that my fingers ached and were sort of frozen in a grip. I was sweating profusely and trembling just a bit. But my mouth spread into a huge grin and, punching the air with my claw-like half-fist, I shouted "yes!"

For the next few days, I confined my outings on Old Blue to my immediate neighborhood. Finally, Phineas coaxed me out for lengthier excursions on busier thoroughfares in the city. The first time I accelerated to 40 miles per hour I thought I had passed the bounds of reason, that 40 was insane. Then I remembered once touching 51 miles per hour on my bicycle on a long, steep downhill segment of a century. By comparison, 40 on a big Harley seemed somewhat less irrational. As I explored more of the circuits Phineas had pioneered, my speeds and confidence grew.

The fall and winter months of 2005–6 were unusually mild, and I was able to spend many afternoons and weekends on Old Blue, sharpening my riding skills and becoming more comfortable with longer and faster rides. On a Saturday in mid-November, after three months of riding in and around Denver, I headed out alone, westbound on US 285 into the mountains, breaching the forbidding barrier of my bicycling youth—and of my bicycling adulthood. I had traveled US 285 between Denver and Fairplay many times by car, but on this trip something happened to me that had never happened on any previous trip. At the top of Kenosha Pass (10,001 feet above sea level), the road goes into a sharp right curve. At the curve's apex, mountain hillside and forest suddenly give way to the seemingly endless vista of South Park. I gasped as I rounded that curve and looked into the long, almost flat mountain valley. Descending the pass and riding into the valley, I realized that I had just had an experience I could not have had any other way. On foot or on a bicycle, the scene would have unfolded gradually and thus lacked the element of surprise I had just experienced. It had never happened, and could never happen, in a car because, seen through car windows, the world might as well be on television. But on Old Blue, that sudden view of South Park was an aesthetic smack in the face. As I rounded that curve, not only the view but also the temperature and even the smell changed. Before I reached the bottom of the pass I wanted that kind of experience again. By the time I reached the town of Fairplay, where I gassed up and turned back toward Denver, I resolved that I would spend as much time as I could traveling by motorcycle, searching for more such smacks in the face.

What follows are accounts of my motorcycling adventures in the American West. I have tried to describe the things I have seen, some of the people I have met, and what those scenes and people prompted me to think about. The first trip began as just a road trip with no purpose in mind other than adventure. As that journey progressed, however, the American West's rich history insisted on riding along. For decades, historians have studied and debated the history of the American West in terms of whether it is a place, a process, or a cultural ideal. Many years ago I penned something called the "Immutable Second Law of History, revised edition," a list of about a dozen silly, yet deeply profound, principles for thinking about history. One of them proclaims, "For any historical question having two or more plausible explanations, the correct interpretation is 'yes.'" By that standard the American West is, yes, a place, many processes, and a bundle of cultural ideals. The West I discovered on these trips is a distinct place, defined by geography and weather; in that place, important processes of human, economic, political, cultural, and environmental development and conflict occurred and continue to occur that both define the region as a place and link its history intimately with the larger history of the United States and the world. Along the way, Americans created deeply and tenaciously held ideas, stereotypes, and values about the West, the people who populated it, and the region's role in building the American nation. The place, the processes, the diverse people, and the ideas of the West were all there for me to see and to think about on Old Blue's Road.

NOTE

1. *Easy Rider*, directed by Dennis Hopper, Raybert Productions, Pando Company, Columbia TriStar Picture Group, Culver City, CA, 1969; Mars Bonfire, "Born to Be Wild," on Steppenwolf, *Steppenwolf* (ABC Dunhill Records, 1968).

1

Family Reunion

Family lore has it that when I was four years old, a visiting aunt asked what I wanted to do when I grew up. Without hesitation, I declared that I would go out West, be a cowboy, and ride horses. A short time later, on my first day of preschool, the teacher asked my name. "I'm the Lone Ranger," I replied. "No," the teacher shot back sweetly, "what is your *real* name?" "I'm the Lone Ranger," I reiterated. The exasperated teacher turned to the girl seated next to me and asked if she knew my real name. Terry, who happened to live across the street from me, assured the teacher that I was, in fact, the Lone Ranger.

Clearly, the cowboy image was a strong motif in my young life, as it was for countless American boys in the mid-1950s. The image of the West and its iconic symbols of manhood were standard fare at the movies, on the radio, and especially on TV and easily gripped young, testosterone-fueled imaginations. American boys, at least those in my neighborhood, aimed to grow up to be sturdy, honest, self-reliant, tough-as-nails, quick-drawing, sharp-shooting, cattle-roping, wagon train–leading, and—all too normal for the era—Indian-killing, genuine American men.

DOI: 10.5876/9781607323273.c001

As an adult and a scholar, I had long since put aside such notions. Or so I thought. I was, after all, the very image of the non-cowboy—a stable, responsible husband, father, and urban professional. Furthermore, I knew that the popular culture image of the American West, and the cowboy's place in it, was not so. Most of the Americans who went west (wherever and whatever that was and is) were not cowboys. Not all of them were men. Not all of them were white. Most of them did not own guns or horses. In fact, most of them lived in towns and cities. Further, the cowboy, whatever his personal quirks and pathologies may have been, was not a monad. Like those other frontier icons—the fur trappers, trail scouts, and Indians—cowboys lived and worked in a complex social and economic setting. They were skilled tradesmen employed in a large, organized, and even technologically advanced industry. Their job was to provide security for, and monitor the feeding and health of, millions of range cattle and, each year, organize them into herds and drive them to railheads in towns such as Dodge City, Kansas, to be loaded onto railroad cars and shipped to their demise at packing plants.

Nevertheless, when my wife suggested (not intending to be taken seriously) that I ride my motorcycle to her forthcoming family reunion in Victoria, British Columbia, visions flashed through my mind of me and Old Blue blasting across the Northern Plains and over the Rockies, the very image of the iconic cowboy. I pulled out an atlas and started looking at routes. That was in February 2006. The reunion was to be in August. I had a lot of time to plan and imagine.

The trip I planned would take me through parts of Colorado, Wyoming, Montana, Idaho, Washington, Utah, and British Columbia. But the route was the only part of the trip I could have planned. The experiences, scenery, people, and history I encountered proved far more interesting than I could have imagined. In all of the planning and for much of the ride, I did not think of the trip as an excursion into the history of the West. Only as the trip progressed did I start to see my journey as a way to become more intimately acquainted with the region where I have lived my entire life.

THERMOPOLIS

My wife and daughter left for the family reunion a couple of days before my departure. With them out of the house, I had little else to do but pack my

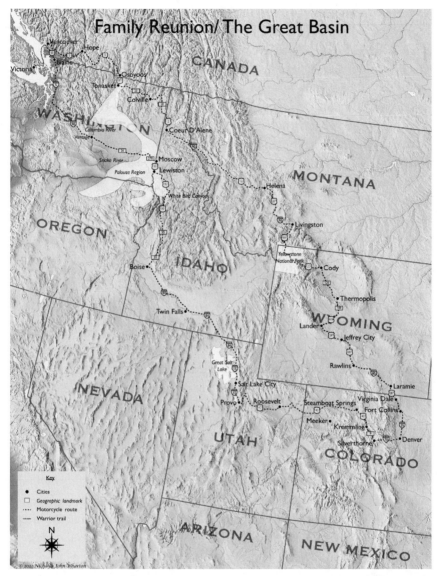

MAP 1.1. Map by Nicholas J. Wharton

bags, polish Old Blue, and think about the trip. But as my departure loomed I began to experience a bit of buyer's remorse, that feeling of being careful about what you wish for because you just might get it. The trip began to seem irresponsible and perhaps a bit dangerous. I would, after all, be in mostly rural areas; even though I would carry a cell phone, a flat tire, break-down, or accident could leave a fellow in a lonely predicament. Plus, I am embarrassed to admit, the final, deadly scene of *Easy Rider* flashed through my mind once or twice. My last thought before I hit the ignition switch was "this is nuts," but away I went.

I rode north on Interstate 25 to Fort Collins, where I picked up US 287. I had not been in the town for almost a decade, but it felt very familiar. My wife and I had gone to college there in the late 1960s and early 1970s, and we lived there again briefly after she finished law school. In the older parts of town the streets are very wide—wide enough, it was said, for a wagon and team of four to make a U-turn. The town, like most of Colorado, is polit-ically and socially conservative, which made for a lot of town-versus-gown hostility in the Vietnam War and counterculture era. Many of us on the "gown" side of the divide referred to Fort Collins as the city of wide streets and narrow minds. Though I sometimes wonder which side of the town-versus-gown divide was really more narrow-minded back then, Fort Collins today is the heart of a congressional district that elected, over and over, a US representative who—in a time of terrorism, war, skyrocketing healthcare costs, four-dollar-per-gallon gasoline, and wholesale exporting of American jobs—believed gay marriage is the greatest threat to the republic. Before this journey ended, however, I encountered political and cultural attitudes that make this part of northern Colorado seem rather liberal.

From Fort Collins, US 287 ascends to the Laramie Plains, following a route well-known to both Indians and fur trappers long before permanent white settlement began. At a spot called Ted's Place, the road begins a long climb past palisades of granite guarding open ranchland and toward the old Overland Stage station called Virginia Dale, 4 miles south of the Wyoming line. Jack Slade, a hard-drinking gunslinger employed by the Overland Stage Company, built Virginia Dale in 1862 and named the station for a lady friend. Mark Twain stopped there on his journey to the Nevada goldfields, sitting down to breakfast "with a half-savage, half-civilized company of armed and bearded mountaineers, ranchmen and station employees." He was surprised to find Slade to be "gentlemanly-appearing, quiet and affable." The stage station and Slade's cabin can still be seen from a nearby county road. Slade's oversight of the station was short-lived, as was he. A Virginia City, Montana, mob, bent on cleaning up the ruffian element in their town, lynched Slade in 1864. It is not known if he had it coming.[1]

At Laramie I turned west on Interstate 80 and headed into an area of southern Wyoming that seemed unattractive at first glance. The highway was clogged with big trucks, and the surrounding land appeared barren and inhospitable. It is always windy on the Laramie Plains, and I was buffeted about pretty roughly. But as I settled in for the ride to Rawlins, I could see mountains far to the north, west, and south. Behind me, in my mirrors, I could see, it appeared, forever. It occurred to me, and not for the last time on this trip, that this was country someone traveling by car, as I had done many years before, would want to get through as fast as possible. But riding on Old Blue, I noticed the subtle textures and hues of the land. What at first seemed a region of uniform pale beige revealed shades of yellow, brown, red, green, and blue in its plants, rocks, and sky.

I left the interstate at Rawlins and rolled northwest toward Lander. The terrain between Rawlins and Lander would qualify under most definitions of "desolate," although, as with the area along I-80, I found it to be a beautiful desolation. The land seemed devoid of cultivated plant life, with gray-blue sage the main flora. Yellow sandstone battlements were the dominant geological feature. As I rode along the stretch of US 287 approaching Jeffrey City, I guessed that I could see at least 20 miles ahead and behind, and for long periods of time I saw no other vehicles. Running out of gas here would make for either a long walk or a long wait. So I decided not to tempt the fuel gauge fairies (notorious little critters well-known to motorcyclists for the tricks they play with the fuel needle) and to stop for gas at Jeffrey City.

Jeffrey City is in the heart of the Sweetwater River stretch of the Oregon Trail. About 20 miles due east is Independence Rock, a massive granite hump rising abruptly from the plains. A party of trappers celebrated American independence there in July 1824, lending the formation its name. Two decades later, Independence Rock became an important landmark for emigrants on the Oregon Trail, who often stopped to engrave names, dates, and messages on the rock before continuing their journey. About 50 miles due west of Jeffrey City is South Pass where the Oregon Trail crosses the continental divide, another important milestone on the westward journey. Travelers in the 1840s and 1850s, who expected to spend days, not hours, crossing the area, were less taken than I with the Sweetwater country's stark beauty. One man in 1858 described it as "a gloomy, God-forsaken country" and "a cheerless picture, made still more so by the numerous human graves" and animal remains spread along the trail.[2]

Jeffrey City today is practically a ghost town, a remnant of the history of boom and bust in the West. The town grew quickly in the 1950s and 1960s, its development supported by uranium mining. By the mid-1980s, though, Jeffrey City went bust. The Cold War petered out, and demand for uranium to fuel power plants plummeted with the discrediting of the nuclear power industry following the Three Mile Island and Chernobyl disasters in 1979 and 1986, respectively. Today, barely fifty people live there.[3]

I guessed that, as with virtually any small town, Jeffrey City's gas station would be on the highway. As I passed the town limits, there on the left was a forlorn-looking café with a single gas pump sitting about 50 feet from the door. I found to my disappointment that the pump had only regular gasoline. The Harley dealer and my owner's manual made it very clear that I should use only premium grade gas in Old Blue's engine, so I pulled back onto the highway intent on stopping at the next station when I got into the center of town. Heading west, I soon saw a few houses and what looked like a school building but no gas station. I kept going, but after a couple of miles it occurred to me that I had seen all I was going to see of Jeffrey City, or least of its gas stations. By now the gas needle was hovering on the red zone, so it was back to the lonely café with its single pump of regular gas.

I parked Old Blue by the pump, walked over to the café, and was not surprised to find it empty except for a couple I took to be the owners—she gaunt and gray and he of ruddy complexion with longish gray hair. Had he been dressed in buckskins, he could easily have been taken for an early-nineteenth-century mountain man. I decided to nickname him Jedediah, though I refrained from addressing him as such. They both were pleasant, though Jedediah was a tad gruff at first when trying to communicate with me before I had removed my helmet and earplugs. Once I was able to hear him, I explained that the twenty-dollar bill I had laid on the counter was for a fill-up. "Oh hell, son, fill your tank first," he commanded. I explained that in Denver, gassing up before paying could get a fellow shot. A faint smile crept across Jedediah's lips, and he said softly, "oh, I don't worry much about somebody driving off without paying." "Cool," I thought to myself, "they still trust people out here." I filled my tank, settled up with Jedediah, and was on my way again. Old Blue did not seem to mind the low-test gas.

Several weeks later I told this story to one of my bicycling friends, Gandhi. An avid fly fisherman, Gandhi's favorite streams are in Yellowstone National Park. He travels there at least a couple of times every summer, so he knows the US 287 route, including Jeffrey City, well. Gandhi explained that Jedediah's trusting attitude toward strangers at his gas pump was undoubtedly genuine. But, he added, that trust was undoubtedly backed up by a high-powered rifle kept under the counter and that he likely could take out a tire or worse at several hundred yards. That, I realized, could very well explain Jedediah's smile when he said he did not worry too much about gasoline thieves.

From Jeffrey City I continued on US 287 to Lander, where I turned onto Wyoming 789, which took me northeastward into the Wind River Reservation. Established in 1868 by the Treaty of Fort Bridger, the 3,500-square-mile reservation is home to the Eastern Shoshone and the Arapaho Indians. Fort Washakie, named for the Shoshone chief who signed the 1868 treaty, is the reservation headquarters. Sacagawea, the Shoshone woman who guided the Lewis and Clark expedition from their winter encampment among the Mandan, in North Dakota, to the Pacific and back, is supposedly buried there.[4]

From Riverton, the highway sweeps around the Boysen Reservoir and then dives into the spectacular Wind River Canyon. The trip through the canyon is a geological wonder, with well-placed signs identifying examples of major phases and processes in the earth's development. Along this stretch, I had my first close wildlife encounter. Coming out of a fairly sharp right curve, which I cut pretty close to the shoulder, I passed a small deer grazing just off the road. The deer seemed unfazed as I roared by, almost within petting distance, but the encounter raised my heart rate considerably and shook me out of my scenery-inspired reverie.

Near the north end of the canyon, at a spot called Wedding of the Waters, the Wind River becomes the Bighorn River. It is the same river; just its name changes. A roadside marker explains that in the early days, mountain men exploring and trapping to the south called it the Wind River. At the same time, those working to the north, in the Bighorn Basin, called it the Bighorn.[5] I suppose it was easier to go on calling one river by two names than to risk the political ruckus choosing one name or the other would cause.

Thermopolis, my destination for the day, sits aside the Bighorn River just north of the mouth of the canyon and boasts two major attractions:

FIGURE 1.1. Wedding of the Waters near Thermopolis, Wyoming, where the Wind River becomes the Bighorn River.

its mineral hot springs and the Wyoming Dinosaur Museum. At the latter, visitors can join paleontologists on digs for dinosaur fossils. The hot springs, located at the northeast edge of town, are a gift of the Wind River Indians. Originally part of the Wind River Reservation, in 1896 the Shoshone and Arapaho agreed to sell the area to the United States, on condition that the public always have free access to the springs. The springs remain free to the public, but you have to pay a fee for towels.

After a shower and a nap, I was as hungry as a Yellowstone bear in March. As I headed out in search of a large, medium-rare portion of a Wyoming cow, I stopped at the desk and asked Paul, the afternoon clerk, for recommendations. Without hesitation, Paul suggested the L'il Wrangler just up the road. Attired in shorts, sneakers, and a T-shirt, I asked Paul teasingly if I was dressed appropriately for the L'il Wrangler. "Oh heck," he replied, "everything is casual in Thermopolis, even at the Safari Club where they serve steak and lobster." Thus reassured, I asked Paul if the restaurant was within reasonable walking distance. Paul now had his revenge for my tease about eveningwear in Thermopolis. "Sure, it is only about three blocks up the street."

So I set out for the L'il Wrangler on foot, happy to get a little exercise after sitting on Old Blue for 438 miles. But after about twenty minutes, with no L'il Wrangler in sight, I decided that when Paul had said it was three blocks, he meant three *Wyoming* blocks. With that realization I turned back to the motel, changed into boots and jeans, and decided to ride to my steak.

Yellowstone

It was warm in Thermopolis the next morning but, factoring in wind chill, I decided to put on my rain jacket over my long-sleeved T-shirt and leather vest. I had thought about bringing my leather bomber jacket, which had served me well on rides the previous fall, winter, and spring months, but decided it was too bulky for my limited luggage and too warm to wear all the time. The long-sleeved shirts, vest, and rain gear surely would be plenty. After all, it was August. Obviously, some important realities associated with the phrases "northern Rocky Mountains" and "southern British Columbia" had not registered fully in my born-and-raised-in-the-American-West brain. As I blew north on the highway out of Thermopolis it got *cold*. My fingers, sheathed in leather gloves, were okay, as were my toes in their heavy boots, but the rest of me was soon freezing. The first town I reached, Meeteetse, offered little relief other than welcome slower speeds. Actually, it was worth slowing down to get a look at the town. This is ranch country, and Meeteetse celebrates its cowboy heritage right down to its wood plank sidewalks.

Cody was my best hope for finding appropriate attire, as I knew there was a Harley store there. I would buy a leather jacket there—at any price. I found the store without difficulty and parked right in front. By the time I got off of Old Blue and removed gloves, helmet, and rain jacket I was sweating profusely. It was already hot in Cody and not yet 10:00 a.m. My frozen despair melted in the warm sunshine, and I began to wonder if I really needed to add a few hundred dollars to Cody's economy. But it was time for a break anyway, and the Harley store was as good a place as any to spend a few minutes off the bike. Fortunately, as I looked through the selection of jackets, reason overcame hubris. I considered that I was going to be heading generally north that day and the following two days and reckoned, as a rule of thumb, that August mornings do not get warmer as one progresses north. I found a jacket that fit comfortably, though it was not the classic Marlon-Brando-in-the-Wild-Ones style I had in mind. However, on the back it had a stylized eagle inlaid in red leather. Very dashing indeed, and it was marked down 40 percent.

Back on the road, well insulated in black and red leather, I headed for Yellowstone National Park. Heading west out of Cody, I made the first of two fortuitous detours on the trip. This one was especially fortunate. My original plan had been to stay on Wyoming 120 until it ran into Wyoming 296. That would take me over the Chief Joseph Highway, reputed to be one of the most beautiful roads in the country, to Yellowstone's northeast gate. Then I would have a short trip across the north edge of the park to Gardiner, Montana, and on to Helena. However, just outside Cody I followed the first sign pointing to Yellowstone. That put me on US 20, headed toward the park's east gate. I finally realized my error when I pulled up to the park gate. I was chagrined, to say the least, that my inattention had taken me well off my intended route. But the prospect of seeing more of Yellowstone than I had planned had consolations. I pulled directly up to the ticket booth, a good omen, I thought. Up ahead I could see a few cars off to the side of the road, their occupants probably looking at park maps before going on. I paid my entry fee, and the friendly park ranger smiled and waved me through. I gunned the engine and rolled into the park. About 150 yards in I reached those cars on the side of the road. The occupants were not checking maps. They were just sitting there. Construction delay. I shut off Old Blue's engine, dismounted, quickly removed my helmet, gloves, and jacket—it was hot—and began walking up and down the road, in part to try to find out how long I would be there and in part because there was nothing else to do. I learned that about 15 miles of the road was torn up and that traffic was being led through in caravans, one in each direction about every 30 minutes. A westbound group had just departed, which explained why I was near the head of the line. I was going to be there for a while.

I surveyed the other vehicles and their occupants. Up ahead was an enormous motor home. "Crap," I thought, "even when we get moving again I'm going to be stuck behind that beast, looking at its rear end instead of the scenery." Behind me I noticed a vintage-looking station wagon carrying a young couple and their two kids. Even though it was only midday, all four looked tired, hot, and ready to explode. The kids wanted to get out and play. "No," the dad snapped at them, "we'll be going any minute." I knew that none of us would be on our way any minute, but the dad was obviously in no mood to hear that. I nodded to them but thought better of approaching, as a dark pall of frustration and gloom seemed to hover around the station wagon. Soon, other folks got out of their cars, trucks, vans, and motor homes (no other motorcyclists had joined the line) and began milling about. The family in the motor home up ahead brought their dog down the line for some exercise and relief. We exchanged greetings as they passed, and they soon turned back to their house on wheels. A couple of minutes later the motor home father, teenage son, and dog were back outside, carrying bottles of cold water and pop. They stopped at the vintage station wagon and handed drinks to the young couple and their kids. With that simple, kind gesture, the evil spirits around the station wagon family fled. The kids asked if they could get out and pet the motor home dog. Their dad, more relaxed, said "okay."

In a few more minutes the motor home father, son, and dog turned back toward their vehicle. I flashed a broad smile at them, acknowledging their kindness to the station wagon family. They stopped to talk for a couple of minutes. They were from Massachusetts, and this was their first trip to the American West. Oh-my-God everything is so big and wide-open and beautiful and they had never seen so much wildlife and they sure hoped they would see some buffalo in the park. I could not bear to correct them on the name of the aforementioned animal. Besides, if "buffalo" was good enough for Lewis and Clark, it ought to be acceptable for anyone who has come this way since. However, "bison" is all right, too.

As we chatted about the West and what we expected to see in the park, the teenage boy was eyeing Old Blue. I asked if he would like to sit on the bike. He looked to his dad, who nodded assent, and then swung his leg over the saddle. Since our temporary parking lot was on a slope, I was not disappointed that the boy did not want to push up off of the kickstand, and after a couple of minutes he dismounted. He wanted to know what it was like to ride all day on a motorcycle. Fun, challenging, tiring, I told him. Then he wanted to know how fast Old Blue could go. I told him I did not know since I never, ever rode faster than the speed limit and explained that speeding was not smart or safe motorcycling or driving. The motor home dad flashed a smile at me.

A few minutes later the construction scout car delivered a line of outbound vehicles to the park gate, made a U-turn, and took its place at the head of our line. Everyone scurried back to their vehicles. I suited up, jumped into the saddle, fired Old Blue's engine, and finally rolled into the park. As I rode along, I found myself somewhat distracted from the scenery, thinking instead about what had just happened at the construction stop and how typically western it had been. Not uniquely western, but typical.

An enduring theme in the history of the American West is the rapid creation and disappearance of communities. People joined together or were forced together by economic opportunity, happenstance, or simple survival; sooner or later, when opportunity or necessity passed, they went their separate ways. Jeffrey City is an example of the process. It is part of the stories of American Indians, of explorers and trappers, of hundreds of mining towns and logging camps. On the plains, Cheyenne and Arapaho bands camped and hunted together and then parted. Lewis and Clark spent the winter of 1804–5 living with the Mandans. In the Colorado Rockies, mining towns appeared overnight and grew to contain hundreds, even thousands of souls in a matter of weeks; when the ore ran out, they emptied just as quickly. Boom and bust, community and ghost town. All of this was a vivid reminder of how different from reality is the mythology and iconography of the American West and the American westerner. The iconic westerners—the Indian, the fur trapper, the cowboy—relied on communities, however transient, for survival and livelihood.

Then I thought about that motor home. Anyone on a motorcycle or in a car who has ever been stuck behind a motor home on a narrow mountain road is part of a community whose motto is "when is that clown going to pull over and let the fifty vehicles behind him pass?" I have been as guilty as anyone of ridiculing these behemoths and their occupants. I have called the motor homes "Waste-a-Begos." Certainly, the sight of some of them loaded with bicycles and ATVs (all-terrain-eating vehicles), towing the family car, with television antennae affixed to roofs invites some ridicule. After all, hauling all the comforts of home, not to mention the consumption of hydrocarbons involved, is not exactly getting away from it all and getting back to nature.

But who decided that motor home travel is, or should be, about getting away from it all and getting back to nature? Is modern motor home travel historically all that different from earlier modes of travel in the West? Cowboys and prospectors traveled with the essentials of life packed in their bags or on their burros. When an Indian band moved from one camp to another, they packed up their lodges and all of their belongings, loaded them onto horses, travois, and their backs, and took it all with them. To be sure, the motives and goals of travel have changed. The cowboys, prospectors, and Indians moved from place to place out of economic necessity, while modern travelers pursue recreation or a change of scenery in their lives. That is a different reason for traveling with all the basics of life, not necessarily a less legitimate one.

I do not camp out. To me, a hotel without room service is "roughing it." I ride with saddle bags stuffed with clothing, toiletries, cameras, notebooks, tools, oil, and so on because I believe the best way to ensure that I will not need something is to have it with me. I have gone on vacations to Hawaii and Europe with less stuff than I take on overnight motorcycle trips. But I have talked with motorcyclists who speak proudly and loudly about how independent they are. They travel with only a toothbrush and a change of underwear. These conversations usually take place in motel parking lots or in restaurants across the street from a motel. Some motorcyclists (very few in my observation) add a sleeping bag to their minimalist travel kit and sleep on the ground, sometimes under lightweight tents. You get the picture. It is a difference of quantity more than quality. The motor home traveler and the motorcyclist alike tote the things they think they need for their trips.

Is one more independent than the other? Both depend on filling stations for gasoline. Motorcyclists also need motels and restaurants or food stores. Memoirs by camping motorcyclists almost invariably record daily vignettes of pitching camp and then going to the nearest town for food.[6] Motor home travelers fill their vehicles' cupboards with food and other supplies and stop at stores only to restock. To get full advantage of the vehicle, however, they must park at a campsite with running water and electricity, though a portable generator will suffice for the latter. So, one form of transportation does not appear to provide greater autonomy than the other. But the motor home traveler does seem to have more in common with the overland migrant in a Conestoga wagon than the motorcyclist has with the cowboy whose horse could graze on the range (assuming the range had adequate edible vegetation).

Shortly after we passed the construction zone, the motor home turned off the road into a campground, and the burning question of "Waste-a-Bego" versus motorcycle travel receded quickly from my thoughts. I began to pay more attention to my surroundings, especially to whatever lay ahead, which I now could actually see.

Yellowstone's scenery—mountains, forests, rivers, lakes, geothermal features, and wildlife—was all I had imagined it would be. In the area along the
northeast shore of Yellowstone Lake and north toward Canyon Village, the
pungent, sulfurous odor from steam vents reminded me that I was in the
middle of the largest active volcanic caldera in North America. The Grand
Canyon of the Yellowstone River with its dramatic falls is one of the most
beautiful places on the planet. Yellowstone's animal life was also on display.
Especially entertaining were the two-legged critters roaming the park.

Since about 1990, the number of visitors to the park each year has hovered
around 3 million.[7] Judging by the number of times traffic slowed to a crawl
or stopped, I guessed that no fewer than half that number were there that day.
In Yellowstone it is considered appropriate behavior, upon sighting a bison,
bear, beaver, or squirrel, to stop one's vehicle right on the road, jump out,
and do one or more of the following: gawk at the animal; attempt to get it to
approach by offering ice cream, popped corn, or candy; or pursue it into the
woods. Meanwhile, other tourists have the option of waiting in their cars or
joining in the gawking, enticing, or pursuit of the animal in question.

At one point, as I pulled to a stop in a long line of cars, I saw a small herd
of bipeds running toward me in the opposite lane. They were pointing into
the woods and jabbering excitedly. The only word I could make out distinctly
was "bear." I am no woodsman, but I have no doubt that somewhere a rule
is written down stating, "Do not chase the bear." I suspect there is also a
corollary to that rule saying something like, "You only think you are chasing
the bear; the bear is running ahead of you until you get too tired to run away
from her when she decides to turn around and chase you."

A bit further up the road I saw my first Yellowstone bison. Several members of a herd of these wonderful beasts had scattered along the roadway
while the group's main body grazed in the meadow a couple of hundred
yards away. As I crept along, a bison occasionally ambled across the road, and,
of course, all traffic came to a stop. I did not mind at all. Through this stretch
of road, the park management has posted roadside signs stating that bison
are large, wild, and sometimes ill-tempered animals and that tourists should
not approach them. Naturally, therefore, some tourists take that warning as
an invitation to approach the bison. A few yards beyond one of these signs
I saw an enormous bull lying on the road, warming himself on the sun-
drenched pavement. Walking toward him, his hand extended in some sort

FIGURE 1.2. Yellowstone's bison can often be observed grazing by the park's road-ways and seemingly inviting human attempts to interact with them.

of inter-species peace gesture, was a man evidently intent on establishing relations with the bull. The great bison eyed him calmly but with a look in his eyes that clearly said, "Do I look like I want you to pet me?" Listening to the television news that evening, I heard no report of a man being trampled by a bison in Yellowstone, so, evidently, either the tourist and the bull safely greeted one another, the bull got up and left, or the tourist thought better of his attempt to touch a wild bison.

KILL, EAT, WEAR

This urge to interact with wild animals is very entertaining to human observ-ers, though the animals doubtless find it less amusing than the humans do. Watching it also touched off a weird line of thought. First, it occurred to me that the urge to interact with wild animals represents a distinctly modern attitude toward them. Two hundred years ago and for most of the succeeding century, humans regarded wildlife in the American West as things to kill, eat, and wear. Indians may well have had a religious regard for animals, especially bison, but I have no sense of them wanting to play with the beasts. White people added another motivation to the kill-eat-wear attitude: profit. They trapped and shot the beaver and bison populations to sell their hides. In the case of the bison, whites also killed for sport until the enormous herds that once roamed the Great Plains were reduced to the edge of extinction.[8]

What to twenty-first-century Americans is a history of wanton destruction was symptomatic of a powerful underlying attitude toward the West and its resources. The animals, gold and silver, coal, trees, water all were there to be used. Their use, in turn, was necessary for the advancement of American Civilization. In 1845 an American newsman, John L. O'Sullivan, declared it to be the "manifest destiny" of the United States and its citizens to "overspread the continent allotted by Providence for the development of our yearly multiplying millions."[9] So, unrestricted exploitation of the West's natural resources was not only necessary but was also God's will. As white Americans overspread the continent, they claimed and used whatever they wanted and needed. Few laws or institutions got in the way. Indeed, most laws and institutions abetted the process. Anything that did get in the way was altered or removed. Anyone who got in the way, that is, Indians, was killed or pushed aside. The government set aside places such as the Wind River area, Pine Ridge, and the Four Corners region, which seemed to have few resources white people might want and where few white people would want to live, for the surviving Indian population.

Two events in the 1890s seemed to signal the completion of the over-spreading of the continent by American Civilization or at least the end of the era of unbridled conquest. The first was the massacre in 1890 of harmless Lakota Indians at Wounded Knee, on the Pine Ridge Reservation in South Dakota. The Lakotas provoked this fate by participating in the Ghost Dance movement, which promised its followers that the time was coming when the white man would disappear and the buffalo would return. After Wounded Knee, Indians never again stood in the way of the advance of American Civilization (see chapter 6).

The second event occurred far from both Yellowstone and Wounded Knee. In 1893 a young scholar named Frederick Jackson Turner gave a talk to a gathering of historians in Chicago. In this talk, which he later published as an essay, "The Significance of the Frontier in American History," Turner pondered how the process of continental conquest had shaped American history, society, and culture. In a nutshell, Turner argued that the existence of the frontier, with its vast spaces and enormous resources, and the processes of its conquest had shaped America and Americans into an energetic, prosperous, individualistic, and democratic people and society. Turner was worried, however, as were other leaders of academia, business, and government. In 1890 the census bureau had concluded that "there can hardly be said to be a frontier line" any longer in the continental United States.[10] The place, resources, and process that, as Turner and many others understood it, had made America the uniquely democratic, prosperous, and powerful country it had become were disappearing. What would become of America when, sooner rather than later, it was all conquered and used up? Indeed, the catastrophic economic depression of the mid-1890s and eruptions of apparent class warfare symbolized by uprisings among industrial workers and farmers (the Populist movement, Coxey's Army, the Pullman strike of 1894) seemed to prove that America was falling apart.

Late-nineteenth and early-twentieth-century Americans came up with various solutions to the growing economic, social, and cultural crises; two of these were imperialism and conservation. Having conquered their North American empire by the late decades of the nineteenth century, Americans in the 1890s turned their attention to creating—by commerce, diplomacy, and war—an overseas commercial and colonial empire. A global empire, backed by American naval power and using a few strategic colonies, would be an extension of the frontier, a source of resources and markets, and an outlet for the country's still powerful expansive energy.

As Americans built their global empire, a small number of intellectuals and political figures also addressed the problem of arresting the environmental damage caused by a century of uninhibited resource exploitation. In 1891 the US Congress enacted the Forest Reserves Act, giving the president authority to withdraw tracts of public land from settlement and exploitation. Between them, Presidents Benjamin Harrison and Grover Cleveland set aside 37 million acres of forest reserves. However, the federal government exercised little management authority over those reserves until Congress passed the Forest Management Act of 1897, giving the US Department of Agriculture's Division of Forestry (later the Forest Service) authority to control access to and utilization of the reserves. Five years later another landmark law, the Newlands Reclamation Act, took the federal government into the business of dam building to promote irrigation and hydroelectric power generation in the West.[11]

These and subsequent conservation laws were both revolutionary and fairly conservative. Up to this time the national government had viewed its role to be that of expediting the disposal, settlement, and development of the West's vast public lands. Henceforth, the federal government began to exercise a powerful role in managing access to and uses of public lands. To business interests accustomed to unfettered use of western lands and resources, this was a radical intrusion into the rights of industry. Now, instead of free access, business would have to gain the permission of bureaucrats, such as Forest Service chief Gifford Pinchot, to extract mineral wealth, fell trees, and run cattle on lands they had come to regard as their own. They did not like it, and they still don't.

Pinchot, Theodore Roosevelt, and other conservationists were not enemies of industrial capitalism. Unlike wilderness preservationists such as John Muir, they did not want to lock up western lands and bar economic development. Indeed, Pinchot liked to say, "wilderness is waste."[12] The conservation ethic emphasized controlled use of land and resources and, where possible, the renewal and increase of those resources (e.g., timber and rangelands, irrigation, and development of hydroelectric power). So, conservation was revolutionary in that it established a powerful role for the federal government in managing the country's natural resources and, in doing so, managing the industrial capitalist economy that depended on those resources. But the conservation concept was also fundamentally conservative in that it aimed to preserve the resources on which America's industrial economy depended to ensure their orderly and sustained use. The goal was not to deny access to resources but to control it. Almost no one has been happy with the arrangement. Cattlemen, mining companies, and lumber interests chafe under what they view as excessive regulation, while environmentalists criticize government agencies for allowing too much development.

America's national parks were not a major product of the conservation movement. Historian Richard White explains that the great parks came into being "not because progressives or western interest groups thought the government could make the lands more productive, but because they believed those lands to be useless in terms of the extractive economy of the West." Instead, White notes, their value lay in their monumental scenery, the preservation of which Americans viewed "as compensation for the cultural riches they lacked." Parks in the West, he continues, "contain only the highest, most rugged and extreme land forms." Otherwise, "any place where a cow could take some comfort was too valuable for a park."[13] In short, America's great national parks system was born of a sentimental attachment to pretty but economically undesirable places that made Americans feel good about themselves and their country. In that spirit, in 1872 Congress established Yellowstone as the nation's and the world's first national park.

It is difficult to conceive that at the time of Yellowstone's creation, anyone would have believed Americans needed to be protected against a national park. Most Americans then, as now, would have said the opposite. Strangely, however, a small but very powerful interest group in Montana claims just that. In 1902, Yellowstone was home to fewer than 50 of America's iconic mammal, the bison. From that low point, with the help of imported stock, Yellowstone's herd grew to almost 1,500 at mid-century. Trapping and hunting reduced that number to fewer than 400 in the mid-1960s, when the National Park Service abandoned those herd-management techniques in favor of letting nature determine the herd's size. By the mid-1990s bison in Yellowstone numbered about 3,500, and that number today is more than 4,000.[14]

Because the bison choose not to confine themselves year-round to the park's boundaries and its sanctuary, they sometimes wander onto neighboring ranch and Forest Service lands in Montana. That, according to some Montana ranchers and the state government, makes them a threat to the well-being of if not the nation, at least Montana's livestock industry. Yellowstone bison tend to migrate northward out of the park during the harsh winter and early spring months and return during the summer. During the summer months, some ranchers graze their stock on the same lands the bison occupied months before. The ranchers and the state believe that, even though bison and cattle almost never intermingle, the bison constitute a danger to the cows by putting them at risk to contract brucellosis.[15] An article in *Montana Outdoors,* a tourism magazine published by the State of Montana, noted in 2004 that this disease, which causes pregnant cows to abort, "petrifies cattle ranchers."[16] It is far from clear, however, whether science supports the ranchers' fears. The disease is transmitted by contact with fluids and tissues produced by calving or abortion of a bison fetus. The Humane Society of the United States notes, "There has never been a documented

case of a wild, free-roaming bison infecting domestic cattle with brucellosis."[17] Nevertheless, the fear of the immediate loss of an infected cow and
the greater fear of Montana losing its status as a brucellosis-free state, which
would require ranchers to test every animal to be shipped out of state, is
enough to lead to demands for strict controls on the Yellowstone bison herd
and to doom about 250 of them to death each year.[18] Yellowstone's bison,
then, are the objects of two very different attitudes. One is represented by
that tourist aiming to pet a lounging bull. The other, more deeply rooted
in historical attitudes about the West's resources, continues to view those
resources as things to be used. If they are not usable or if they threaten other
uses, they should be eliminated.

As I thought about the Yellowstone bison representing conflicting images
and attitudes about the West, I cruised north through the last several miles of
the park past Roaring Mountain (it roars because of steam escaping from its
many vents) and the Mammoth Hot Springs, with their enormous, garishly
colored mineral formations. I exited the park through the stone arch of the
Roosevelt Gate, at Gardiner, Montana, and zigzagged northwest to Helena.

Helena, Coeur d'Alene, Colville

Montana's capital is a pretty place, rising on slopes from the broad Helena
Valley to the east. After settling in at a motel, I joined a parking lot community of fellow motorcyclists. We stood around, admiring one another's bikes
and telling lies about our machines and what we had done on them. The next
morning, as I breakfasted on the motel's coffee and muffins, a trucker from
Idaho warned me off of my intended route, Montana Highway 200. Long
stretches of the road were torn up, he said, and there were major construction delays. That meant that after a short run on US Highway 12, I would be
on Interstate 90 all the way to Coeur d'Alene, Idaho. Pat, a fellow I met in
the parking lot, suggested that he and I ride together that day. Pat was from
Sacramento, California, and was on his way, via Montana, to visit family in
Coeur d'Alene. The ride to Coeur d'Alene was only about 225 miles, and we
were there by noon. In between, the highway passes through the forested
mountains and valleys of the Lolo National Forest and the city of Missoula,
Montana. Just a few miles southwest of Missoula is Lolo Pass, over which
Lewis and Clark traveled in September 1805.

We stopped in Missoula for gas, and as I filled Old Blue's tank I noticed a middle-aged man eyeing the bike and me. The man approached, nodded toward the bike, and asked "from Colorado, eh? Where're ya headed?" I explained that I was going to Victoria, British Columbia. The man's eyes widened and, looking again at Old Blue, he exclaimed "on that?" For an instant I thought he was insulting my motorcycle, but then I realized his expression came from envy. My journey now seemed even more of an adventure.

By the time Pat and I rode into Coeur d'Alene, my nose told me that I had entered the Pacific Northwest. The spicy, pungent aroma of freshly milled lumber filled the air. As pleasant as that aroma was, it reminded me that this is an industrial region where timber and mining interests wield great power and where major social conflicts have played out.

Coeur d'Alene was the scene of major battles in the industrial labor wars at the end of the nineteenth and beginning of the twentieth centuries. On the evening of December 30, 1905, Idaho's former governor, Frank Steunenberg, died in a bomb attack at his home in Caldwell, about 30 miles west of the state capital, Boise. Steunenberg had been elected governor in 1896 with strong backing from Idaho's working people, especially the miners. Four years before, a violent strike in the Coeur d'Alene district had ended badly for the miners, in part because of anti-union intervention by the state government. With Steunenberg in the governor's chair, miners and their militant new union, the Western Federation of Miners (WFM), hoped for better treatment. Mine owners in the Coeur d'Alene area, however, were dead set against dealing with the union and in 1899 began firing workers who had joined the WFM. In response, the union led the miners out on strike. The strike soon became violent, and when strikers occupied and destroyed properties of the Bunker Hill and Sullivan Mine, Governor Steunenberg asked for US Army troops to intervene. The miners and union leaders never forgave Steunenberg, and that December night in 1905 one of them, Harry Orchard, exacted his revenge.[19]

Once in custody, Orchard confessed to murdering the former governor and claimed that William D. "Big Bill" Haywood, the leader of the WFM, had commissioned the assassination. That year, Haywood had played a major role in creating another new union, the Industrial Workers of the World (IWW), a radical organization that sought not only better working conditions but also a socialist transformation of American society. Pinning the Steunenberg murder on Haywood would have been a serious blow to the IWW and to political radicalism. However, Haywood was in Denver and seemed beyond the reach of Idaho law enforcement.[20]

Undeterred by legal niceties such as extradition laws, not to mention the flimsiness of the case against the IWW leader, Pinkerton detectives (a private detective agency notorious for its union-busting activities) traveled to Denver, kidnapped Haywood, and spirited him back to Idaho for trial. Clarence Darrow, the greatest trial lawyer of the era and a union sympathizer, led Haywood's defense team and ultimately secured his acquittal.[21]

The Coeur d'Alene strike and the Haywood trial were a warning. The growing ranks of industrial workers had real, legitimate grievances. The future would hold only more violence and chaos unless American business and government addressed their demands. Over the next three decades, reform sentiment and more rounds of strikes and social warfare, such as the Colorado coalfield war of 1913–14, contributed to American workers winning the right to organize unions and to bargain collectively with their employers with at least some protection from government.

From Coeur d'Alene, I headed north into the Pend Oreille (pondo-ray) country, which extends across northwestern Montana, northern Idaho, and northeastern Washington. Pend Oreille is the name early French inhabitants hung on the Kalispell Indians in the region; it referred to their shell ear pendants. It is an area of verdant mountains and valleys, lakes and streams; the varied greens of the vegetation all seemed to vibrate in the August sun. From Newport, Washington, I rode for 50 miles along the west bank of the Pend Oreille River until the road turned southwest toward Colville, where I stopped for the night.

Colville is located about 10 miles east of the site of Kettle Falls on the Columbia River and 30 miles south of the Canadian border. Once a spectacular, turbulent 50-foot cataract, Kettle Falls disappeared in 1941 under the rising waters of Roosevelt Lake. Kettle Falls was an important fishing and trading site for the area's Salish Indians. Explorer David Thompson, whose travels opened much of the Pacific Northwest to white penetration, visited Kettle Falls in the summer of 1811 and witnessed the annual gathering of area Indians to harvest the salmon, celebrate the great fish in ritual, and trade among themselves and with other Indian visitors from as far away as the northern Great Plains of Montana. In little more than a decade, the arrival of white people and their commercial empire built on beaver pelts began the long process of conquest and displacement that led to the Salish Indians' confinement to the nearby Colville Indian Reservation. The reservation, established in 1872, is home to the Colville Confederate Tribes, the governing body of the twelve bands who live there.[22] The last group to move onto the reservation was the remnant of Chief Joseph's Wallowa Nez Perce band, who arrived in 1885.

The long, heroic, and ultimately disastrous odyssey of Joseph and the Wallowa began in 1877 when they agreed reluctantly to removal from their homelands in Oregon's Wallowa Valley to the Lapwai Reservation in Idaho. During the journey to the reservation, young dissidents attacked and killed a number of white settlers. Joseph and the band's war chiefs decided they must flee the violent retribution they knew was coming. When US troops caught up with them in White Bird Canyon in western Idaho, the Wallowa stood, fought, and soundly defeated the American forces.

After their victory at White Bird Canyon, Joseph and his band of about 800 set out on a 1,700-mile flight for freedom in Canada. They almost made it. After crossing the Bitterroot Mountains they turned north through the Yellowstone area and came to within 40 miles of the Canadian border. In late September 1877 a US Army force commanded by General Nelson A. Miles found them, and the sides fought a five-day running battle. Finally, Joseph accepted defeat and in his famous surrender statement vowed that he would "fight no more forever." Of the 800 who set out from White Bird Canyon in June, just over 400 band members survived to surrender with Joseph. A small group evaded surrender and managed to escape into Canada.[23]

General Miles promised to return Joseph and his people to the Nez Perce Reservation in Idaho. Instead, the army exiled them to Fort Leavenworth in Kansas. It was not until 1885 that the United States allowed the Wallowa to return to the Pacific Northwest and then to the Colville Reservation, not that of the Nez Perce. When they arrived at the Colville Reservation they numbered only about 270. Chief Joseph is buried there in a private cemetery.[24]

LUNCH IN HOPE

Riding west out of Colville the next morning, I crossed the Columbia River at the town of Kettle Falls. The river there today is placid, and the great granite stones that once churned its waters into a roaring waterfall lie deep beneath the surface of Roosevelt Lake. Washington State's official folk song is Woody Guthrie's paean to the river and the Grand Coulee Dam, "Roll on Columbia, Roll On."[25] The song's refrain is ironic since the Columbia above the dam oozes more than it rolls.

West of the river, Washington 20 winds its way into beautiful, misty, thickly forested country. The unmistakable smell of freshly sawn lumber filled the air. Unfortunately, another unmistakable odor, smoke, also filled the air as I rode west. I had planned to follow Washington 20 all the way across the state, but by the time I reached the town of Tonasket my sinuses were swollen shut from the smoke, which was now quite visible in the air. I decided to stop for coffee at a gas station in Tonasket and try to find out if the fire was burning on my intended route. I pulled into a parking spot next to a Dodge beater of uncertain vintage. Inside it was a fellow I immediately took to be Tonasket's resident character. My first guess was that he lived in his car, but I quickly realized that could not be the case because he had so much stuff crammed into it that he could only have slept, very awkwardly, sitting up and with his head hanging out the driver's door window.

I locked both the ignition and the fork lock on Old Blue before going into the gas station store for coffee. When I walked back outside, the Tonasket Character was out of his car and walking around Blue. I leaned back on the rustic pine log railing along the store's porch and eyed the Character with no small amount of suspicion. After he circled the bike a second time he looked up at me, smiled a huge semi-toothless grin, and exclaimed, "Colorado. Helluva long ride. Good for you!" I nodded and smiled back. "I used to live there myself, after 'Nam, in Nederland." "So, do you live around here?" I inquired. "Yep, I have a little trailer a few miles south of town. Came into town to get away from the smoke." I concluded from this comment that the smoke was worse south and west of Tonasket, where I was headed. I told the Character that I planned to ride Highway 20 all the way over to I-5. "You're gonna be in smoke all the way," he said. "There's a couple of big burns along 20 and it might be closed in places, too." I recalled from my map studies that US 97 ran north from Tonasket into British Columbia and that I could follow British Columbia's Highway 3 to Vancouver. I asked the Character if he knew anything about the Canadian route. "Yep, great road, beautiful scenery, nice people up there." That decided the question. I would head north and then west across British Columbia. It proved to be one of the best choices I made on the trip.

The ride from Tonasket to the Canadian border was only about 20 miles and took me into the Okanagan Valley. *Okanagan* is a Salish term meaning "transport to the head or top end," referring to the northward course of the Okanagan River to the Columbia River.[26] As I approached the border, the road rose up the side of the valley and I gained a spectacular view of Lake Osoyoos and the border towns of Oroville and Osoyoos straddling the international boundary. Pulling up to the border checkpoint, I observed that the Canadian facility looked like highway tollbooths, while the adjoining American post, a forbidding-looking two-story techno-blockhouse, could easily serve as a county jail.

My welcome to Canada came in the person of a friendly young border agent who examined my passport, then asked where I lived and my occupation. When I answered that I was a history professor from Colorado, the agent brightened and explained that she had recently graduated from the University of British Columbia with a minor in history. I asked what history courses she had taken and which were her favorites, and she replied that she really liked US history. This surprised me a bit, and I asked her why. American history, she explained, was so "busy" and full of contradictions and surprises. She was fascinated by America's diversity and how Americans have grappled with it. I reminded her that Canada, as a multilingual society with large Indian, European, Asian, African, and, lately, Latin American populations, was pretty diverse itself. Then I asked if her interest in US history was unusual among Canadian students. Not especially, she said, explaining that the power of America's economy, culture, and technology was too influential to ignore. It occurred to me that while this young Canadian woman seemed well educated in US history, a student at my university could not take a course on Canadian history. In a quarter-century of college teaching, I had only one student who had done any work on Canadian history, and she was a Canadian expatriate who returned to Toronto to pursue a PhD in North American studies. We chatted for ten or fifteen minutes until another vehicle pulled up behind me. I rolled through the parking lot and into Osoyoos. I had not been taking tourist-type photos on the trip but could not resist taking a picture of Old Blue in front of the large, colorful "Welcome to British Columbia" sign.

FIGURE 1.3. Old Blue at the US-Canadian border.

From Osoyoos, Highway 3 meanders west to the town of Hope through terrain ranging from the arid region of the southern Okanagan to the densely forested mountains of the Fraser River region. In the three hours or so it took to cover that distance I experienced three seasons—summer, spring, and winter. In short stretches I rode through misty rain, snow, then warm sunshine. Pressing westward, cloud-shrouded valleys and canyons occasionally gave glimpses of thickly forested slopes and sheer granite walls.

One of the prettiest areas is the Similkameen Valley, west of the village of Keremeos. The village's Greek-sounding name is actually an Indian term meaning, according to the village website, "meeting of the winds."[27] I stopped in Keremeos to exchange currency. As I entered the town bank, the teller's eyes grew big. Evidently, few large, leather-clad motorcyclists stop in, and I sensed she was concerned that I might be there to rob the bank. I smiled as broadly as I could, said my most effusive "hi," and announced the purpose of my visit. Thus reassured, the teller changed my George Washingtons into a handful of Elizabeth IIs of equal value, less the inevitable exchange fee.

Much of the region between Osoyoos and the town of Hope, 150 miles to the west, is wine and fruit-growing country. Riding through the mountain valleys, I noticed lots of roadside fruit stands. They looked pretty much like fruit stands everywhere, with one exception—no one was tending them. They are honor system fruit stands. The growers stock them in the morning and set out a price list alongside a box for customers to deposit their money. After passing several of these stands, my historian's sense of the darkness and depravity of human nature finally made me stop at one to investigate. I saw that the stand's display boxes were nearly empty, suggesting that most of its stock had been purchased or taken. What I really wanted to see, however, was the cash box. It was full of money. Indeed, customers had been careful to place a small rock on top of the currency to keep it from blowing away. Looking around in all directions I saw no house or other buildings anywhere in the immediate vicinity. Anyone who wanted to could have taken the money and the remaining fruit without being seen. Even though I live in a very safe neighborhood in Denver, it would never occur to me to leave anything of real value sitting out, day or night, unattended or unshackled. But here in southern British Columbia, they leave the fruit of their labors unguarded by the roadside.

By the time I reached Hope, I was ready for gas and a cup of hot coffee. I found both plus another encounter with Canadian hospitality. Hope is a small town with a population of about 6,500 in a setting that can be described as at least idyllic. The town occupies a thumb of land bounded on three sides by the Fraser River. To the west the river flows into a broad plain leading to Vancouver. Mountains rise behind the town in the other three directions. I pulled into a combination gas station, fast-food restaurant, and coffee shop. After I filled my tank, I surveyed the parking lot for an open space. There was only one, but as I took aim on it, a rider on a small Suzuki motorcycle pulled into it. I took a chance and rolled in next to him and, without killing my engine—so as not to be *too* presumptuous—asked the gentleman if he minded sharing his parking space. "Be my guest," he replied cheerfully.

By the time I had dismounted and removed my helmet, the man had noticed my Colorado license plate. "You rode all the way from Colorado?" he inquired. "Yes," I replied, and he asked which way I was headed. I told him I was going west, toward Vancouver, to catch the ferry to Victoria. "Ah, Victoria, and the island is lovely," he said, "you'll like it there." He told me he was riding an overnighter from Vancouver, where he lived, to Osoyoos. I explained that I had just come from there and that he should expect light rain, a little snow, and periods of sun. He thanked me for the information, and we turned to go into the fast-food/coffee shop.

As we stood in line, the man introduced himself as Robert and asked if I would join him for lunch. I was startled but gladly accepted in hopes of gathering intelligence about the ride ahead, as well as welcoming some company and a little more time off the bike. Once settled at our table, Robert began quizzing me about my trip. I answered his questions as economically as I could until he asked what I thought of "BC" (British Columbia). I replied that what I had seen of it was gorgeous and that I intended to return someday and see a lot more of it. Then I told him that, despite the honor system fruit stands, the colorful currency, and the funny speed limit signs that required me to use my limited math abilities to convert the posted speed from kilometers to miles per hour, in some ways I really did not feel as though I was in another country. Robert agreed and observed that American popular culture had long ago crept across the border without even showing a passport.

Sitting there in a fast-food restaurant—an icon of American culture—I felt I had to find some way to assure Robert that I did not view Canada and Canadians as mere appendages of the United States. "There are differences," I opined; "for one thing, you folks speak better English. And you don't go about gratuitously bombing people who have done you no direct harm." Robert did not agree entirely, noting that as American pop culture penetrated Canada, so, too, had the American dialect. He found the language of hip-hop especially baffling. On that point I assured him that Americans over the age of forty also find it unintelligible. As to my point about bombing people, Robert said that, much to his regret, he agreed. He could not understand why the United States had invaded and occupied Iraq. "You see," I replied, "we aren't so different. Most Americans can't figure it out either." "Still," he continued, "you Americans have done a lot of good in the world. Just look at all the money you raised for tsunami relief in South Asia." I agreed but observed that the people of New Orleans had been waiting a year for that sort of American generosity, especially since their government had failed them so completely in its response to Hurricane Katrina's devastation. "Be that as it may," Robert replied, "I think you are being too hard on your country." That touched a nerve of American pride in me.

It was my turn to say something nice about Canadians. Canada, like the United States, is a racially and ethnically diverse society. Unlike Americans, I observed, "you folks don't seem to spend a lot of energy squabbling about it. Some of our jingo birds want to ban the use of any language other than English in government offices and documents. Here, people don't seem to get worked up over using English and French." Robert agreed, though he said I was probably overestimating the depth and breadth of ethnic and linguistic harmony there, pointing out that Canadians in the eastern provinces squabble a lot over language. Then he said something that really surprised me: "I sometimes think we Canadians are too polite."

"I don't know how courtesy can be a bad thing," I replied, all the while thinking to myself "no shit, man. You let this big American and his Hog take over your parking spot and then invite him to lunch!" "I think we Americans don't think about the graces and the niceties enough," I said. "We're always in a big hurry. Problem is, though, most of the time what we're rushing around about isn't terribly important. But whatever it is we're doing, we have to do it or get there right now so we can get on to the next damned thing. We're always going somewhere but never seem to get there. I guess it's the going that we care most about. I suppose we're afraid that if we actually get to where we're going, wherever that is, then there will be nowhere else to go."

"Interesting," Robert said with a chuckle. "You realize that you managed to take my comment about Canadian manners and turn it into a soliloquy on American competitiveness." "Yep," I replied, "pretty American of me."

With that, we made our goodbyes, and I left Hope behind. I never did ask Robert about the road and traffic into Vancouver or for directions to the ferry.

VICTORIA

Highway 3 merges with the Trans-Canada Highway just outside of Hope, and the route into Vancouver becomes a four-lane highway. I did not ride all the way into Vancouver, however, but left the highway a few miles east of the city and followed secondary roads through the southern suburbs to the ferry terminal at Tsawwassen. The terminal itself is on a small island accessed from the mainland by a long causeway. I arrived in plenty of time for the next ferry and enjoyed sitting in the sun with the sea breeze blowing in from Puget Sound. In a single day I had ridden in two countries, through logging territory, a fruit- and wine-producing region, alpine vistas, deep canyons, rain, snow, and sunshine and now found myself on a small speck of land off the shore of the North American continent. What a great day.

After about a thirty-minute wait, the ferry arrived and disgorged a seemingly endless stream of cars, trucks, buses, RVs, and a few motorcycles. The loading attendant waved me and the other four motorcyclists in line over to a holding area, where we waited for yet another seemingly endless stream of vehicles to roll up the ramps into the ferry. Finally, he waved us forward. We would be the last on and the last off.

Once we were parked and our motorcycles secured with bracing blocks shoved under the frames, we motorcyclists took a quick measure of one another. There was a German couple touring Canada on matched BMWs and a young Alberta couple on their honeymoon. The latter had ridden two-up (i.e., on one bike) from their home in Red Deer (midway between Calgary and Edmonton in Alberta) and planned to spend several days exploring Vancouver Island.

The ferry was the biggest vessel I had ever been on. It had five decks, three for vehicles and two with passenger lounges, restaurants, bars, and observation decks. I guessed that departure and docking would be the bumpiest part of the voyage and stayed by Old Blue until we were well away from the dock and up to speed, just in case some jolt might knock it over. I did the same as we approached the Swartz Bay dock on Vancouver Island. I need not have worried, however, because the trip was smooth as glass and I barely felt the ship's motion.

Once I felt sure Old Blue would remain upright during the crossing, I headed up to the passenger decks. The trip to Vancouver Island took about an hour and a half. I found a seat in one of the lounges but almost immediately felt restless. It seemed a shame to sit indoors and watch through windows as the wooded channel islands slipped by, so I wandered out onto the deck. As I leaned against a deck railing and looked about, I noticed two young Japanese women taking turns photographing one another with the water and islands behind them. I gestured to them in universal "would you like me to take a picture of you together" sign language. They looked at me with wide-eyed suspicion and conferred for a moment. I guessed that the conversation was along the lines of "should we take the risk? Will this big, leather-clad biker steal our camera?" At length, they decided to chance it, smiled shyly, and handed me the camera. I took two or three photos, smiled, bowed slightly, and handed the camera back. With relief on their faces, they smiled, bowed, and scurried away. After that, I strolled around the passenger decks, had a snack in one of the restaurants, and decided to go back below to check on Old Blue and my luggage. I spent the rest of the trip on the ferry's fantail, which I found to be the most pleasant spot on the ship, protected from the wind but with the afternoon sun streaming in and a wonderful view of the channel and the receding coastline and city of Vancouver.

Old Blue and I were the last off the ferry, which was fine as I did not want to be at the head of a line of traffic headed into a strange city. Instead, I had the luxury of staying under the speed limit as I navigated my way to Victoria. Following directions I had to the house my wife's family had rented for the week, I turned west into the mountains above the city. Perched on a hilltop, the house had a spectacular view of the city and harbor below, which compensated in part for the rodent population scurrying about the place.

In the morning I rode Old Blue to the Harley dealership in Victoria to get a quick inspection. Riding into town the previous day, I thought I heard a strange sound coming from the engine and wanted to get it checked. This led to my only encounter with a semi-surly Canadian. I found the mechanic, explained the problem, and asked him to take the bike for a test ride. The mechanic refused, saying it had been raining that morning and he was not going out on wet streets. I pointed out that the sun was shining and that I had just ridden into town on perfectly dry streets. The mechanic realized that the only way to get rid of me was to ride the bike. He donned his helmet and rode away. Ten minutes later he reappeared and, using my lip-reading skills, I could discern him muttering something to the effect of "crazy damned Americans." However, by the time he crossed the parking lot to where I waited, he had put on a small smile and assured me that there was nothing wrong with the bike. I had probably heard some engine pinging because of being at sea level. Thus reassured, I bought a souvenir T-shirt from the dealership to commemorate the visit to Victoria and to prove that I had been there.

My wife is a patient and tolerant soul, but by the time I arrived in Victoria she had had more than enough extended-family togetherness. So after my visit to the Harley shop, we decided to spend the rest of the day touring the southern part of the island, *sans* cousins and kids. We spent the afternoon wandering around the Butchart Gardens, a fifty-five-acre botanical wonder that fills the walls and floor of a worked-out quarry. The original Butchart family home has been converted into an elegant restaurant where we stopped for afternoon tea, a sort of light lunch including tiny appetizers, tiny desserts, and no actual lunch. Instead, little silver trays offer up small, crust-less sandwiches invariably made with some form of cucumber. All of the ladies and the one other man in the dining room seemed to enjoy it, but as I munched on the cucumber sandwiches I thought about various cuts of American beef.

The next morning my wife and daughter headed to the airport in Seattle, and I took the ferry back to the mainland and headed south to the border.

NOTES

1. Charlene Tresner, "Fort Collins—Its History in a Nutshell," at http://history.poudrelibraries.org/archive/cityhistory.php, accessed July 27, 2014; "People of the Poudre, Native Americans in Larimer County, Colorado, 12,000 y.a.–1878, Native American Occupancy (Ceramic, 150 AD–1850," at http://history.poudrelibraries.org/archive/ethnic/native4.php, accessed July 27, 2014; "Fort Collins History and Architecture: Euro-American Explorations, ca. 1540–1858," at http://history.poudrelibrar ies.org/archive/contexts/euroexplorations.php, accessed July 27, 2014; Mark Twain, *Roughing It* (Harford, CT: American Publishing, 1891), 87.

2. T. A. Larson, *Wyoming: A History* (New York: W. W. Norton, 1984), 46–47.

3. Mike Jamison, "Jeffrey City—Wyoming Ghost Towns [*sic*]," at http://www.bootsnall.com/articles/08-08/september-2001-jeffrey-city-wyoming-ghost-towns.html, accessed July 27, 2014. A Colorado company, Energy Fuels, has acquired rights to the uranium mines near Jeffrey City and plans to start work there by 2016. Adam Voge, "Energy Fuels to Open Uranium Mine Near Jeffrey City by 2016," at http://

trib.com/business/energy/energy-fuels-to-open-uranium-mine-near-jeffrey-city-by /article_3318c77d-3513-5011-9bOc-d9c7c94c6bdo.html, accessed July 27, 2014.

4. Thomas H. Johnson, *Also Called Sacajawea: Chief Woman's Stolen Identity* (Long Grove, IL: Waveland, 2007), argues convincingly that Sacagawea is not buried on the Wind River Reservation.

5. A photo of the roadside marker can be viewed at http://thermopoliswyoming .blogspot.com/2008/08/wedding-of-waters.html, accessed July 27, 2014.

6. Peter Egan, *Leanings: The Best of Peter Egan from Cycle World* (St. Paul: Motorbooks, 2002); Peter Egan, *Leanings 2: Great Stories by America's Favorites Motorcycle Writer* (St. Paul: Motorbooks, 2005); Garri Garripoli, *Tao of the Ride: Motorcycles and the Mechanics of the Soul* (Deerfield Beach, FL: Health Communication, 1999); Gary Paulsen, *Zero to Sixty: The Motorcycle Journey of a Lifetime* (San Diego: Harvest Books, 1997, 1999); Neil Peart, *Ghost Rider: Travels on the Healing Road* (Toronto: ECW Press, 2002).

7. National Park Service, Yellowstone National Park, "Visitation Statistics," at http://www.nps.gov/yell/planyourvisit/visitationstats.htm, accessed July 27, 2014.

8. The bison population may already have been declining before the slaughter of the 1870s and 1880s. Historian Richard White argues that "drought, habitat destruction, competition from exotic species, and introduced diseases" were pressuring bison herds by the mid-nineteenth century. Especially ironic, in view of the twenty-first-century controversies over Yellowstone bison, was the damage caused by the introduction of brucellosis by range cattle. Richard White, "Animals and Enterprise," in Clyde A. Milner II, Carol A. O'Connor, and Martha A. Sandweiss, eds., *The Oxford History of the American West* (New York: Oxford University Press, 1994), 249.

9. John L. O'Sullivan, *United States Magazine and Democratic Review* (New York City), July 1845, quoted in Clyde A. Milner II, "National Initiatives," in Milner, O'Connor, and Sandweiss, eds., *Oxford History of the American West*, 166.

10. Frederick Jackson Turner, "The Significance of the Frontier in American History: Address Delivered at the Forty-First Annual Meeting of the State Historical Society of Wisconsin, December 14, 1893" (Madison: State Historical Society of Wisconsin, 1894), quoted in Clyde A. Milner II, "America Only More So," in Milner, O'Connor, and Sandweiss, eds., *Oxford History of the American West*, 3.

11. William Cronon, "Landscapes of Abundance and Scarcity," in Milner, O'Connor, and Sandweiss, eds., *Oxford History of the American West*, 607–8; Richard White, *It's Your Misfortune and None of My Own: A New History of the American West* (Norman: University of Oklahoma Press, 1991), 407–9.

12. White, *It's Your Misfortune and None of My Own*, 409.

13. Ibid., 410.

14. National Park Service, Yellowstone National Park, "Yellowstone Bison," at http://www.nps.gov/yell/naturesciencebisoninfo.htm, accessed July 27, 2014.

15. The Humane Society of the United States, "Yellowstone Bison Hazing and Slaughter," at http://www.humanesociety.org/issues/lethal_wildlife_management /facts/yellowstone_bison_hazing_slaughter.html, accessed July 27, 2014.

16. Tom Dickson, "Buffaloed," *Montana Outdoors* (November-December 2004), at http://fwp.mt.gov./mtoutdoors/HTML/articles/2004/Buffaloed.htm, accessed July 27, 2014.

17. Humane Society of the United States, "Yellowstone Bison Hazing and Slaughter."

18. Dickson, "Buffaloed."

19. J. Anthony Lucas, *Big Trouble: A Murder in a Small Western Town Sets off a Struggle for the Soul of America* (New York: Simon and Schuster, 1997); Richard Maxwell Brown, "Violence," in Milner, O'Connor, and Sandweiss, eds., *Oxford History of the American West*, 411–14.

20. J. Anthony Lucas, *Big Trouble: A Murder in a Small Western Town Sets off a Struggle for the Soul of America* (New York: Simon and Schuster, 1997); Richard Maxwell Brown, "Violence," in Milner, O'Connor, and Sandweiss, eds., *Oxford History of the American West*, 411–14.

21. Lucas, *Big Trouble*; Richard Maxwell Brown, "Violence," in Milner, O'Connor, and Sandweiss, eds., *Oxford History of the American West*, 411–14. Haywood and the IWW went on to lead strikes all across the United States, and Haywood became a fan of the Bolshevik revolution in Russia. He moved to the Soviet Union after serving time in a federal prison for his vocal opposition to the US entry into World War I. He died there in 1928 and is buried in the Kremlin.

22. United States Department of Agriculture, Forest Service, "Colville National Forest: History," at http://www.fs.usda.gov/main/colville/learning/history-culture, accessed July 27, 2014; HistoryLink.org, "Kettle Falls," HistoryLink.org Essay 7577, at www.historylink.org/index.cfm?DisplayPage=output.cfm&file_id=7577, accessed July 27, 2014; City of Colville, Washington, "History," at http://www.colville.wa.us /history.htm, accessed September 5, 2007; Confederated Tribes of the Colville Reservation, "A Walk through Time: This Is Our True Story," http://www.colville tribes.com/past.htm, accessed September 5, 2007.

23. White, *It's Your Misfortune and None of My Own*, 107–8, quotation on 108; Jerome A. Greene, *Nez Perce Summer, 1877: The U.S. Army and the Nee-Me-Poo Crisis* (Helena: Montana Historical Society Press, 2000); u-s-history.com, "Wars and Battles: The Nez Perce War, 1877," at http://www.u-s-history.com/pages/h1549.html.

24. White, *It's Your Misfortune and None of My Own*, 107–8; Greene, *Nez Perce Summer, 1877*; u-s-history.com, "Wars and Battles."

25. Netstate, "The Washington State Folk Song," http://netstate.com/states/symb/song/wa_roll_on_columbia.htm, accessed September 23, 2007.

26. "Okanagan Nation Alliance—History and Culture," at http://syilx.org/who-we-are/the-syilx-people/, accessed July 28, 2014.

27. "The Official Village of Keremeos Website: Area History," at http://www.keremeos.ca/content/our-community, accessed July 28, 2014.

2

The Great Basin

I arrived at the Blane, Washington, border crossing at about 10:00 a.m. Leaving the United States three days before had been an easy and pleasant experience. Never having had airliners crashed into any of their major buildings, Canadians evidently do not worry as much about terrorism as Americans do. Plus, the Blane border crossing sits astride Interstate 5, the main north-south highway in western Washington and into Canada, a setting quite different from the rural border station at Osoyoos. As I approached the customs station, my heart sank. I pulled to a stop at least a quarter of a mile from the station, one in a crowd of several hundred vehicles waiting to go through. It was a pleasant day, but the morning mist I had ridden through from the Tsawwassen ferry terminal soon burned off and the sun began to heat up the asphalt. After idling for several minutes, Old Blue's air-cooled engine began to protest and I had to shut it down. Fortunately, the approach to the customs station was on a slight slope, so I was able to coast most of the way as the line inched forward. Finally, at 11:30 a.m., I pulled up to the station. The surly customs agent took my passport, went into his cubicle for several

DOI: 10.5876/9781607323273.c002

minutes and entered my identity into a computer, returned, still frowning, and handed back my passport.

"How long have you been in Canada? Where did you stay? Where is your home? What is your occupation? Who is your employer?" I sensed that he already knew the answers and was relieved when I seemed to pass the examination and he could wave me back into my own, my native land.

I had intended to stay on the interstate only as far as Everett, Washington, and from there follow US 2 to Wenatchee, in the middle of the state, then zigzag south and east on state roads to my destination for the day—Moscow, Idaho. But because of the long delay at the border, I decided to stay on I-5 and I-90 most of the way to make up some time and ensure that the long, 450-mile ride ended in daylight. I left I-90 where it crosses the Columbia River, turned onto Washington Highway 26, and rode into a region of modern historical importance and unexpected scenic beauty.

THE PALOUSE

Washington 26 passes a few miles north of the US Department of Energy's Hanford Site. The federal government took over this 660-square-mile patch of farm and ranchland in 1943 to build the Hanford Engineer Works, part of the Manhattan Project. Hanford suited the project's requirements for a location remote from significant population centers but with abundant water and electric power sources. The Columbia River, which flows across the Hanford Site's northern section and along its eastern boundary, provided both water and electric power from the Grand Coulee and Bonneville Dams. Around 1,500 families had to pack up and leave within a month to make way for the project's plutonium research and manufacturing facilities. Here, scientists and engineers produced the plutonium used in the Trinity test device detonated at Alamogordo, New Mexico, in July 1945 and in the weapon exploded over Nagasaki, Japan, on August 9, 1945. Production of the small quantity of plutonium used in those devices consumed all of the power from two of Grand Coulee's three hydroelectric generators. Hanford's plutonium operations continued after the war and expanded as the Cold War set in. Plutonium produced there was shipped to other facilities to be manufactured into weapons components. One of those facilities, the Rocky Flats plant (built in 1952), was about 25 miles from my home in Denver. In the early 1990s both Hanford and Rocky Flats stopped weapons production (in the latter case, after years of environmental and anti–nuclear weapons protests). Today, operations at the former weapons sites are devoted to cleaning up a half-century of nuclear waste and preserving the sites as Cold War–era museums.[1]

The terrain around the Hanford Site reminded me of the plains of eastern Colorado. Not far to the east, however, the landscape changes dramatically as the plains of the Columbia Plateau give way to a land of rolling hills known as the Palouse region. Over many millennia, southwesterly winds deposited dusty soil, called loess, to depths of as much as 200 feet atop the underlying basalt. The result was the area's dome-like dunes. Because of the wind action, the domes' northeast slopes are much steeper than the southwest sides. Unlike desert dunes, the mounds of this semiarid region are fertile, and with irrigation the Palouse became a rich wheat-producing area. The rivers and streams flowing through the Palouse, including the Snake and the Palouse, have cut through the soil down to bedrock, creating spectacular scenes such as the 200-foot-high Palouse Falls.[2] In the late afternoon the Palouse hills cast dramatic shadows, making the area a favorite of landscape photographers. As I rolled through the area in mid-August, many farmers were harvesting their wheat crops, and I saw several photographers along the road capturing images of the contrast of brown soils of harvested fields next to fields still heavy with golden stands of wheat. Historian and geographer D. W. Meinig writes vividly of the area that it can "with little imagination appear to be in motion—a heavy sea rolling into high crests, breaking into concave slopes."[3]

After I returned home, I asked my brother-in-law, a native of the region, what the term *Palouse* means. He said he did not know for certain but had always believed it means "bumps." Though his answer is descriptively accurate, brothers-in-law are, of course, always wrong. The term is actually from the Sehaptin Indian word *palus*, the name of the main Palouse Indian village, which was located at the junction of the Snake and Palouse Rivers. It means "something sticking down in the water" and refers to a large rock in the river. The Palouse Indians believed the rock was the fossilized heart of Beaver, a major figure in their religion. In the Palouse tradition, Beaver fought a great battle with four brothers. The brothers speared Beaver five times, and each time he thrashed about and gouged out a canyon. The fifth time the brothers speared Beaver, he tore out an especially large chasm that became the Palouse Falls.[4]

The Palouse region lends its name to another important element in the history of the Indians of the Columbia region: the Appaloosa horse. Represented in artwork from prehistoric French cave paintings and in third-century BCE Chinese drawings, this ancient breed, with its distinctive spotted coat, spread throughout Europe and Asia long before its introduction to the New World. Spanish conquerors brought the animal to North America in the sixteenth century, and it had spread to the Columbia River region by the early eighteenth century. The Nez Perce and other indigenous people of the region adopted the horse and made it a mainstay of their societies, altering their cultures, economies, and warfare. By the time Americans began to penetrate the region, the native people of the Columbia Basin and western Rocky Mountains—including the Nez Perce, their cultural relatives the Palouse, and the Shoshones—had substantial herds.[5]

Lewis and Clark knew the Indians had horses. Indeed, they staked the success of their journey out of the mountains to the Columbia on finding the Shoshones and trading with them for horses. Meriwether Lewis wrote in his journal on July 27, 1805, "We begin to feel considerable anxiety with rispect [sic] to the Snake [Shoshone] Indians. If we do not find them or some other nation who have horses I fear the successful issue of our voyage will be very doubtful or at all events more difficult in it's [sic] accomplishment." Lewis echoed that concern in his entry for August 8, 1805, noting that "without horses we shall be obliged to leave a great part of our stores, of which, it appears that we have a stock already sufficiently small for the length of the voyage before us." With Sacagawea's guidance the expedition found her people, the Shoshones, and acquired the needed horses.[6]

By the mid-nineteenth century, white settlers in the Columbia Basin referred to the local Indians' horses as "Palousey horses" and as "Appalouseys," and those terms evolved into *Appaloosa*. White settlers were quick to appreciate the horse's importance to the Nez Perce and Palouse peoples, especially as the animal contributed to their independence and power. In 1858, in an early eruption of the long series of conflicts that finally led to the Nez Perce War in 1877, a US Army force, bent on punishing area bands for raids against white settlers in the Spokane area, slaughtered 800 Indian horses. Two decades later, in the aftermath of the Nez Perce War, the government dispersed the remaining Indian horse herds.[7]

MOSCOW

Moscow, Idaho, is a pleasant city of about 22,000. As the home of the University of Idaho, it has the look and feel of a socially and culturally progressive college town with an impressive variety of galleries, theaters, programs, and festivals, including the annual Lionel Hampton Jazz Festival. In the 2004 presidential election Democrat John Kerry won 53 percent of Moscow's vote, compared with about 45 percent for George W. Bush. In 2008 Barack Obama carried the city with 51 percent of the vote, suggesting a progressive slant to the town's political culture. More than half the town's population has a bachelor's degree or higher, compared with only 22 percent statewide. Like all of Idaho, Moscow's population is overwhelmingly white. Minorities—mainly African Americans, Asians, and Hispanics—constitute only about 10 percent of the population.[8]

Beneath its progressive, college town appearance, Moscow has a less appealing cultural underside. In late 2003 two University of Idaho professors exposed that underside by publishing in the local press a review of a then seven-year-old book titled *Southern Slavery as It Was*. A local evangelical minister, Douglas Wilson, and coauthor Steve Wilkins self-published the book in 1996. Wilkins was a founder of the League of the South, an evangelical secessionist group devoted to leading the states of the Confederacy out of the American union and establishing a society governed by their notions of biblical law. *Southern Slavery as It Was* made two assertions, one merely biblical and the other quite astonishing. One was that the Bible sanctions slavery, including American slavery. The second was that slavery was not the vicious, racist institution represented in most historians' treatments but instead was a generally benign and beneficent system. Both of those preposterous assertions are easily dismissed by reference to the Bible and to the legitimate scholarly literature on the history of American slavery.[9]

Northern Idaho did not need another group or episode adding to the region's reputation as a haven for some of the most extreme fringe elements in American culture. In addition, *Southern Slavery as It Was* does not reflect the humane and democratic traditions and character of evangelical Protestantism in the United States. In fact, the overwhelming majority of Moscow community members repudiated the book. The local newspaper, while defending the authors' right to their views, denounced their "misguided message." Unfortunately, however, even as it stated forthrightly that "slavery is wrong, was wrong and always will be wrong," the paper praised the community for discussing the issue in a responsible manner, given that the subject was "as controversial as slavery."[10] Controversial?

The true purpose of *Southern Slavery as It Was* was not to defend the institution of slavery. Instead, the tract and its authors represent cultural and ideological themes deeply rooted in American history that can be summed up as a recurring ill-ease with the ever-changing character and quality of our culture. Early in the twentieth century it inspired many states to pass laws forbidding the teaching of evolution in public schools. The contemporary religious, cultural, and political movement known as the "religious right" is the most recent resurgence of this revolt against modernity. Today, many religious folks demand that "creationism" be taught alongside evolution in science classes. Others, especially men, who find their social status and power threatened, look to the Bible for authority to undo a century of legal and political progress in the status and power of women. Others see a mortal danger from homosexuals who in recent decades, vocally and with growing success, have pressed their demands to be acknowledged as human beings and citizens. Throughout the nineteenth century and the early decades of the twentieth century, anti-modernism included nasty features of religious and ethnic bigotry. Groups and individuals whom historians refer to as "nativists" saw in eastern and southern European immigrants, large numbers of them Roman Catholics and Jews, a dire threat to American culture and democracy. It is no small irony that today the descendants of those onetime pariahs are found among the ranks of those demanding the removal and exclusion from the United States of illegal immigrants, especially those from Mexico. One of the shrillest such voices has been that of Colorado politician Tom Tancredo, a descendant of Italian immigrants who, while serving in Congress and during a quixotic third-party run for governor, espoused an anti-immigrant platform.

Tancredo represents Colorado's own unfortunate history of nativism and anti-modernism, showing that northern Idaho is far from unique in that regard. In the 1920s the Ku Klux Klan, the quintessential nativist group, enrolled thousands of members and had the political muscle to control the state government and the city governments of Denver and other Colorado towns. In Denver, Klan members were especially fond of parading in their robes and hoods through the city's Italian and Jewish neighborhoods. Their preferred brand of cigar was the CYANA (Catholics, You Are Not Americans). In the statehouse, Klan-controlled governor Clarence Morley proposed and nearly won passage of legislation to ban the sacramental use of alcohol, a measure aimed blatantly at Catholics. The Colorado Klan's downfall began when its leader, Dr. John Galen Locke, attempted to defend Colorado womanhood and traditional family values by kidnapping and threatening to castrate the nineteen-year-old father (himself a Klansman) of a child born out of wedlock.[11]

Klan activity occurred throughout the West in the 1920s, with especially virulent eruptions in Texas, Oklahoma, Kansas, Montana, and Oregon. In Texas, the Klan's national leader, Imperial Wizard Hiram Wesley Evans, led 80,000 Klansmen. Oregon voters, seduced temporarily by the Klan's anti-Catholic message, enacted a measure requiring all children in the state to attend public schools, a clear assault on Catholic schools. The Klan sickness seemed to fade by the late 1920s, but nearly a century later *Southern Slavery as It Was*, the anti-immigrant movement, homophobia, and the campaign to turn back the clock on American women demonstrate the persistence of the underlying pathologies of anti-modernism and nativism.

BETTY BOOP AND THE GOLD WING MAN

As I loaded my luggage onto Old Blue and prepared to leave Moscow, I had a brief encounter with a local woman whom I doubt anyone has ever bossed around. A white pickup truck pulled into the motel's covered portico where I had parked for the night. I did not look up but heard the driver exit the truck and walk toward me. Then I felt a slap on my back and a strong female voice declared, "Nice bike, son." I God blessed her for insinuating that I was young enough to be her son, though I guessed that she was seventyish and hence only a decade or so my senior. I also told her that I liked the Betty Boop mud flaps on her truck. It turned out that she owned the motel and was delivering fresh muffins for the continental breakfast, for which I also God blessed her. Thus greeted and fortified, I made my way out of Moscow bound for Twin Falls.

The ride to Twin Falls was about 440 miles, two-thirds of it on two-lane mountain roads. It was a long day and I made few stops other than for gas. Thirty miles south of Moscow I pulled into the Confluence Overlook, which affords a spectacular view of the towns of Lewiston and Clarkston and the meeting of the Clearwater and Snake Rivers, a thousand feet below and 8 miles away. Lewis and Clark followed the Clearwater out of the mountains to the Snake, which took them to the Columbia River. Eight years later, in 1812, fur trapper Donald MacKenzie built a trading post, 5 miles upstream on the Clearwater, for John Jacob Astor's Pacific Fur Company. Astor's fur enterprise established a strong, permanent American presence in the Pacific Northwest. It was also the foundation of a personal fortune that made him, for a time, the wealthiest American.[12] From the Confluence Overlook, US 95 passes through the Nez Perce Reservation. A few miles south of the town of Grangeville, another pullout overlooks White Bird Canyon where the Nez Perce War began in 1877. Intrigued by the site's historical marker and recalling what little I knew of the Nez Perce War and Chief Joseph and the Wallowa band's heroic flight, I stayed long enough to take a few photographs. As I rode away, it occurred to me that I should have been taking a lot of pictures and making notes on this trip. The historian in me was beginning to stir.

At Meridian, a suburb of Boise, I rolled onto Interstate 84. I had not been out of the saddle for hours and, after 300 miles of mountain riding, decided a gas and rest stop was in order before taking on the 130 or so miles of interstate riding to Twin Falls. As I filled Old Blue's tank, I noticed another motorcyclist at a pump about 30 feet away fueling his Honda Gold Wing, the land yacht of touring bikes. I was taken, however, not so much by the motorcycle as by what I initially thought was tall, strange-looking luggage on the bike. It looked sort of like a lumpy duffle bag with a helmet strapped to the top. On closer inspection, the duffle bag turned out to be a 6-foot stuffed gorilla wearing a helmet and strapped into the Gold Wing's passenger seat. I could not resist going over for a closer look and engaged Gold Wing Man in a brief conversation. Gold Wing Man and his gorilla were on their way from Salt Lake City to Wyoming, obviously taking an indirect route (which I did not bother to point out). I did not ask Gold Wing Man about his gorilla, nor did he seem inclined to explain his companion. After a few minutes, I wished Gold Wing Man and his friend a safe and pleasant journey, he wished me the same, and we parted.

For months afterward I told no one about Gold Wing Man and his gorilla, thinking I had probably been hallucinating. Then I decided that a tall tale about meeting a motorcyclist riding with a helmeted, 6-foot stuffed gorilla

FIGURE 2.1. White Bird Canyon, Idaho, where the Nez Perce War began in 1877.

was a great story, so one evening the following spring I told the story to a group of strangers at a charity dinner. As I finished the tale, a man seated directly across the table from me said, "I've seen him! Last summer. On I-25 going through downtown Denver." My hallucination gets around.

THE DAMMED SNAKE

Taking my leave of Gold Wing Man and his primate companion, I rolled onto Interstate 84 for the trip to Twin Falls. Boise, Idaho's capital city, is in a broad valley between the Owyhee and Boise Mountains. By the time I reached Mountain Home, 50 miles to the southeast, the setting had changed dramatically. While the mountains remained in view to the north, the terrain in all other directions turned to the sagebrush plains of the Great Basin. Bounded by the Sierras to the west, the Rockies and the Colorado Plateau to the east, the Mojave Desert in the south, and the Columbia Plateau to the north, the Great Basin is a 113,000-square-mile desert and semiarid zone extending from southern Idaho to southern Nevada and including parts of California and much of Utah.[13]

The northern Great Basin's natural resources were sufficient to sustain the native Shoshone and Paiute peoples, but the area must have seemed daunting, if not forbidding, to nineteenth-century white Americans passing through. That accounts for Idaho's comparatively delayed and sparse settlement. US Highway 30 and Interstates 15, 86, and 84 approximate the route of the Oregon Trail across Idaho. Thousands of settlers passed through on their way to the Pacific Northwest and California; few stopped in Idaho. Significant white settlement awaited the combination of capital and technology needed to raise the waters of the Snake River to irrigate the land. Historian F. Ross Peterson has called the Snake Idaho's "most unifying geographical feature," providing a "cord of cohesion" tying together farms, factories, and cities.[14] The river rises in Yellowstone National Park, flows across southern Idaho in a great arc, then turns north near Caldwell to form the border between Idaho and Oregon and southern Washington.

The city of Twin Falls is a product of the combination of land, water, money, technology, and public policy. In the late nineteenth and early twentieth centuries, the federal government set out to water and populate the West's arid lands. The National Reclamation Act of 1902, or the Newlands Act (so-called after its principal sponsor, Nevada congressman Francis G. Newlands), is the best-known and most important of the early federal irrigation and hydroelectric dam–building measures for the West. Less well-known was the Carey Act of 1894. Sponsored by another western politician, Wyoming senator Joseph M. Carey, this measure granted 1 million acres of federal land to states willing to irrigate it themselves or in partnership with private water developers. The states sold land to settlers for fifty cents per acre and water shares, sold by developers, cost twenty-five dollars per acre. Historians have judged the Carey Act as largely a failure, but it had significant impact in Idaho where between 1900 and 1920, Carey Act projects increased irrigated land from 40,000 acres to 600,000 acres. The rapid transformation of south-central Idaho's sagebrush desert into productive agricultural land earned the region the nickname of the Magic Valley. With the rapid expansion of irrigation, the area's population also rose. Idaho's population more than tripled from 1890 to 1910, and that of the six counties along the Snake River grew from 5,700 to 40,000 between 1900 and 1920.[15]

US Highway 93, which links Twin Falls with I-84, passes over the Perrine Bridge, a 1,500-foot-long span that crosses a chasm 500 feet above the Snake

River. The bridge is named for Ira B. Perrine, a settler who arrived in Idaho in 1883. In 1900 Perrine, who tried his hand at mining, dairy farming, and surveying, organized a group of investors as the Twin Falls Land and Water Company to develop Carey Act projects on the Snake. In 1903 the State of Idaho awarded the company a contract to develop 270,000 acres south of the river. The company built the Milner Dam, named for its chief investor, Utah businessman Stanley Milner, and began diverting the river into its main irrigation canal in March 1905.[16] Milner Dam was the second dam built on the Snake; the Swan Falls Dam, built in 1901 south of Boise, was the first. Today, a score of irrigation and hydroelectric dams calm the Snake's flow through Idaho, and the river irrigates more than 3 million acres. Twenty percent of that acreage is watered by the Milner Dam, which in the summer months diverts virtually the entire flow from the river, reducing to a trickle the once powerful Shoshone Falls and Twin Falls.[17]

Dried-up waterfalls are not the most serious environmental consequences of damming the Snake River. Far downstream from Twin Falls, as the river approaches its junction with the Columbia, four dams built between 1961 and 1975 harnessed the Snake, transformed the region's economy, and set in motion environmental problems that today defy technological and political solutions. Together the four dams generate about 5 percent of the electric power used in the Pacific Northwest. The dams also turned the lower Snake into a 140-mile-long lake, permitting barge traffic to the Columbia and on to the Pacific Ocean and making the town of Lewiston, Idaho—more than 300 miles inland from the Pacific—a seaport. Area farmers and industries use the barges instead of highways and railroads to ship their products to world markets.[18]

Environmental problems linked to the lower Snake dams are summed up in two words: silt and salmon. Miles of levees protect Lewiston from the waters rising behind the Lower Granite Dam. The US Army Corps of Engineers built the levees to stand 5 feet higher than any foreseeable flood. However, 100 million cubic yards of sediment flow into the reservoir each year, and the accumulated muck has raised the water level and reduced the levees' safety margin to only 1½ feet. Grain-laden barges that once had easy passage down the channel now get stuck in the sediment. Possible solutions include raising the levees, dredging, flushing the reservoir, and, most dramatically, removing the dams. Each approach provokes strong opposition.

The city of Lewiston, which the levees protect, opposes raising the barriers because doing so would disrupt recreational facilities that have been built on and around them. Raising the levees would also require raising several bridges, a very expensive task. Dredging the reservoir and shipping channel does not appear to be a practical solution since the US Army Corps of Engineers has been able to remove only 300,000 to 500,000 cubic yards of silt every five years, a fraction of the 500 million tons that build up in that period. Environmentalists oppose dredging because they claim the operation would harm fish in the river and reservoir. Opening the dam's floodgates would flush the silt out of the reservoir, but the barge companies and their customers oppose that solution because it would make the barge channel temporarily unusable.[19]

The question of the future of salmon in the Snake River both complicates and may point to the ultimate outcome of the silt problem and the dams' future. Annual runs of salmon in the river once numbered in the millions, but in recent years the fish have been counted only in the tens of thousands. The salmon are considered endangered species. Wildlife and environmental groups argue that the dams are the cause of the reduction in salmon stocks and that no amount of technological tinkering can repair the damage. The dams, they say, must be removed. However, all of the business interests dependent on the dams, as well as the Bonneville Power Administration, strongly oppose that argument, saying that the economic loss to the region—including loss of the dams' electric power capacity—would be unacceptable. Removal advocates counter that eliminating the dams and restoring the Snake as a free-flowing river would trigger an economic resurgence based on recreation and tourism. And, they argue, the costs of building new highway and railway transportation, or simply paying farmers and industries to compensate them for increased shipping costs, would be cheaper for taxpayers than the current annual investment of hundreds of millions of dollars in futile efforts to mitigate the dams' harm to the salmon.[20]

In 2005, environmental groups sued the federal government after the Bush administration made the astonishing claim that the dams do not threaten the survival of endangered salmon and that habitat restoration plans would increase fish stocks without requiring removal of the dams. The government argued, in fact, that the dams were an immutable part of the landscape and so could not be removed. The federal judge in the case rejected the government's mitigation plans and its argument for the immutability of the dams. In late 2007 the judge seemed ready to reject yet another government mitigation plan and in a letter to the litigants chastised the government for failing to include removing the dams as a possible measure in their planning. "I instructed Federal Defendants to consider all mitigation measures necessary to avoid jeopardy [to the fish], including removal of the four lower Snake River Dams, if all else failed," Judge James Redden wrote. "Despite those instructions, the [government's plans] again appear to rely heavily on mitigation actions that are neither reasonably certain to occur, nor certain to benefit listed species within a reasonable time." Moreover, he concluded, "Federal Defendants seem unwilling to seriously consider any significant changes to the status quo."[21]

That commitment to the status quo describes not only federal policy but also the intractability of the problem, rooted as it is in the determination of all of the interests involved—except those advocating removing the dams—to avoid hard choices. Litigation of the issue continues, and neither Congress nor the executive branch of the federal government has the political will to decide on a course of action in opposition to the demands of the federal agencies, state and local governments, and business interests concerned.[22] Indeed, any decision, whether by Congress, the executive, or the courts, to remove the dams would run against a more than century-old commitment to develop (i.e., dam) the West's rivers. Unless the court takes decisive action, the silt will continue to accumulate and the fish will continue to die off until some disaster—a flood in Lewiston or the extinction of a salmon species—forces a decision.

TWIN FALLS

As work proceeded on their dam and canal system, Ira Perrine and his associates also began building the town of Twin Falls and incorporated it in April 1905, just a month after the dam and canal began operations. By the end of the year Twin Falls had a population of at least 2,000 and a full complement of stores, saloons, a six-room school, a newspaper, and several churches. The company, which donated land for the school, a courthouse, and a public park, dominated the new town. The first building was the home of the Twin Falls Investment Company, the land sales arm of the irrigation operation. Perrine owned the largest hotel and a general store. The hotel's electric sign, said the town newspaper, "shone like a beacon of progress far across the desert." The first mayor was the company's chief engineer, and another employee held the job of town clerk.[23]

This instant city's creation underscores important themes in the history of the agrarian American West. First, agricultural development of the Great Plains and, later, of the Great Basin and Columbia Plateau required federal money to make low-cost land and water available for development by states, business interests, and—only last—individual settlers. Congress passed the Homestead Act in 1862, granting 160 acres of federal land to settlers who could occupy and develop that land within five years, but family farmers could hope to survive and prosper only when the costly infrastructure of railroads, dams, and towns was in place. So the promise of free or cheap land meant little without federally subsidized railroad and dam construction. Second, town development accompanied and more often preceded agricultural settlement. Towns provided the economic and social infrastructure— the banks, railheads, stores, and churches—necessary to build and sustain a farm economy. So the sturdy independent farmer, an icon of American culture older and even more important than the cowboy, could not have existed in the American West without a complicated and interdependent foundation of federal policy and subsidized capitalism.

Twin Falls today is a city of about 40,000 and serves, as it has from its beginnings, as the key urban center of the Magic Valley's farming and cattle industry. The city's most imposing structure, a 29,000-square-foot Mormon Temple topped by a 159-foot spire and a golden statute of the angel Moroni, serves approximately 50,000 Mormons living in the Magic Valley area.[24] Southeastern Idaho is very much a Mormon domain. Mormons founded Idaho's first permanent settlement, Franklin, in 1860 (the original 13 settlers believed they were in Utah Territory). Franklin's 600 residents seem to revel in their remoteness, noting on their town website that its location between Logan, Utah, and Preston, Idaho, makes for but a "short drive to civilization."[25]

As I rolled out of Twin Falls the next morning, I rode toward the historical, religious, and political center of one of America's most interesting communities: the Mormons.

One of the first tasks Brigham Young and his followers set for themselves when they arrived at the Great Salt Lake was to begin construction of a temple for their new settlement. Young laid out the site in the summer of 1847, though construction did not begin until 1853. Forty years later the Mormons opened their 253,000-square-foot temple in the heart of what was becoming a substantial western city of about 45,000.[26] The temple, now surrounded by modern high-rise buildings, remains the city's focal point.

During the era of the Second Great Awakening in the early nineteenth century, religious fervor was especially heated in western New York, earning the region the sobriquet of "the Burned over District." Participants in revival meetings often had profound experiences, such as speaking in tongues and seeing visions. Mormonism, institutionalized as the Church of Jesus Christ of Latter-Day Saints, traces its origins to this setting. According to Mormon belief, around the year 1820 Joseph Smith Jr., a teenage farm boy living with his family near Palmyra, New York, had a vision in which God and Jesus warned him that all existing religions were errant. Three years later an angel named Moroni directed Smith to a hill where the angel told him he would find a cache of engraved gold plates bound together as a book. The gold plates contained the story of a band of ancient Hebrews who fled the Holy Land around 600 BCE, ahead of the Babylonian captivity. God led them to the New World, where they built a powerful civilization. Jesus visited them shortly after his death and resurrection and brought them to Christianity. After a few centuries, however, they fell into division, conflict, and decay. Moroni's father, Mormon, authored their story. Moroni, the last patriarch of these Israelites in America, hid the gold plates in the Hill of Cumorah until the time came to reveal them again to the world. Smith published the *Book of Mormon* in 1830 and started building his new church. From the beginning, Smith and his followers saw themselves as a people apart from the rest of American society.[27]

We Americans admire people who live by their values, stand up for their beliefs, and stick together—that is, unless they are too good at those things. Then they get into trouble. They find themselves in conflict with other, more widely accepted values and beliefs and with other communities and institutions. The Mormons' claim to represent a restored Christianity seemed heretical and arrogant. Their growing numbers challenged established denominations. Their solidarity threatened established business and political interests, since they preferred to trade and hire among themselves and they tended to vote as a block according to their leaders' instructions. There were suspicions that they provoked Indian unrest and opposed slavery. And some of them practiced plural marriage.[28]

Joseph Smith called his followers to gather in 1831 at Kirtland, Ohio. From there they soon moved to Jackson County, Missouri, and in 1839 to Commerce, Illinois, which they took over and renamed Nauvoo. They hoped that by controlling their own city, they could escape the harassment and violence that plagued them in Ohio and Missouri. It was not to be. In 1844 the Mormons fell victim to a wave of violence that culminated in the mob murder of Smith. They tried for a time to hang on in Illinois, but continued threats and violence convinced their new leader, Brigham Young, to seek a new home for them. Young found it in John C. Frémont's recently published account of his 1842–44 journeys to Oregon and the Great Basin, *Report of the Exploring Expedition to the Rocky Mountains* (1845), in which the "Pathfinder" described the Great Salt Lake area as "truly a bucolic region." On the strength of this report, Young chose the Salt Lake Valley as the new Zion. Young and his followers chose the Great Basin as their new home because it seemed so remote from the American society and government that had caused them so much pain. Poet William Clayton put that aspiration into verse during the early days of the migration west:

> We'll find the place which God for us prepared,
> Far away in the West,
> Where none shall come to hurt or make [us] afraid.[29]

The Mormon migration began in earnest in the spring of 1847. They followed the Oregon Trail along the Platte River. To avoid contact with non-Mormon emigrants, they kept to the north side of the Platte. (In the summer of 2007 I was in a delightful coffee/art shop in Bluff, Utah, in the southeast corner of the state. In a conversion with the owner I described a planned future motorcycle tour of the Oregon Trail. A customer sitting nearby quickly corrected me, declaring the route's proper name to be the Mormon Trail. Uncharacteristically, I obeyed my inner diplomat rather than argue the point.)

The Salt Lake Valley was not the Eden some members of Young's party expected. Instead of the bucolic place Frémont had described, they found what one of the immigrants called "a broad and barren plain hemmed in by mountains . . . the paradise of the lizard, the cricket and the rattlesnake." Nevertheless, only Brigham Young's opinion mattered at the moment, and he was pleased with what he saw. Young is said to have declared, "This is the place whereon we will plant our feet and where the Lord's people will dwell."[30]

The pioneer party immediately set to work to prepare the ground for the thousands coming behind them. They put up a stockade, laid out the first streets and town lots of Salt Lake City, with the temple site at the center, and began assigning farmland and digging irrigation ditches. Three months later the settlement numbered about 2,000, and in 1850 it had grown to more than 11,000. Utah's population grew rapidly over the succeeding half-century and topped a quarter million by 1900.[31]

As their numbers grew, the Mormons and their leaders worked to acquire economic self-sufficiency, political autonomy, and more territory. As soon as sufficient numbers had come to ensure Salt Lake City's survival, church elders began sending out groups to plant colonies, first in the canyons to the north and south of Salt Lake and eventually throughout the Great Basin and as far away as Mexico and Canada. By 1900 around 500 settlements stretched from Alberta, Canada, to Sonora, Mexico.[32] The Mormons claimed political suzerainty over the Great Basin region long before their numbers and settlements supported the claim demographically. In March 1849 the Mormon hierarchy proclaimed the establishment of the State of Deseret and quickly applied for American statehood. Deseret's territorial claim was enormous, encompassing all of modern Utah and Nevada; most of Arizona; southeastern California, including the San Diego area; Wyoming, Colorado, and New Mexico west of the continental divide; and the southeast corner of Idaho—more than 200,000 square miles in all.

The long years of persecution and the exodus to the Great Basin created among the Mormons a powerful sense of themselves as a people apart. But in applying for admission to the American union, they acknowledged that their refuge could not exist separate from the United States. After all, Deseret included much of the territory the United States had only recently seized from Mexico. In 1850 Congress asserted federal authority over the region by rejecting statehood and instead establishing a new Utah Territory within borders significantly smaller than those the Mormons had claimed for the State of Deseret. Eleven years later Congress carved the Nevada Territory from Utah, confining the Mormon realm to Utah's modern boundaries. Nevada became a state in 1864, but Utah, more settled and better organized, waited three more decades.[33]

During the territorial period and beyond, the church and its leaders remained Utah's real government. Indeed, the territorial governorship remained in Mormon hands. The federal government dispatched a long line of non-Mormon political appointees to Utah, but they found themselves either ignored or subjected to harassment. Most did not stay very long. As humorist Mark Twain put it, "There is a batch of . . . officials here, shipped from Washington, and they maintain the semblance of a republican form of government—but the petrified truth is that Utah is an absolute monarchy and Brigham Young is king."[34]

This flaunting of federal authority alone was enough to incite powerful animosity toward the Mormons, but it was a cultural issue—plural marriage, sanctioned as church doctrine in 1852—that delayed statehood and nearly provoked armed conflict with the national government. Once the Mormons brought plural marriage out of their doctrinal and cultural closet, those forces determined to assert national control and to break the church's virtual monopoly on political and economic power in Utah could mount their crusade under the twin banners of federal sovereignty and traditional family values.

But the struggle between the Mormons and the national government was about much more than plural marriage. It was the Mormons' success in building and sustaining a community, within but set apart from the rest of American society, that provoked the hostility of the "gentiles." In a moment of candor, a territorial judge told the Mormons what the battle was really about. "We care nothing for your polygamy," said Judge Elliot F. Sanford. "It's a good war-cry and serves our purposes by enlisting sympathy for our cause . . . What we most object to is your unity; your political and commercial solidarity; the obedience you render to your spiritual leaders in temporal affairs."[35]

The Mormons held out on the issue of plural marriage until September 1890, when the church abandoned the practice as official doctrine. That denied the Mormons' opponents their best weapon and spelled the end of the federal government's harassment of the church and its leadership. In surrendering on plural marriage, the Mormons won the larger struggle. Utah achieved statehood in 1896, with the Mormon hierarchy in firm control of the new state and the Mormon community very much still in control of its cultural and economic life.

The church's official about-face on plural marriage did not end the practice, as families and communities devoted to it either went underground or removed themselves to remote areas on the periphery of the Mormon empire. Polygamists and the Mormon Church denounced one another as apostates guilty of straying from the faith's true doctrines. Even today, polygamist communities live more or less openly in rural areas of southern Utah and northern Arizona, and two polygamist breakaway sects together claim more than 17,000 members. However, as the Mormons learned more than a century ago, polygamist communities have found that American culture and law can reach into the most remote areas of the republic. A Utah jury in 2007 convicted the leader of one of the sects on felony charges of being an accomplice to rape in the forced marriage of a fourteen-year-old girl. Ultimately, legal and political pressures may not be the most powerful force against the polygamists as population growth associated with tourism and developing extractive industries bring their communities into more frequent contact with outsiders.[36]

HOME

As I rode through the Salt Lake Valley, I found myself admiring all that the Mormons had endured and all they achieved in building their desert empire. I thought about how their experience underscores the importance of community in the history of the American West, the struggles of the weak against the powerful, and how sometimes the weak become powerful. But after days of riding in sparsely populated rural areas, it was something of a shock to find myself in a bustling urban center, so thoughts about the Mormon experience gave way to focus on staying out of trouble on the construction-clogged freeway. That made it easy to miss my exit from the interstate. The first clue that I had gone astray was a friendly sign saying "Welcome to Provo." As I cruised past that clue, the realization set in that I was about 40 miles off course. I pulled into a gas station, filled Old Blue's tank, and bought two bottles of cold water, one of which I poured over my head.

Thus refreshed, I walked toward two young men—they had the look of carpenters—standing by a pickup truck. They regarded the large, leather-clad, dripping-wet motorcyclist approaching them with looks of bemused alarm. Sensing their distrust, I flashed my best chagrined smile and explained that I was lost (a neat trick, given that I was within sight of an interstate highway). I asked if there was some way to get to US 40 and my destination, the town of Roosevelt, without backtracking all the way through Salt Lake. Relieved that I was not hitting them up for spare change or worse, the carpenters relaxed and provided idiot-proof directions. I pulled out of the gas station onto Provo's main street and followed it north, past Brigham Young University. Soon, the road veered right into Provo Canyon.

The ride up Provo Canyon ends at Heber City in the Heber Valley, a broad basin between the Wasatch and Uintah Mountain ranges. From Heber City I rolled off the last 80 miles of the day, arriving in Roosevelt as the sun began to set. Roosevelt is located in the middle of the Uintah and Ouray Indian Reservation. At least ten Ute Indian bands once occupied the vast territory from central Utah to the eastern foothills of the Rocky Mountains in Colorado and from southern Wyoming to northern New Mexico. Most Ute bands were nomadic, though some interrupted their migrations long enough to plant and harvest corn. Before the Mormons settled in the Great Basin, the Utes weathered and even profited from contact with whites. The Spanish introduced the horse to Ute culture, expanding the range of their territory and travels; and French and American trappers brought new weapons and implements. Contact with the Mormons, however, triggered an era of conflict that resulted in the Utah Ute's confinement to a reservation in the desolate Uintah Basin. In 1860 Brigham Young dispatched a survey party east across the Wasatch Mountains into the Uintah Valley. The surveyors reported that the area was not suitable for Mormon settlement because it could not support farming. It was, they noted, "one vast contiguity of waste, and measurably valueless, excepting for nomadic purposes."[37] It was, in short, a good place to which to remove the Utes. Within two decades Colorado had also banished most of its Ute population to the same area.

The Utes did not go readily or willingly to their desolate new home, but by the early 1870s most had given up resistance. The struggle to scratch out the barest of lives took its toll. By 1930 fewer than 1,000 full tribe members remained. In recent decades, however, their fortunes changed with the development of the reservation's significant oil, gas, oil shale, tar sand, and Gilsonite resources. Tribal members now number about 3,300.[38]

My motel was on the eastern edge of Roosevelt and was very quiet. I fell asleep early and slept late. In the morning I walked to the motel's restaurant to get breakfast. As I ate, I noticed an elderly Indian woman seated a couple of booths away. I enjoyed watching the young Ute women working in the restaurant wait on her with a doting respect we see too little of today. They took turns bringing her small plates of food and refilling her orange juice. Soon, a second woman joined the first and she received the same attention. After a while the ladies stood up and strolled out of the restaurant. No check for them.

After breakfast, I headed east toward Colorado and the last day of my adventure. As I rode into northwestern Colorado, I was still in country rich in the history of the Utes. The town of Meeker is about 60 miles east of the state line and just a few miles from the site of the Utes' last stand in Colorado. In 1868 the Ute bands in Colorado agreed reluctantly to a treaty confining them to the western third of the territory. Though they lost access to the Eastern Plains and much of the mountains, they still had a sizable domain that included the mighty San Juan and West Elk Mountain ranges and the valleys of the Uncompahgre, Colorado, White, and Yampa Rivers. Unfortunately, like almost every other treaty between Indians and the United States, the 1868 agreement was not worth the paper it was written on. The gold and silver excitements that swept Colorado in the 1860s and 1870s brought hordes of whites to the territory who were not about to let any Indians or treaties stand between them and their dreams of mineral riches. In 1873 the government forced the Utes to surrender much of the San Juan Mountain region. Worse was to come.[39]

Into the volatile mix of Utes determined to defend their lands and whites determined to take what they wanted entered Nathan Meeker, an evangelical Protestant reformer determined to save the Utes from themselves. Meeker had come to Colorado in 1870 as a leader of Horace Greeley's Union Colony. The colony succeeded in founding the city of Greeley, but Meeker went broke. In 1877 he secured the job of federal agent to the White River Ute Indians in northwest Colorado. Meeker arrived at his post in the summer of 1878 and set out to force his wards to abandon their nomadic ways, settle down, and take up the plow. The White River Utes resisted Meeker, whose efforts to coerce them included withholding treaty rations, which he believed were harmful to the Indians since they made them dependent on the government.[40]

In September 1879, after a year of failed attempts to pastoralize his Indians, Meeker decided to force the issue. He ordered his agency farmer to plow up the Utes' best horse pasture and threatened to do the same to their horse racing grounds. The Utes correctly took these actions as threatening their way of life. Meeker seemed to expect trouble. In a report to his superior, he expressed his determination to go forward with the plowing, "but whether unmolested I cannot say. This is a bad lot of Indians. They have had free rations so long and have been flattered and petted so much that they think themselves lords of all."[41] In succeeding days, Meeker's relations with the Indians went from bad to worse, at one point resulting in a shoving matching between the agent and a Ute leader named Canalla and, worse, someone taking a shot at the agency farmer. Finally, on September 10, Meeker asked the army to send troops to protect him. The troops approached the reservation boundary on September 29 and ran into a Ute war party that killed the force's commander and thirteen of his men and pinned the rest down for a week. That same day another group of Utes attacked Meeker's headquarters, killed the agent and eleven others, and took his wife, daughter, and three other people captive.

The Ute victory in this White River Uprising was temporary. The fighting enraged Colorado's white population, and politicians and newspapers took up the cry "The Utes Must Go!"[42] More federal troops poured into the area to restore order, and the government demanded that Chief Ouray, the leader of the Uncompaghre Utes—who played no part in the uprising—agree to negotiate a new treaty binding almost all of Colorado's Ute bands. The resulting treaty, signed in 1880, stripped the Utes of all but a small parcel of inhospitable land in the southwest corner of the state (today's Southern Ute and Ute Mountain Ute Reservations) and forced the White River and Uncompaghre bands to relocate to a new reservation just east of the Uintah reservation in Utah. The northwest corner of Colorado, where the Utes once roamed, became and remains a domain of ranches, farms, mines, and recreational areas. Coal mines and the enormous Hayden Generating Station are both economic mainstays and environmental concerns in the area.

East of Craig, Colorado, the broad Yampa River Valley enters a large geologic box bounded on the north by the Elkhead Mountain range, on the south by the Flat Tops, and on the east by the Park Range. With almost no traffic to watch out for, my thoughts about the Utes gave way to a blank, scenery-induced reverie, the kind that gets motorcyclists killed. Somewhere near the town of Milner, however, two objects caught my eye. One was a big red semi rig coming toward me; the other was a pronghorn antelope trotting down a roadside berm on my side of the road, clearly intent on crossing the highway. It took a couple of seconds to shake off my pleasant, deadly reverie and calculate that, at our relative speeds, the pronghorn and I were about to occupy the same space at the same moment. By the time that realization soaked in, the distance between us had narrowed considerably. I rolled off of the accelerator, applied light pressure on the brakes, and remembered reading somewhere that I should not swerve to avoid animals in the road. The pronghorn evidently made its own calculations and began to run faster toward the road as I slowed. It seemed as if I could have reached down with my left hand and patted the critter on its butt as I whizzed by. I also expected to hear a loud thud because the animal was running directly into the path of the oncoming truck. Instead, I heard a loud blast from the truck's horn but no thud. I glanced back in the mirror and saw the pronghorn running, apparently unscathed, across the field toward the Elkheads. Winston Churchill is said to have quipped, "Nothing in life is so exhilarating as to be shot at without result."[43] I, and no doubt the pronghorn, understood the sentiment.

My heart rate was just about back to normal as I rode through Steamboat Springs, one of the birthplaces of recreational skiing in Colorado. Legend has it that early white settlers thought one of the area's many hot springs made a chugging sound reminiscent of a steam engine, hence the name Steamboat Springs. Damage caused by railroad construction silenced the spring about a century ago. White settlement in the area began in the 1870s with the arrival of ranchers and, later, miners. Many of those ranchers and miners probably skied, but for them skiing was not a sport. Instead, early mountain settlers relied on their skis when winter snows made horse and foot travel impossible. Preachers, doctors and midwives, and mail carriers skied regular circuits to deliver their services. By the mid-1880s, however, mountain dwellers began to organize downhill skiing clubs. From that time on, skiing became more and more a recreational and social activity emphasizing vertical descent over horizontal travel. By the 1920s ski clubs and entrepreneurs began installing various contraptions, often powered by automobile engines, to haul skiers up mountainsides, saving them the exertion of climbing on foot. Businessmen and ski enthusiasts began to think bigger in the 1930s, with plans to build ski resorts. The first efforts to transform Aspen, then a virtual ghost town about 90 miles to the south, into a resort began to bear fruit in the mid-1930s. Meantime, Denver skiers began to ride the Denver and Rio Grande train to the West Portal of the Moffat Tunnel (originally a railroad tunnel whose pioneer bore became a diversion tunnel carrying water from the western slope to Denver), where in 1940 the city of Denver opened the Winter Park ski area. World War II interrupted ski-area development, but in the postwar era businessmen—including many veterans of the Tenth Mountain Division, the army's elite ski troops who had trained in Colorado during the war—launched the era of large-scale development. The results included Vail, Aspen, Arapahoe Basin, and Steamboat Springs.[44]

Steamboat Springs's modern identity as a destination resort took root with the arrival of a Norwegian immigrant named Carl Howelsen. Howelsen came to the United States in 1904 and worked for a time for the Ringling Brothers and Barnum & Bailey Circus as the "Flying Norwegian," skiing down a wooden scaffold and jumping over various obstacles including circus elephants. He arrived in Colorado in 1911 and two years later was in Steamboat Springs supporting himself as a ski instructor and part-time stonemason. Howelsen built a ski jump and began dazzling the town's young people with his leaps. Reports of a flying man soon brought a delegation of parents to investigate. Rather than try to explain himself, Howelsen simply gave an on-the-spot demonstration with a 70-foot jump. The townsfolk were satisfied that nothing supernatural was going on and, with their blessings, Howelsen was soon busy teaching Steamboat Springs youngsters the art of ski jumping. Howelsen Hill, located across the Yampa River from the center of town, is still used to train ski jumpers.[45]

From Steamboat Springs I rode on to Kremmling and turned south on Colorado 9 bound for Interstate 70. Kremmling is the locale of one especially disturbing memory of my Cold War–era childhood. One weekend, probably in the mid- to late 1950s, my parents decided to drag my sister and me away on an all-day drive in the mountains. We must have been on US 40 because construction of I-70 through the mountains did not begin until the

1960s.[46] At some point in that endless, boring day trapped in the car with my parents and sibling, my mother declared that we should go to Kremmling. I spent the next few hours in a state of terror because I had not until that moment realized that the headquarters of the dreaded Soviet Union was so close to my Denver home. Further, I was frightened and confused that my heretofore flawlessly patriotic parents would be taking me there. Even at age seven or eight I had heard of Senator Joe McCarthy and knew that the most normal-appearing people—even my parents—might be communist subversives. Would I have to report them? If I did, would I be a hero? Where would I live if they went to prison? I decided to keep the dreadful secret to myself and bear my family's shame in silence.

Colorado 9 parallels the Blue River all the way to Silverthorne, which straddles I-70. Silverthorne is a bedroom town serving the nearby Dillon Reservoir and the Breckenridge and Keystone ski areas. The town's spectacular setting cannot disguise the fact that it is densely urbanized, packed with condominiums, apartment buildings, fast-food restaurants, and that holy grail of the serious recreational shopper: an outlet mall. Once I arrived there and rolled onto I-70, I felt that my adventure was over.

I had been dreading the ride on I-70 to Denver. The interstate is the main route linking Denver and the rest of eastern Colorado to recreational sites, including the Summit County ski resorts, along its corridor all the way to Grand Junction. Traffic is especially heavy in the winter months and sometimes moves at a crawl. Summer traffic on the highway is lighter but more dangerous because lower volume means higher speeds. I confess to enjoying the fast ascent on Old Blue up the steep, 7-mile climb from Silverthorne to the Eisenhower-Johnson Tunnels, flying by cars struggling to sustain even moderate speeds on the slope. The 1.7-mile-long tunnels, named for President Dwight Eisenhower (westbound) and former Colorado governor and US senator Edwin Johnson (eastbound), cross the continental divide at 11,000 feet above sea level, making them world's highest vehicular tunnels. I enjoyed the sound from Old Blue's engine reverberating off the tunnel walls, but the air inside was thick with exhaust fumes (more than 1 million vehicles went through the tunnels in August 2006 and every August since).[47] Exiting the tunnel, I gulped some fresh air and steeled myself for the really scary part of the ride: the steep, fast, 12-mile descent to Georgetown. Gravity and lead feet on accelerators result in most cars and trucks running down the hill far too fast. Add to that the standard Colorado driver's "me first" attitude, and the image that comes to mind is of a high-speed slalom race with all the racers on the course at the same time. I decided to stay out of the fray by getting into the right lane and staying there all the way to the bottom. It was slower—only slightly over the speed limit—but I was in no great hurry since nothing more exciting than my garage awaited me.

I rolled off I-70 and onto US 6 just outside Golden and headed into Denver. A few minutes later I pulled into the garage, cut the engine, and checked the odometer. I had ridden 3,314 miles. It had been the adventure of a lifetime. I had been in six states and one Canadian province. I had seen, touched, and smelled the Great Plains, the Rocky Mountains, the Puget Sound, river valleys, forests, deserts, farmland, ranchland, small towns, and great cities. I had seen the geological wonders of the Wind River Canyon and of Yellowstone. I had experienced close encounters with wildlife and watched people trying to connect with wild animals. I had ridden over historic trails and past battlefields. I had watched an essential western American historical process, the formation and dissolution of community, take place on the side of a road. I had seen what faith, devotion, and ideals can build. And I had seen what self-righteousness, greed, and fear can do.

I began to understand that the personal and intellectual distance I had covered was greater than the miles ridden. When I set out ten days earlier, it was just a road trip, albeit unlike any I had ever taken. Once home, however, I realized that I also had stumbled upon a new (for me) way of encountering history. I began giving myself moral head slaps. Why had I not taken more pictures? Why had I not made notes about the places I had seen and the people I encountered and all they made me ponder? I began reconstructing the journey in my mind and then in notes and then in text. And I began thinking about the next trip.

Notes

1. Bruce Hevley and John M. Findlay, eds., *The Atomic West* (Seattle: University of Washington Press, 1998), 3–89; US Department of Energy, Hanford Site, Hanford Cultural and Historic Resources Program, History and Archaeology, at http://www.hanford.gov/doe/history/?history=archaeology, accessed October 7, 2007; US Department of Energy, Hanford, "Hanford Overview and History," at http://

www.hanford.gov/page.cfm/hanfordoverviewandhistory, accessed July 30, 2014; US Department of Energy, Hanford Site, "Environmental Report for Calendar Year 1997," at http://msa.hanford.gov/files.cfm/PNNL-11795_1997.pdf, accessed July 30, 2014.

2. State of Washington, Department of Transportation, "Palouse Scenic Byway Application Visual Analysis Discipline Report, October 2002," at http://contextsensitivesolutions.org/content/reading/a-methodology/resources/method_byway/, accessed July 30, 2014; Palouse Prairie Foundation, "The Palouse Prairie," at www.palouseprairie.org/display, accessed October 19, 2007; Washington State Parks and Recreation Commission, "Palouse Falls," at www.parks.wa.gov/559/Palouse-Falls," accessed July 30, 2014.

3. D. W. Meinig, *The Great Columbia Basin: A Historical Geography, 1805–1910* (Seattle: University of Washington Press, 1968), 11.

4. State of Washington, Department of Transportation, "Palouse Scenic Byway Application Visual Analysis Discipline Report, October 2002"; Washington State Parks and Recreation Commission, "Palouse Falls"; Latah [Idaho] County Historical Society, "Origin of the Word 'Palouse,'" at http://www.latahcountyhistorical society.org/#!histories-of-latah-county-communities/cmx6, accessed July 30, 2014.

5. Francis Haines, *Appaloosa: The Spotted Horse in Art and History* (Austin: Amon Carter Museum of Western Art and University of Texas Press, 1963), 69–73.

6. Bernard DeVoto, ed., *The Journals of Lewis and Clark* (New York: Houghton Mifflin, Mariner Books, 1981 [1953]), 168–69, 182, 323.

7. Haines, *Appaloosa*, 91–95; Department of Animal Science, Oklahoma State University, "Appaloosa," at http://www.ansi.okstate.edu/breeds/horses/appaloosa/index.htm, accessed October 22, 2007; American Appaloosa Association Worldwide, "Appaloosa History," at http://www.amappaloosa.com/history/story.htm, accessed July 30, 2014; Appaloosa Museum, "History of the Appaloosa," at http://appaloosamuseum.org/default.asp?contentID=521, accessed October 24, 2007; HistoryLink.org, "U.S. Army Colonel George Wright Slaughters 800 Palouse Horses on September 8, 1858," HistoryLink.org Essay 5142, at http://www.history link.org/index.cfm?DisplayPage=output.cfm&File_Id=5142, accessed July 30, 2014.

8. Latah County, Idaho, "General Election, November 2, 2004, United States Offices, President of the United States," at http://www.latah.id.us/Elections/2004 Gen/CANV0001.HTM, accessed October 31, 2007; Latah County, Idaho, "Latah County 2008 General Election Results," at http://www.latah.id.us/elections/2008 /2008Gen/index.php, accessed July 30, 2014; US Census Bureau, "State and County Quick Facts, Idaho," at http://quickfacts.census.gov/qfd/states/16000.html, accessed November 3, 2007; US Census Bureau, "Profile of General Demographic

Characteristics: 2000; Geographic Area: Moscow City, Idaho," at http://censtats .census.gov/data/ID/1601654550.pdf, accessed November 3, 2007.

9. Steve Wilkins and Douglas Wilson, *Southern Slavery as It Was: A Monograph by Steve Wilkins and Douglas Wilson* (Moscow, ID: Canon, 1996), at http:// reformed-theology.org/html/books/slavery/southern_slavery_as_it_was.htm, accessed July 30, 2014. Biblical denunciations of slavery include Deuteronomy 23:15–16, 24:7, and Exodus 21:16. On the history of American slavery, slave-master relations, and slave resistance and rebellion, see David Brion Davis, *Inhuman Bondage: The Rise and Fall of Slavery in the New World* (New York: Oxford University Press, 2006); Peter Kolchin, *American Slavery, 1619–1877* (New York: Hill and Wang, 1993).

10. *Moscow-Pullman Daily News*, October 17, 2003, text provided to the author electronically by the source, October 29, 2007.

11. Carl Abbott, Stephen J. Leonard, and Thomas J. Noel, *Colorado: A History of the Centennial State*, 4th ed. (Boulder: University Press of Colorado, 2005), 271–78; Stephen J. Leonard and Thomas J. Noel, *Denver: Mining Camp to Metropolis* (Niwot: University Press of Colorado, 1990), 189–202.

12. National Park Service, "Nez Perce National Historical Park and Big Hole National Battlefield Site Guide," at http://nps.gov/nepe/historyculture/confluence -overlook.htm, accessed July 30, 2014.

13. United States Geological Survey, "The Great Basin and the Columbia Plateau," at http://greatbasin.wr.usgs.gov, accessed July 30, 2014.

14. F. Ross Peterson, *Idaho: A Bicentennial History* (New York: W. W. Norton, 1976), 7–8.

15. Malone and Etulain, *American West*, 16; Allen G. Bogue, "An Agricultural Empire," in Clyde A. Milner, Carol A. O'Connor, and Martha Sandweiss, eds., *The Oxford History of the American West* (New York: Oxford University Press, 1994), 301; William Cronon, "Landscapes of Abundance and Scarcity," in Milner, O'Connor, and Sandweiss, eds., *Oxford History of the American West*, 607.

16. Peterson, *Idaho*, 130–31; Pisani, *Water and American Government*, 67–68.

17. Richard A. Slaughter, "Institutional History of the Snake River, 1850–2004," 3, at http://cses.washington.edu/db/pdf/Slaughter_InstitutionalHistorySnake241. pdf, accessed July 30, 2014; WaterfallsWest.com, "Shoshone Falls," at http://water fallswest.com/id_shoshone.html, accessed December 22, 2007; WaterfallsWest .com, "Twin Falls," at http://www.waterfallswest.com/id_twinfalls.html, accessed December 22, 2007.

18. Center for Columbia River History, "Dams of the Columbia Basin and Their Effects on the Native Fishery," at http://www.ccrh.org/comm/river/dams7.htm, accessed July 28, 2014; Bonneville Power Administration, "Power Benefits of the Lower Snake River Dams," at http://www.bpa.gov/news/pubs/FactSheets

/fs200901-Power%20benefits%200f%20the%20lower%20Snake%20River%20dams
.pdf, accessed July 28, 2014; Felicity Barringer, "On the Snake River, Dam's Natural
Allies Seem to Have a Change of Heart," *New York Times*, May 13, 2007, at http://
www.nytimes.com/2007/05/13/us/13dam.html?ex=13336795200&en=9406844d3ed
f46a&ei=5124&partner=newsvine&exprod=newsvine, accessed December 23, 2007,
July 28, 2014.

19. Erik Robinson, "Pressure Builds on Snake River Dams," *The Columbian*, April
15, 2007, at http://www.bluefish.org/pressure.htm, accessed July 28, 2014.

20. Ibid.; William Yardley, "Removing Barriers to Salmon Migration," *New York
Times*, July 29, 2011, at http://www.nytimes.com/2011/07/30/us/30dam.html?page
wanted=all&_r=0, accessed July 28, 2014; "Snake River Barging Drop: New Factor
in Dams Debate," *Seattle Times,* at http://seattletimes.com/html/localnews/2021
636038_snakeriverxml.html, accessed July 28, 2014.

21. "Judge Rejects Salmon Opinion; Environmentalists See Hope of Breaching Dams," *The Columbian*, May 27, 2005, at http://www.columbian.com/
links/05272005.cfm, accessed December 29, 2007; "Waterway for Trade: Lewis and
Clark Rode a Wild Snake River; Today It Is an Avenue of Commerce," *The Columbian*, October 9, 2005, at http://www.columbian.com/links/10092005.cfm, accessed
December 29, 2007; "Pressure Builds on Snake River Dams," *The Columbian*, April 15,
2007, at http://infoweb.Newsbank.com/iw-search/we/InfoWeb?p_action=doc&p...
MTI1Mi4yOTcwMTE6MT04OnjmLTEwNTEx&&p_multi=VCBB&s_jsEnabled=
true, accessed December 23, 2007; Redden quoted in "Judge: Salmon Plan Isn't
Looking Good," *The Columbian*, December 8, 2007, at http://www.columbian.com
/news/localNews/2007/12/12082007_Judge-Salmon-plan-isnt-looking-good.cfm,
accessed December 29, 2007; Barringer, "On the Snake River." For a detailed history
of the lower Snake River dams and their environmental consequences, see Keith
Petersen, *River of Life, Channel of Death: Fish and Dams on the Lower Snake* (Corvallis:
Oregon State University Press, 2001).

22. Maria L. LaGanga, "Groups Sue U.S. Agencies, Saying Plan to Protect Salmon
Falls Short," *Los Angeles Times*, June 17, 2014, at http://www.latimes.com/nation
/nationnow/la-na-nn-salmon-lawsuit-20140617-story.html, accessed July 29, 2014.

23. *Twin Falls News,* December 22, 1905, quoted in Pisani, *Water and American
Government*, 69.

24. Utah.com, "Salt Lake City History," at http://www.utah.com/cities/slc_
history.htm, accessed July 30, 2014.

25. "An Early History of Franklin," at http://franklinidaho.org/History2.
htm, accessed December 23, 2007; "Franklin, Idaho," at http://franklinidaho.org,
accessed December 23, 2007.

26. "Salt Lake Temple," at http://www.ldschurchtemples.com/saltlake/, accessed January 16, 2008; Utah.com, "Salt Lake City History."

27. George Brown Tindall and David E. Shi, *America: A Narrative History*, 3rd ed. (New York: W. W. Norton, 1992), 479–86, provides an overview of the Second Great Awakening and the early history of the Mormons. Leonard J. Arrington and Davis Bitton, *The Mormon Experience: A History of the Latter-Day Saints* (New York: Alfred A. Knopf, 1979), is a good, if dated, introduction to Mormon history.

28. Arrington and Bitton, *The Mormon Experience*, 48–49.

29. Ibid., 95, 102; William Clayton, "Come, Come, Ye Saints," at https://www.lds.org/music/library/hymns/come-come-ye-saints?,lang=eng, accessed July 29, 2014; Tindall and Shi, *America*, 485; Richard White, *"It's Your Misfortune and None of My Own": A New History of the American West* (Norman: University of Oklahoma Press, 1991), 123.

30. Frémont quoted in Tindall and Shi, *America: A Narrative History*, 486; Young quoted in Arrington and Bitton, *The Mormon Experience*, 101.

31. Glen M. Leonard, "A Place in the West, 1847–1877," at https://www.lds.org/liahona/1979/10/a-place-in-the-west-18471877?lang=eng, accessed July 30, 2014; US Census Bureau, "Population: 1790 to 1990," tables 16, 27, at http://www.census.gov/population/censusdata/table-16.pdf, accessed January 24, 2008.

32. Ibid., 108, 117–21.

33. William P. MacKinnon, "'Like Splitting a Man up His Backbone': The Territorial Dismemberment of Utah, 1850-1896," *Utah Historical Quarterly* 71, no. 2 (Spring 2003): 99–124.

34. Quoted in White, *It's Your Misfortune and None of My Own*, 169.

35. Ibid., 356; Sanford quoted in Arrington and Bitton, *The Mormon Experience*, 182–83; Carol Cornwall Madsen, "Woman Suffrage," the Encyclopedia of Mormonism, at http://eom.byu.edu/index.php/Woman_Suffrage, accessed July 31, 2011.

36. *New York Times*, November 21, 2007, http://wwwnytimes.com/2007/11/21/us/21jeffs.html, accessed February 16, 2008; *New York Times*, September 10, 2007, at http://www.nytimes.com/2007/09/10/us/10jeffs.html?_r=0, accessed July 30, 2014; Church of Jesus Christ of Latter-Day Saints, LDS Newsroom, "Polygamy: Latter-Day Saints and the Practice of Plural Marriage," at http://www.mormonnewsroom.org/article/polygamy-latter-day-saints-and-the-practice-of-plural-marriage, accessed July 30, 2014; "Jeffs' Preaching Will Be Dissected Word by Word," *Salt Lake Tribune,* at http://www.sltrib.com/polygamy/ci_4698070, accessed February 15, 2008; "Declaration of Alvin S. Barlow, Sr.," at http://www.scribd.com/doc/2626320/Declaration-of-Alvin-S-Barlow-Sr, accessed July 30, 2014.

37. Clifford Duncan, "The Northern Utes of Utah," in Forrest S. Cuch, ed., *A History of Utah's American Indians* (Salt Lake City: Utah State Division of Indian Affairs/Utah State Division of History, 2000), 189.

38. Ibid., 209; "Ute Nation," at http://www.utah.com/tribes/ute_main.htm, accessed February 3, 2008.

39. Abbott, Leonard, and Noel, *Colorado*, 113–14; James Whiteside, *Colorado: A Sports History* (Boulder: University Press of Colorado, 1999), 1–3.

40. Abbott, Leonard, and Noel, *Colorado*, 115; Whiteside, *Colorado: A Sports History*, 3–5.

41. Quoted in Whiteside, *Colorado: A Sports History*, 4.

42. Ibid., 5.

43. http://www.notable-quotes.com/c/churchill_sir_winston.html, accessed March 17, 2008.

44. Whiteside, *Colorado: A Sports History*, 29–40, 89–143.

45. Ibid., 91–94.

46. Colorado Department of Transportation, "The History of I-70 in Colorado," at http://www.coloradodot.info/about/CDOTHistory/50th-anniversary/interstate-70, accessed July 30, 2014.

47. Colorado Department of Transportation, "Eisenhower Tunnel Traffic Counts," at http://www.coloradodot.info/travel/eisenhower-tunnel/eisenhower-tunnel-traffic-counts.html#2006%20Traffic%20Counts, accessed July 30, 2014.

3

Four Trails, Two Rivers

Phineas had planned to go with me to Victoria but bailed at the last minute, pleading some nonsense about finishing a grant proposal that would pay his salary for the next couple of years. Over the following months I rarely passed up an opportunity to rub it in, regaling him with tales of the scenery, wildlife, characters, and harrowing escapes I had experienced. When I told him I intended to start my next trip right after classes ended in May, it was clear that he would happily risk unemployment rather than endure another round of my taunting. By then, I was thinking deliberately about motorcycling as a way to connect with the American West's history, and so I warned him that if he came along there would be many stops at historical sites.

Since the last trip had gone north and west, my thoughts wandered south and east. Santa Fe was an obvious and historically rich destination, but it was only a day's ride from Denver. We could easily spend a couple of days riding around northern New Mexico, but both of us wanted to pound out a lot of miles and see a wide variety of geographies. Still, Santa Fe and northern

DOI: 10.5876/9781607323273.c003

New Mexico stayed on the agenda. Thinking about Santa Fe drew my attention to the Santa Fe Trail, the route nineteenth-century traders and trappers followed from Missouri to Santa Fe, following the Arkansas River much of the way. But the ride to the trail's jumping-off point, in Franklin, Missouri, would take two days and then three or four more days to get to Santa Fe; that was too long for the time we had.

When I finally pulled out a map, a route that met all of our criteria almost jumped off the page. We would head south and east from Denver, following the route of the Cherokee and Smoky Hill Trails, then zigzag across the rest of eastern Colorado and into western Kansas to Dodge City. From there we would turn back west and southwest along the Santa Fe Trail to its end at the plaza in New Mexico's capital. Finally, we would head north, following the route of the Old Spanish Trail along the Rio Grande through northern New Mexico, into southern Colorado, and through the San Luis Valley, leaving the old trail where it turns west and heading across South Park to Denver. The route offered everything we wanted: lots of history, Santa Fe, and varied scenery from the Great Plains to the mountains and valleys of northern New Mexico and southern Colorado.

THE CHEROKEE TRAIL

We left early on a late May morning in 2007. A diamond blue sky with just a few cotton puff clouds was almost enough to make me forget the lousy winter we had endured. Almost. Deep snows from a series of blizzards still lay on the slopes of the Front Range mountains. To the east, however, only the greening plains were ahead of us.

We rode southeast out of Denver, following the route of one of the oldest of Colorado's pioneer trails, known both as the Trappers Trail and the Cherokee Trail. By the 1830s, beaver trappers were working a route extending from Taos north through the San Luis Valley, over the Sangre de Cristo Mountains, and along the Front Range of the Rocky Mountains. The Front Range segment of the route became part of the Cherokee Trail in 1849 when Cherokees from Oklahoma, following the lure of California gold, trekked along the Santa Fe Trail and the Arkansas River to the foot of the Rockies and then turned north. Some followed the Cache La Poudre River west into the mountains and over the Medicine Bow range into southern Wyoming

MAP 3.1. Map by Nicholas J. Wharton

to the Oregon Trail, while others continued north to Fort Laramie and the Platte River before turning west.[1]

A century and a half ago the Cherokee Trail was a link on a major immigrant route from the Great Plains to the Rocky Mountains, and by the mid-1860s it was a well-established stagecoach route with stations set up every 4 miles or so. Two of those stations are still standing. Four Mile House, a living history museum in Denver, and Seventeen Mile House, near Parker, are registered landmarks. Today, the Cherokee Trail is a heavily traveled commuter route linking suburban bedroom communities to Denver. At one of those suburbs, Franktown, we turned east onto the route of the Smoky Hill Trail.

THE SMOKY HILL TRAIL

In the summer of 1858 a group of prospectors led by William Green Russell of Auraria, Georgia, found gold in the South Platte River a few miles upstream from its confluence with Cherry Creek. News of the find spread quickly, and by the end of the year other gold seekers turned up at the settlement, called Auraria, taking shape at the point where the South Platte and Cherry Creek meet. A rival town popped up across Cherry Creek, and the two eventually became Denver. Migrants to the region came so quickly and in such large numbers that in 1861 the federal government established Colorado as a new territory.[2]

Fortune hunters traveled to Colorado on three routes. The northern route followed the Oregon Trail along the Platte River across Nebraska. At the site of present-day North Platte, Nebraska, they turned off the main route and followed the South Platte River to Denver. The southern route followed the Santa Fe Trail and the Arkansas River to the foot of the mountains and the Trappers/Cherokee Trail on to Denver. By 1859 these were well-worn and relatively easily traveled routes. The central route, the Smoky Hill Trail, was a different story.[3]

The Smoky Hill River rises in eastern Colorado, a few miles northwest of the town of Cheyenne Wells, and flows east to the Fort Riley, Kansas, area, where it joins the Republican River to form the Kansas River. The Smoky Hill offered travelers the shortest, most direct route across the plains to the gold diggings. That was the route's only advantage. For most of its course the Smoky Hill is not much of a river, and by the time travelers reached its source the streambed often offered only sand. A little farther west, the stands of trees travelers had found along the eastern reaches of the river disappeared, and the plains grasses turned short and sparse. Without water, fuel, and adequate pasturage, poorly equipped travelers could find themselves in dire trouble. The final 150-mile trek came to be known as the Starvation Trail. Those who made it across in 1859 told tales of privation, sickness, and death. Graves and unburied corpses were common sights. Daniel Blue and his two brothers left their home in Illinois to chase the dream of quick riches. At Topeka they joined a small group, sixteen in all, and set out along the Smoky Hill. Of the Blues, only Daniel made it to Denver, and he survived by eating his brothers. An Arapaho man found him, near death, and saw to it that he reached white settlement.[4]

Word of the Smoky Hill Trail's hazards got out fast. An item in the *Rocky Mountain News*, Denver's fledgling newspaper, noted in April 1860, "Three roads will be traveled next summer. The Arkansas by those from the south and southwest, the Smoky Hill by the foolhardy and insane, and the Platte by the great mass of migration."[5] Travel on the Smoky Hill Trail became safer in the mid-1860s when the Butterfield Overland Company started stagecoach service, and in 1870 the Kansas Pacific Railroad ran tracks on the route into Denver, linking the territorial capital to Kansas City.

Daniel Blue's ordeal and rescue exemplifies much that happened on the Colorado plains during and after the gold rush. Mid-nineteenth-century white Americans thought of the Great Plains and the rest of the American West as unoccupied and unused. Certainly, the experiences of those who hazarded the Starvation Trail did little to challenge that idea. But the Great Plains was occupied. For hundreds of years, a well-ordered society lived there and thrived on its precious resources. The Arapaho man who rescued Daniel Blue was a member of that Indian society composed of Arapaho, Cheyenne, Kiowa, and Comanche peoples. Occasionally, Apache, Ute, and Lakota bands also came into the area. As historian Elliott West shows in his wonderful book *The Contested Plains*, they organized their lives around the water, trees, grasses, and especially the bison. Though they were nomadic, their migrations were not aimless. They knew the best places to make their camps, where water, grass, and wood were plentiful—spots like the Big Timbers on the Smoky Hill and Arkansas Rivers and Sand Creek.[6]

Today, the Indians are gone and the Smoky Hill Trail region is an area of towns, farms, and ranches. Nevertheless, as we rolled southeast out of Franktown, traffic and settlement thinned out quickly. Soon I could erase from my mind's eye the few signs of modern settlement and imagine the Colorado plains as the Indians and the gold rush migrants had seen it. The plains grasses shimmered deep green and were punctuated with yellow, coral red, and pale blue wildflowers; eroded arroyos showed the power of plains thunderstorms to carve the landscape.

We reached Interstate 70 a few miles west of Limon and then picked up US 40 and continued along the Smoky Hill route through the towns of Hugo and Kit Carson. Hugo is a grain elevator town that originally grew up as a division point for the Kansas Pacific Railroad. The Union Pacific built a large roundhouse there in 1908; it is the only one of its type still standing in Colorado and remains the town's most prominent building.[7] Just off the highway, a long-abandoned service station's fading sign still promises repairs on anything "from daybreak to heart break." Like Hugo, Kit Carson—named for the famous scout, trapper, and soldier Christopher "Kit" Carson—also began as a Kansas Pacific stop. Today, the restored railroad station houses a museum. Across the street, at an outdoor museum of antique farm imple-ments, a local artist has fashioned a 30-foot tower out of sundry farm tools. We left the Smoky Hill Trail at Kit Carson and headed south to the town of Eads where, at a welcome rest area, we admired a lovely bronze statue titled *Kindred Spirits*, a tribute to the shared experiences of Indian, Hispanic, and white women who passed through and sometimes settled in the area. I did not realize it then, but art, artists, and the cultures they reflect would be an important feature of this journey.

SAND CREEK

John Chivington was a physically powerful and charismatic man. A Methodist minister, he could be described in modern terms as an evangelical fundamen-talist of the most rigid and self-righteous order—with guns. In the 1860s this "Fighting Preacher" became an officer in Colorado's territorial army and a cen-tral character in one of the great crimes in American history. On the morning of November 29, 1864, soldiers of the First and Third Colorado Regiments, composed mostly of poorly trained 100-day volunteers under Chivington's command, attacked an encampment of Cheyennes and Arapahos at Sand Creek. The attack caught the Indians completely by surprise because they believed their camp was under the protection of the US Army at nearby Fort Lyon (near the present-day town of Lamar). When the attack began, the Cheyenne chief Black Kettle, who flew an American flag on his lodge,

FIGURE 3.1. A fanciful tower of farm tools, Kit Carson, Colorado. Art was a major feature of this journey.

FIGURE 3.2. *Kindred Spirits*, in Eads, Colorado, honors southeastern Colorado's Indian, Hispanic, and white women.

frantically waved a white flag. The troops answered his signal of submission with intensified gunfire.[8]

The Indians, mainly old men, women, and young children, had few arms with which to defend themselves. The men used their few weapons to try to cover the others fleeing north along the creek, but they were no match for the well-armed troops with their rifles and artillery. Several hundred yards to the north, terrified people tried to protect themselves by digging holes in the sandy, dry creek bed, while others continued running to the northeast toward another Cheyenne camp near the Smoky Hill. Those who were not run down and shot were blasted by artillery fire. The soldiers' murderous rampage continued into the afternoon; when the shooting stopped, at least 150 Cheyennes and Arapahos lay dead. The soldiers spent the rest of the afternoon and the next day mutilating bodies and destroying everything of use in the camp. To their credit, one unit of the First Colorado, under the command of Captain Silas Soule, refused to participate in the rampage.[9]

What had the victims of Sand Creek done to provoke the attack? The simplest answer is that they were there. Sand Creek is a place you really have to want to go to. The site is about 15 miles northeast of Eads and is reached by an 8-mile rutted, washboard dirt road. By any common sense measure, it is a remote spot in a sparsely settled area. (The population density of Kiowa County today is only 0.8 persons per square mile.)[10] From the bluff overlooking the massacre site you can look out onto the plains to the east, north, and south all the way to the horizon and see no evidence of human activity. But even here, on land most white people in 1864 thought of as a place to get through, Black Kettle and his people could not be left alone. Colonel Chivington, to his everlasting infamy, really wanted to go to Sand Creek.

But that does not answer the question of why Chivington or anyone else cared that the Cheyenne and Arapahos had made camp there. Remote as the area was and is, the Sand Creek Massacre site is only 30 miles north of the busy transcontinental highway that was the Arkansas River and the Santa Fe Trail. Before the gold rush, Black Kettle more than likely would have chosen a much more hospitable site to camp, such as the Big Timbers near the confluence of Sand Creek and the Arkansas River. But in 1861 the US Army built Fort Wise at that location to protect the trail and the gold seekers headed for Denver and the central Rockies. (The army later renamed the post for Nathaniel Lyon, the first Union general killed in the Civil War.)

Conflict between the Plains Indians and the territory's rapidly growing white population had been a constant since 1859, but until 1864 it had generally been limited to small-scale raids and retaliation. Two treaties, both as worthless to the Indians as almost every other treaty they agreed to or were forced to accept, supposedly governed relations between Indians and whites on the plains. In the 1851 Treaty of Fort Laramie, the Plains Indians granted white travelers safe passage along the Oregon Trail and agreed to apportion the region among themselves, with the Cheyennes and Arapahos controlling the plains of what became Colorado and western Kansas. A decade later the gold rush rendered that solemn agreement meaningless, and most of the Cheyennes and Arapahos accepted a new arrangement, spelled out in the Treaty of Fort Wise (1861), restricting their territory to the area bounded by the Arkansas River, Sand Creek, and the Front Range of the mountains. The federal government also promised, but never fully delivered, annuities, supplies, farm equipment, and training to sustain the Indians and help them become farmers.[11]

Many Cheyenne and Arapaho leaders wanted peace and saw the 1861 treaty as the best they could hope for, but some bands and individuals refused to accept it. Among them were the *Hotamitaneos*, the Cheyenne Dog Soldiers. Determined to fight to preserve their control of the plains and their way of life, they stepped up raiding against migrants, farmers, and ranchers. During the spring, summer, and fall of 1864, the pattern of raiding and retaliation gave way to organized warfare as the territorial government set out to extinguish the Indians' claim to the plains of eastern Colorado. Politicians and newspapermen wanted blood. William Newton Byers's *Rocky Mountain News* demanded a campaign of "active extermination of the red devils."[12] In June, Governor John Evans ordered all Indians to report to military posts. It was summer and the Cheyenne and Arapaho bands were spread out across the Colorado plains; weeks passed before Evans's order reached all of them. On August 10, in a second proclamation, Evans declared war. Noting that most Indians had not followed his June directive, the governor authorized Colorado's white citizens to take up arms to hunt down and kill hostile Indians who, by his definition, were any who had not yet turned themselves in at military posts.[13]

While Evans and Chivington prepared for war, Black Kettle and US Army Major Edward Wynkoop, one of the few whites who wanted to prevent war, tried to defuse the crisis. In September Wynkoop traveled to Denver with Black Kettle and seven other Cheyenne and Arapaho chiefs and convinced the reluctant Evans and Chivington to meet with them. The conference began with Black Kettle begging for peace. Black Kettle told the governor, "We want to take good tidings home to our people, that they may sleep in peace. I want you to give all these chiefs of the soldiers here to understand that we are for peace, and that we have made peace, that we may not be mistaken by them for enemies."[14]

Evans replied by rehearsing all of the white population's grievances against the Indians and then washed his hands of the matter, telling the chiefs that they must make peace with the military. To underscore that point, Evans asked Chivington to state his views. The commander of the Third Colorado Regiment told the chiefs he would fight them until they laid down their weapons and surrendered to military authority. Since Black Kettle and the others were "nearer to Major Wynkoop than anyone else, they can go to him when they are ready to do that."[15]

The peace chiefs could not be blamed for wondering whether they had made peace. They also could not be blamed for believing that if they traveled to Fort Lyon and turned themselves over to Major Wynkoop's authority, they would not be subject to attack. However, Governor Evans and Colonel Chivington had other ideas. Despite Black Kettle's plea for peace, Evans notified federal authorities that the Indians remained hostile and must be dealt with by force. "The winter," he noted, was "the most favorable time for their chastisement." For his part, Chivington still believed what he had told Wynkoop months before about dealing with the Indians: "to kill them is the only way to have peace and quiet."[16] Chivington, however, did not intend to go after the Dog Soldiers or any other Indians who might actually offer a serious fight. Instead, he intended to wage war against the essentially defenseless people heading toward Fort Lyon.

In mid-November, Black Kettle and other Cheyenne peace chiefs and their people were camped on Sand Creek, north of Fort Lyon, and Black Kettle went to the fort to ask for the US Army's protection. By then, however, the army had relieved Major Wynkoop of his command there, yielding to pressure from politicians like Evans who found him too sympathetic to the Indians. Wynkoop's replacement, Major Scott Anthony, who was much more to the territorial leaders' liking, approved of the Sand Creek campsite.

FIGURE 3.3. A simple granite marker, decorated with prayer offerings, overlooks the area of the Sand Creek Massacre.

However, when he informed his superiors of the Sand Creek encampment, he said he would "try to keep the Indians quiet until such time as I receive reinforcements," suggesting his intent to attack them.[17] Those reinforcements, of course, were Chivington and the Third Colorado, who moved out of Denver on November 14. Fifteen days later they were at Sand Creek.

After the massacre, the Cheyennes and Arapahos retaliated by stepping up attacks on farms, ranches, and emigrant trails. In January 1865 they sacked Julesburg. They controlled the South Platte for a time and isolated Denver from the rest of the world. Federal officials finally approached Black Kettle, who had taken the surviving remnant of his band south of the Arkansas to avoid the fighting, offering yet another treaty. By the time the treaty council gathered at the Little Arkansas in central Kansas in October 1865, congressional and army investigations had revealed the truth about Sand Creek. The federal peace commissioners apologized for the "gross and wanton outrages" committed at Sand Creek and offered the Cheyenne and Arapaho survivors a new reservation south of the Arkansas River. Historian Dee Brown writes of this Treaty of the Little Arkansas, "Thus did the Cheyennes and Arapahos abandon all claims to the Territory of Colorado. And that of course was the real purpose of the massacre at Sand Creek."[18]

But that was not the end of the sordid tale. Two years later an even larger peace council met at Medicine Lodge Creek in southern Kansas. In the resulting Treaty of Medicine Lodge Creek (1867) the Cheyennes, Arapahos, Comanches, Kiowas, and Plains Apaches agreed to move to a reservation in the western reaches of Indian Territory. Neither the Little Arkansas nor the Medicine Lodge Treaty brought peace to the plains. Some Cheyenne groups, especially the Dog Soldiers, refused to accept them. Even among the bands that did accept the treaties, including Black Kettle's, it proved difficult to keep members—especially young men—on the reservation, particularly when promised rations and supplies did not materialize. Fighting spread across central and western Kansas during 1868, and the area's military commander, General Philip Sheridan, became determined to punish the Indians with a Chivington-esque strategy. Once again, Black Kettle and his people were the targets. On the morning of November 27, 1868, two days short of the fourth anniversary of Sand Creek, an army force commanded by George Armstrong Custer attacked Black Kettle's encampment on the Washita River, on the reservation in Indian Territory. This time Black Kettle did not escape. The Cheyenne peace chief, his wife, and more than 100 others died in this reprise of Sand Creek. Of the Cheyenne dead, only 11 were warriors.[19] The following summer the army brought the Central Plains war to its end with the Battle of Summit Springs in northeastern Colorado, this time engaging and defeating actual Indian warriors: the Dog Soldiers.

RETURN TO SAND CREEK

When I arrived at Sand Creek in the spring of 2007, the site was closed. From the locked entry gate I could see the grove of cottonwood trees standing near the site of Black Kettle's camp. I could have climbed over the gate and walked to the site and probably not been noticed. But it is a sacred place for the Cheyennes and Arapahos and anyone else with a conscience, and going in uninvited seemed wrong. So I contented myself with looking at the site from afar.

During the following winter, I read and thought a lot about Sand Creek and decided I had to go back, spend some time at the site, and fix it and what happened there more clearly in my mind. One of the first things I noticed when I arrived was how deceptive the plains geography can be. Seen from the gateway, the terrain at Sand Creek appears perfectly flat, but once I parked at the brand-new National Park Service office and began walking toward the cottonwood grove, I found it to be a half-mile uphill hike to the edge of a steep bluff overlooking the streambed and the area where Cheyenne and Arapaho tradition places Black Kettle's village. Chivington and his men attacked the village from this point. A granite marker, placed there in 1950, identifies the scene as the Sand Creek "battlefield." The marker and the area immediately around it have become a shrine, and I was taken with the variety of offerings left there, including blankets, moccasins, sneakers, a knife, basketry, coins, storage tins, silver and beaded jewelry, pottery sherds, and a prayer stick with leather braiding and other decorations. The fence surrounding the overlook was festooned with red, yellow, and blue Cheyenne prayer cloths. As I looked out over the scene, I kept thinking about two things: that the place has a profound, stark beauty and that there is no place to hide. The best the fleeing Cheyennes and Arapahos could do was dig pits in the creek bed or keep running.

A few years ago, a multidisciplinary team of historians, archaeologists, and ethnographers surveyed the site and reviewed all of the extant records, maps, and accounts of the massacre. The study concluded that Black Kettle's camp and the site of the defensive creek bed pits, where most of the murders occurred, are actually several hundred yards north of the marker site.[20] Both areas can be seen from the overlook. The Cheyennes and Arapahos insist that the traditional site is the true location of the massacre. I wonder if it really matters.

I spent the night in Eads. That evening I had dinner at the best restaurant in town, the K & M Ranch House. The place was about half full with local folks, mainly farmers and ranchers. The men had powerful arms; they spoke quietly about their day's work, where there had been rain, and how they wished it would rain at their places. They were tired in ways that defy description. Life on Colorado's eastern plains is still hard on body and soul.

Dodge City

Phineas did not ride with me to Sand Creek. He took one look at the dirt road and bid me adieu. His bike had a very expensive custom paint job, which he refused to subject to the indignities of gravel. We agreed to meet at the first town across the state line in Kansas, the village of Tribune. By the time he arrived there, Phineas was hungry. Unfortunately, the only culinary opportunity he found in Tribune was a gas station convenience store. His snack got off to an unpromising start when he went to the vending machine outside the store and found it was sold out of everything but orange soda. He nevertheless purchased a bottle and as soon as he opened it found himself surrounded by a large percentage of Tribune's bee population. Fleeing into the safety of the store, Phineas found his quest for food fulfilled. There, on the counter next to the cash register, was a display case full of large slices of cherry, berry, and apple pies. Phineas asked for a slice of berry pie. As the clerk handed him the gold-crusted prize, Phineas asked if the pie was homemade. "No sir," she declared, "we make it right here." He decided that he would rather not know where in the gas station store they prepared and baked the pies.

As he ate his snack, Phineas notice a couple of local men looking over his bike and, braving the bees, went outside to greet them. "Must be windy riding on that," one of them said. "Yes," Phineas affirmed, it was indeed windy riding a motorcycle in Kansas. The Tribune men expected him to follow with a keen observation of his own and so, pointing to their ramshackle pickup truck, he said, "Must be windy riding in that." "Yep," the second man said, "sure is." Just then, I blew by. I did not see Phineas or his motorcycle, as both were well concealed by the windy pickup truck. Several miles down the road, I pulled into a rest stop and called Phineas. I left a message telling him where I was and that I would wait for him there for a while. Just as I hung up, Phineas rode up the ramp to the rest stop. Thus reunited, we continued east to Scott City.

Scott City is a prosperous-looking agricultural town. Riding along Main Street, I was taken with the beautiful yellow and cornflower blue bisque ornaments on the facade of the high school, which I took to represent corn, the area's major crop. White settlement at Scott City began in the 1880s, but the area was home to human occupants long before then. Just north of town, in Lake Scott State Park, are the ruins of El Cuartelejo (the old barracks or old settlement), the northernmost known Pueblo Indian site. Spanish documents mention El Cuartelejo, but its location remained unknown until the late nineteenth century when homesteader Herbert Steele found some intriguing artifacts beneath the surface of a small mound on his property. Scholars soon identified the site as the place the Spanish called El Cuartelejo.

In the 1660s and 1690s, groups of Pueblo Indians from New Mexico, flee-ing oppressive Spanish rule, settled at El Cuartelejo and lived alongside the area's native Apaches. Both times, Spanish troops tracked the Puebloans to El Cuartelejo and forced them back to New Mexico. Later, as Spain tried to push the boundaries of its New World empire north and east to meet the advancing French empire in North America, El Cuartelejo became a poten-tial military outpost. However, more powerful forces also aimed to control the area; in 1720, when Comanche warriors slaughtered Pedro de Villasur's expedition in Nebraska, the Spanish withdrew from the central plains. By 1730 the Apaches had yielded El Cuartelejo to the Comanches, Utes, and Pawnees. So El Cuartelejo has historical significance belied by its small size for, as archaeologist Robert Hoard has noted, it was "a hub around which revolved the interests of Plains and Pueblo Indians, the Spanish, the French, and early American settlers."[21] El Cuartelejo thus symbolizes the role of the American West as one of the world's great human meeting places.

From Scott City we rode south to Garden City and turned east onto US 50 toward Dodge City. This is cattle country. The feedlots around Garden City generate great wealth and amazing odors. Underscoring the cattle industry's importance, the State of Kansas has placed a scenic overlook beside the high-way there, providing an expansive view of the feed operations.

Motorcyclists riding on the Great Plains must expect to encounter two phenomena: wind and more wind. They should also expect to experience thunderstorms with rain, hail, and tornadoes. And there are bugs, especially grasshoppers, to coat the surfaces of windshields, headlamps, helmets, and exposed human body parts. As we turned onto US 50, I saw not far to the west the roiling cloud of a thunderstorm. Dark, gray-blue and black and out-lined in lurid green, it looked like an enormous deep tissue bruise on the sky. As I watched it in my rearview mirrors, the storm seemed to be chasing us. Soon, wind buffeted us from all points of the compass and made keeping the bikes upright and moving in more or less straight lines a struggle. When the wind blew from the north, we leaned to the left to maintain an upright attitude. As soon as we made that adjustment, the wind would change direc-tions and, coming now from the south, push us into a steeper leftward lean and dangerously close to the centerline. With each cycle we made the proper adjustment just in time to repeat the process in reverse. Adding to the excitement were the sounds—plink, pop, thwap—of sundry Kansas bugs meeting their colorful (predominantly yellow) demise on my windshield, helmet visor, and jacket. Later, I found bug splatter on the back of my helmet and jacket.

After a shower and a nap, Phineas and I decided to take a look at Dodge City, with the major goal of locating a couple of large steaks. As we set out, however, the weather still looked threatening, so we decided to stay off the motorcycles and keep within running distance of the motel. The desk clerk pointed us in the direction of a local steakhouse, and after a walk of a few Kansas blocks we were at its door. It was only about 6:00 p.m., so we did not think much of the fact that the place was three-quarters empty. We soon found out why. A young waitress asked if we would like to order drinks, which we most certainly did. I ordered my usual large iced tea, and Phineas asked what kinds of beer the restaurant served. "Oh, we have about sixty beers," the waitress replied. Phineas brightened and asked for an expensive-sounding Czech pilsner. "Okay," the waitress said, "I'll be right back with you guys's drinks." I hoped the phrase "you guys's" was a local colloquialism; I also hoped it was not. The waitress disappeared for several minutes and returned bearing only my iced tea. Unfortunately, she explained, the bar did not have Phineas's expensive-sounding Czech beer; would he like something else? Slightly disappointed, Phineas asked for another brand, this one sounding Dutch and expensive. After a few minutes the waitress returned, again empty-handed, with the news that the bar did not carry the Dutch-sounding beer either. It turned out that the restaurant's sixty beers included twenty Coors, twenty Budweisers, and twenty Miller Lites. Phineas settled for a large glass of iced tea. The waitress then promised to be right back with "you guys's salads," which were somewhat limp. Fortunately, however, they were small. So, too, were the leathery steaks when they finally arrived. We learned that evening a valuable lesson for eating on the road: a mostly empty steak house in a cattle town does not bode well for a good dinner.

The US Army established Fort Dodge in 1865 to protect traffic on the Santa Fe Trail. Seven years later Dodge City was flourishing 5 miles west of the fort. The town's fortunes grew when the Santa Fe Railway arrived, even as the steel rails heralded the great trail's last days. Dodge City prospered for the next dozen or so years as a cattle town. Each year those skilled industrial

FIGURE 3.4. Dodge City celebrates its cow-town heritage in sculpture aside US Highway 50.

laborers, the cowboys, drove herds of hardy, grass-fed Longhorns from Texas to railheads in Abilene, Caldwell, Wichita, and Dodge City. The 1959 television series *Rawhide*, which propelled actor Clint Eastwood to stardom, celebrated the cattle drive and the cowboy as icons of American individualism, manliness, and heroism. By then, too, another series, *Gunsmoke*, which premiered on radio in 1952 and became a television mainstay from 1955 to 1975, made Dodge City an icon of what Americans believed a western frontier town was like. At the beginning of each episode, the heroic, stone-faced Marshall Dillon strode onto Front Street for a showdown with a gunslinger; with deadly certainty, the gunslinger lost and law and order prevailed.[22]

Modern-day Dodge City works hard to capitalize on this image of the western town. On the outskirts of town a large steel-plate sculpture of ten hard-riding cowboys, lassos at the ready, stands silhouetted against the Kansas sky. In town, a reconstruction of Front Street, as it supposedly appeared in the mid-1870s, is a kind of frontier town amusement park complete with the famous Boot Hill Cemetery (all of the bodies were moved to the more restfully named Maple Grove Cemetery in 1889).[23]

During the era of the cattle drives, roughly 1872–86, Dodge City was a pretty rowdy place when the cowboys came to town. Young men, their pockets filled with pay from the long drives, headed for the town's saloons, gambling halls, and brothels to get drunk, get fleeced, and get laid. Sheriffs Bat Masterson and Wyatt Earp really did patrol the streets, though they were as likely to be seen clearing them of dead animals as depositing dead gun-slingers on them.[24] Gunfights, as represented by Marshall Dillon's weekly showdown, were rare. That does not mean violence was not common, but most of it was personal and drunken and usually involved fisticuffs, not six-shooters. Far more likely in the American West was the organized vio-lence of the strong against the weak, like the massacre at Sand Creek. Other places reminded me of that fact as we rolled west on the Santa Fe Trail.

THE SANTA FE TRAIL

Early the next morning we headed west along the Santa Fe Trail. Nine miles out of Dodge City we pulled off the highway at a small historical park to view some well-preserved trail ruts, imprints left in the plains sod by the passage of thousands of wagon wheels. For more than half a century the Santa Fe Trail was the principal route to the Southwest. In 1821 a Missouri trader, William Becknell, pioneered the trail from his hometown of Franklin, Missouri, to the New Mexican capital. Becknell timed his adventure well. Prior to 1821, American traders were not welcome in Spanish New Mexico. However, the Mexican Revolution that year ended Spain's rule, and the new government welcomed trade with the northern neighbor. From Franklin the trail followed the Missouri River to Independence, which soon displaced Franklin as the trail's jumping-off point. At Independence the trail struck west and south across Kansas until it reached the Arkansas River at the northern apex of the river's Great Bend. From there the trail generally followed the river to the Dodge City area, though many travelers favored a shortcut from Larned.[25]

At three fords of the Arkansas River, one east of Dodge City and two to the west, the Santa Fe Trail divided into two branches, the Mountain Route and the Cimarron Cutoff, or the Desert Route, which struck southwest across the Oklahoma panhandle and northeastern New Mexico. The Cimarron Cutoff was several days faster than the Mountain Route, but it was also risk-ier because water could be in short supply. Nevertheless, by the late 1830s most travelers were taking the Cimarron Cutoff. Santa Fe trader Josiah Gregg, who traveled the trail in the 1830s, wrote in his memoir that "owing to

FIGURE 3.5. Santa Fe Trail ruts are still visible in the grassland just west of Dodge City.

continuous rains" in 1834, "a plain trail was then cut in the softened turf," and from then on the Cimarron Cutoff was "the regular route of the caravans."[26] Phineas and I stayed on US 50, the Mountain Route, which continued along the Arkansas River to La Junta, Colorado, where it left the river and turned southwest toward Trinidad, Colorado.

Pushing west in mild winds, we crossed back into Colorado and passed through the town of Holly. It was a weekday morning, but Holly was strangely quiet, even for a small town of 1,000, with no traffic on the streets or people on the sidewalks. A tornado had struck Holly a few weeks before, killing 2 people. Much of the damage had been cleaned up, but blue tarps still covered many roofs and the shattered remnants of once stately elms and cottonwoods, now stripped of their limbs, stood as mute evidence of the storm's fury. A sign at a church said "We're okay; we're Holly," but despite that resolute and optimistic note, the sadness seemed palpable as we rode through.

Ten miles west of Holly, at the town of Granada (pronounced Gran-nay-duh), is a place called Amache, another of the West's sad places where the powerful imposed their will upon the weak. There, during World War II, the US government—the American people—in the name of national security imprisoned 10,000 American citizens and their non-citizen relatives for no other reason than the belief that their Japanese ancestry made them inherently a threat to the nation.

Japan's attack on Pearl Harbor prompted an understandable sense of rage among Americans. It also provoked a wave of racist hysteria directed against Americans of Japanese ancestry and their non-citizen kin (collectively called the Nikkei). The West Coast states had the largest concentration of Asians in the United States, including Japanese. Within days of Pearl Harbor, a cry went up to punish, confine, and relocate these suspect "aliens." Two months after the attack, President Franklin D. Roosevelt signed Executive Order 9066 authorizing the military to exclude anyone from designated military areas. Roosevelt's order did not specify the West Coast Japanese, but they were the people it was targeting. The military quickly ordered all persons of Japanese ancestry to leave the West Coast. They had a brief period during which they could leave voluntarily, and some did, but in March 1942 the War Relocation Authority ordered those who had not departed to report to relocation centers for assignment and transport to what were called relocation camps or internment camps. They could take with them only what they could carry. From the relocation centers, trains transported them to the camps. There were ten camps in all, eight of them in western states. Amache, named for the daughter of a Cheyenne chief killed at Sand Creek, was one of them.[27]

The people and governments of the interior West did not want or welcome the internees. The governor of Wyoming warned that if any came to his state, "there would be Japs hanging from every pine tree." Idaho's governor complained that the Japanese "live like rats, breed like rats, and act like rats. We don't want them becoming permanently located in our state." Utah's governor did not want Japanese settlers in the Mormon Kingdom either but suggested that he would accept some as forced laborers if the federal government promised to remove them at the war's end. In Colorado, the *Denver Post* joined the frenzy of venomous rhetoric, asserting that "every Jap in this country is either an actual or potential enemy" and screaming "TO HELL WITH THE JAPS! KEEP COLORADO AMERICAN!"[28]

Colorado's governor, Ralph Carr, stood virtually alone against the hatred. When he read Executive Order 9066, Carr exclaimed, "Now that's wrong!"[29] Carr saw to it that Colorado received the unwilling migrants, if not with open arms, at least without overt acts of hostility. He did so because it was the right thing to do, because he believed the state and its citizens had a duty to go along with federal measures during wartime, and because he feared what might happen to American prisoners of the Japanese. In Durango in early 1942, Carr faced down an angry audience, telling them, "Let's have no more loose talk. Let's have no more threats of what we would like to do to the Japs. For every idle threat that gets publicity, a hundred Americans may suffer. For God's sake, shut up!"[30] Carr's principled stand likely damaged his political career. He chose not to run for reelection in 1942 and instead challenged Colorado's most popular Democrat, Edwin Johnson, for the US Senate. He lost that election and never held public office again. Many years later, Colorado's Japanese community erected a memorial to Carr in the garden of downtown Denver's Sakura Square.

Whatever price Ralph Carr paid, it paled in comparison to Amache's prisoners, who lost their homes, their livelihoods, and their dignity. The scene that greeted them in southeastern Colorado must have been shocking and depressing. One internee recalled, "It was bleak, very, very bleak. No trees. No grass, nothing. Just a bare hill with a bunch of barracks on it and lots of sagebrush and other Japanese."[31]

Despite the indignities and hardships, the Nikkei set to work building a community at Amache. They set up schools, recreation centers, and churches; they planted gardens and published a newspaper. When diminished hysteria permitted and military manpower needs demanded it, their sons enlisted or submitted to the draft in large numbers to fight for the country that treated them as pariahs and imprisoned them. The 14,000 men who served in the 442nd Regimental Combat Team earned 9,486 Purple Hearts, twenty-one Medals of Honor, and eight Presidential Unit Citations, making them one of the most highly decorated units in the history of American warfare.[32]

The last of the internees left Amache in October 1945. Forty-three years later the federal government apologized. Today, only the concrete foundations of the barracks and other buildings remain, and the native grasses and cacti are gradually reclaiming them. Nature seems to be trying to cover and heal an ugly scar on the land and on history. However, students and teachers at the nearby Granada High School have taken up the task of preserving the site.

Back on US 50 we headed toward the town of Lamar, located just west of the confluence of Sand Creek and the Arkansas River in the Big Timbers area where Fort Lyon once stood. As we approached the town I saw to my left a

FIGURE 3.6. Camp Amache, Colorado. One internee described the scene as "bleak, very bleak."

large bird flying perhaps 100 feet away and about that high. Soon, the bird flew closer and lower until it was almost overhead and only about 30 feet up. I could see that it was an American Bald Eagle, and it flew along with me for about a quarter of a mile. Its company thrilled me.

In Lamar we stopped at the town's visitor center, which also serves as a local history museum. I noticed two gentlemen deeply engrossed in a game of checkers. They appeared to belong there but took no notice of Phineas and me. Instead, a very nice lady greeted us and offered to show us around the exhibits commemorating the Santa Fe Trail, the Sand Creek Massacre, and Amache. After the brief tour we went outside to inspect a well-preserved Atchison, Topeka, and Santa Fe Railway steam engine and the *Madonna of the Trail*, a statue honoring women who traveled west on the trail. The statue depicts a white pioneer woman, bonneted and wearing a long dress and clod-crushing boots, walking over stones and prickly pear cactus. In one arm she cradles a baby and in the other she carries a flintlock rifle. Clinging to her skirt is a young boy. Where the more modern *Kindred Spirits* at Eads pays tribute to all women in the history of the American West, *Madonna of the Trail* is as much a monument to the process of white American expansion westward as a celebration of women as agents of that expansion and, as such, is also a celebration of American conquest and empire building.

There are actually twelve identical *Madonna of the Trail* statues scattered across the country from Baltimore, Maryland, to Upland, California. They were a joint project of the Daughters of the American Revolution (DAR) and the National Old Trails Ocean-to-Ocean Highway Association. Both groups aimed to preserve and mark the great trails to celebrate American history. The DAR began marking the Santa Fe Trail in 1906, placing small granite markers at important trail sites. Eventually, the markers spanned the entire 900 miles of the trail from Franklin, Missouri, to Santa Fe; and the *Madonna of the Trail* project supplemented it. Dedication ceremonies for ten of the monuments took place in 1928 and 1929. A little-known Missouri politician, Harry S. Truman, spoke at the ceremonies in Lamar.[33]

About 45 miles west of Lamar we took a secondary road to the Bent's Old Fort National Historic Site, one of the most important places in the history of the nineteenth-century American West. Missourians Charles and William Bent entered the Santa Fe Trail trade during the 1820s and soon became major figures not only in the commerce of the plains but also in the region's complex political and military affairs. In 1830 the Bents and their partner, Ceran St. Vrain, built a small stockade on Fountain Creek, at present-day Pueblo, Colorado, with the intention of establishing a presence along the Trappers Trail and near the Santa Fe Trail. William Bent supervised the stockade and began to cultivate friendly relations with the Cheyenne Indians. A Cheyenne chief, Yellow Wolf, soon suggested to Bent that he move to a spot more favorable for trading with the Plains Indians, about 100 miles down the Arkansas. Bent chose a spot on the riverbank about 10 miles northeast of present-day La Junta. The new outpost was an imposing fortress with thick adobe walls standing 14 feet high, enclosing a compound of more than 15,000 square feet. Watchtowers with small artillery pieces anchored two corners. Inside were a store, blacksmith and carpenter shops, warehouses, a communal dining room, laborers' quarters, and private quarters for Bent, St. Vrain, and visiting dignitaries. Outside the walls were a corral and stables for the livestock. To build his fortress, Bent recruited laborers from New Mexico, which was still Mexican territory. This may be the first recorded case of an American employer importing undocumented workers from Mexico.[34]

FIGURE 3.7. *Madonna of the Trail*, Lamar, Colorado.

FIGURE 3.8. Santa Fe Trail sojourner Susan Shelby Magoffin likened Bent's Fort to an ancient castle.

When Bent's Fort opened in 1833, it immediately became the most import-ant American outpost in the Southwest, a rest stop for weary travelers on the Santa Fe Trail, a rendezvous for mountain men, a venue for trade with Indians, and, eventually, a military staging point for the invasion of New Mexico. Travelers approaching the fort likened it to a castle. "At a distance," an American soldier noted in 1846, "it presents a handsome appearance, being castle-like with towers at its angles . . . the design . . . answering all pur-poses of protection, defense, and as a residence." Susan Shelby Magoffin, the eighteen-year-old wife of a prominent trader, also visited Bent's Fort in 1846 and wrote in her journal that it "exactly fills my idea of an ancient castle."[35]

The day had turned hot when we arrived at Bent's Fort. A large bull was doing sleepy sentry duty under a tree near the entry gate. Once inside the fort, we found the interior rooms pleasantly cool. The place seemed almost abandoned—just me, Phineas, the National Park Service staff members dressed in period clothing, and, in the store, two young cats napping on a buffalo robe. Such quiet was contrary to the spirit of the fort, which had bus-tled with activity year-round. Lewis H. Garrard, who visited in 1846, found "a mélange of traders and employers, government officers and subordinates, Indians, Frenchmen, and hunters."[36]

Garrard and Magoffin visited Bent's Fort at an important moment, the summer of 1846, and witnessed the gathering of General Stephen Watts Kearny's Army of the West for the invasion of New Mexico. Kearny's initial conquest of Mexico's northeastern province was virtually bloodless. However, the Bent family and the people of the Taos Pueblo later paid a terrible price for it. Before he left New Mexico to participate in the invasion of California, General Kearny appointed Charles Bent as territorial governor. Bent was already a major political and business figure there because of the wealth he commanded from the Santa Fe Trail trade and as a major land grant holder. In January 1847, resentful New Mexicans and Pueblo Indians in the Taos area rebelled and killed Bent and several other Americans. In response, the army slaughtered scores of women, children, and some rebel men, holed up in the pueblo's San Geronimo church. The old adobe church's battered bell tower is still standing, and birds make their homes in holes left by the Americans' rifle and artillery fire.[37]

William Bent operated his fort until 1849, but by then friction with Comanche and Arapaho Indians and disease among the Cheyennes had all but ruined the buffalo trade. Bent abandoned the fort for a smaller post downstream at the Big Timbers of the Arkansas and spent his remaining years trying to bridge the growing, menacing gap between the Indians and the rapidly growing white presence. Bent's son, George, was living with the Cheyennes and Arapahos at Sand Creek when Chivington's force carried out its murderous attack in 1864.[38]

By the time travelers on the Santa Fe Trail reached Bent's Fort, they could see in the distance the Rocky Mountains, especially the twin Spanish Peaks, which dominate the mountain skyline of southeastern Colorado. To the Indians they were *Wahatoya*, the Breasts of the Earth. In his memoir of his 1846 adventure on the Santa Fe Trail, *Wah-to-yah and the Taos Trail*, Garrard recalled viewing the peaks from the fort, "apparently fifteen miles distant—in reality one hundred and twenty." He could also see the "faint outline" of Pike's Peak far to the north. Like the Santa Fe Trail travelers of old, Phineas and I kept the Spanish Peaks on our right shoulders all the way to Trinidad.[39]

This part of southeastern Colorado is valuable ranchland and worth fighting over, and signs dotting the highway indicated that landowners in this normally placid, conservative area were hopping mad. The US Army wanted to take over more than 400,000 acres to expand its Piñon Canyon Maneuver Site along the Purgatoire River. The plan was a legacy of the war in Iraq, as the army wanted more territory for practicing tank warfare. Opposition to the plan proved strong enough to get the army to back away from its original plan in favor of a scheme to acquire only 100,000 acres from landowners willing to sell or lease voluntarily. That concession did not placate opponents, who remained dead-set against any expansion of the maneuver site. Plus, the army could find no landowners willing to sell or lease their property. In May 2009 the army appeared to throw in the towel. While not explicitly giving up on its plan to expand the Piñon Canyon site, it shifted money for land acquisitions to other uses, a decision reiterated in 2011.[40]

We rolled into Trinidad mid-afternoon and checked into a motel. Trinidad did not exist as a town when Susan Magoffin passed through the area in 1846. However, a large grove of cottonwoods on the banks of the Purgatoire River in what is now downtown Trinidad provided a welcome campsite for Santa Fe Trail travelers as they prepared for the arduous trek over Raton Pass. Fisher's Peak, the distinctive flattop mountain that looms over Trinidad, did not yet bear that name. Magoffin's husband called it "wagon mound" because to him it resembled another Wagon Mound far down the trail in New Mexico. Lewis Garrard called the mountain "Raton Peak."[41]

Permanent settlement began in Trinidad in 1862 when Felipe Baca and a group of families from northern New Mexico arrived to farm and raise sheep. Baca was a major business and political figure in southern Colorado until his death in 1874. Trinidad's economic fortunes grew rapidly in the late nineteenth century when it became the center of southern Colorado's Kingdom of Coal. Coal mines in the area supplied fuel for railroads, smelters, and blast furnaces in Colorado and elsewhere. One of the country's wealthiest and most powerful families, the Rockefellers, owned the largest coal company, the Colorado Fuel and Iron Company. The mines required a large workforce and attracted laborers by the thousands from eastern and southern Europe and Mexico.[42]

After we unpacked the bikes, I told Phineas that I wanted to make a short side-trip. He had experienced all the history he could take for one day and opted for a nap. I got back on Old Blue and headed north on Interstate 25 about 13 miles to Ludlow, yet another place in Colorado where the powerful imposed their will upon the weak. On the morning of April 20, 1914, a unit of the Colorado National Guard opened fire on a tent colony of striking coal miners and their families. The soldiers raked the camp with machine gun fire and by the end of the day burned it to the ground. Nineteen men, women, and children died in the inferno; eleven of them suffocated in a shelter pit dug into the ground below a tent. Elvira Valdez was only three months old. A monument, erected by the United Mine Workers in 1915, stands over this death pit. The names of the dead—Tikas, Fyler, Bartolotti, Costa, Rubino, Valdez, Petrucci, Snyder, Pedregone—are like a roster of the nations that sent their excess population to work, and sometimes to die, in America's mines and mills. The miners went on strike in September 1913, demanding that the coal companies recognize their union, pay better wages, implement better safety practices, and allow more economic and social freedom in company-owned residential camps. The Ludlow Massacre was the State of Colorado's and the coal industry's answer to them.[43]

Phineas and I hit the road early for our final day on the Santa Fe Trail. Within a half hour we had ridden over Raton Pass into New Mexico. We enjoyed the curves on the pass after two days on the arrow-straight roads of the Great Plains. Nineteenth-century travelers in wagons, on horseback, or on foot did not have such an enjoyable time on the pass. Susan Magoffin's crossing in 1846 took five days. She walked much of the way because wagon travel was both uncomfortable and dangerous on the rocky trail. At times the teamsters had to unhitch mules and oxen and manhandle the wagons over especially dangerous stretches rather than risk losing both livestock and rolling stock to an accident.[44]

Travel over Raton Pass improved dramatically in 1865 when Richens Lacy "Uncle Dick" Wootton, a well-known buffalo hunter, rancher, teamster, and storekeeper in Colorado, built a toll road over it. Interstate 25 roughly parallels the route of "Uncle Dick's" road. Wootton earned a comfortable living from his toll road, exempting from his fees only Indians and posses chasing horse and cattle thieves. Wootton sold his right-of-way to the Santa Fe Railway in 1878 when, he said, "I got out of the way of the locomotive." By 1880 the railroad was approaching Santa Fe, bringing to its end the story of the great trail.[45]

Coming off the pass, we rolled past the city of Raton and out into the dry plains of northeastern New Mexico. The trail in this area stayed close to the foothills, more or less along the route of US Highway 64 southwest from Raton. Several miles down the road I turned off to visit the long-abandoned coal town of Dawson. The road to Dawson is marked by a very small, hard-to-spot sign immediately north of a low bridge. If you reach the railroad tracks, you have gone too far. The road is very narrow and the old pavement

FIGURE 3.9. The Ludlow Monument near Trinidad, Colorado.

FIGURE 3.10. Cemetery at Dawson, New Mexico. Identical crosses mark the graves of the victims of the 1913 and 1923 coalmine explosions there.

is rapidly giving way to gravel and grass. Dawson was the site of two of the worst industrial catastrophes in American history. In October 1913 an explosion of gas and dust in the Phelps Dodge Company's Stag Cañon coalmine killed 263 miners. A decade later another 120 miners died in another explosion. The Dawson disasters underscored the western coal miners' very real grievances. After the 1913 blast, striking Colorado miners hurried over Raton Pass to try to help in the rescue and recovery effort. The mine plant and the camp disappeared long ago, but you still can visit the cemetery maintained by descendants of those buried there. The victims of the 1913 and 1923 disasters are buried under identical steel crosses. Many of the dead are buried in ethnic clusters; the Greeks, Italians, Poles, and other ethnic groups laid to rest among their countrymen, making the cemetery at Dawson another monument to the great human meeting place that is the American West.[46]

Phineas did not ride to Dawson with me, refusing again to expose his bike's paint to the indignities of gravel. We agreed to meet a short distance down the road, at the town of Cimarron. Cimarron in the 1870s was the archetype of a Wild West town. There used to be a historical marker near the junction of US 64 and New Mexico 58, quoting a *Las Vegas* [New Mexico] *Gazette* report from the late 1870s: "Everything is quiet in Cimarron. Nobody has been killed in three days."[47] I was disappointed to find that the sign had been replaced with one less colorful. The *Las Vegas Gazette* report referred to something more complex than stereotypical cow-town violence. Instead, it was about one of the American West's most complex, protracted, and violent conflicts between the powerful and the weak: the Colfax County War.

The origins of Cimarron and the Colfax County War lay in an enormous Mexican land grant given in 1841 to Guadalupe Miranda and an associate of the Bents, Charles Beaubien. Mexican law at the time limited land grants to 92,000 acres, but the territory encompassed by the Beaubien-Miranda Grant, when finally surveyed in the 1870s, turned out to be 1.7 million acres. When the United States seized New Mexico in the 1840s, it agreed to recognize the legitimacy of Mexican land titles. That, however, left undecided the question of whether the original grant was legitimate under Mexican and US law.[48]

Beaubien entrusted management of the grant to his son-in-law, Lucien Bonaparte Maxwell, who acquired all of the grant's shares after Beaubien's death in 1864. Maxwell established Cimarron as the headquarters of his landed empire and set about developing it. He started his own ranch and sold land to friends, including Kit Carson and John Dawson. The Stag Cañon coalmine was on what had been Dawson's ranch. Cimarron quickly became a busy rest stop and supply center on the Santa Fe Trail, accounting for the deep trail swale just north of town. Maxwell earned a reputation for generosity to friends and guests, especially if they were white. However, he was also known for his brutal treatment of his Mexican employees.[49] By the late 1860s prospectors had found gold nearby, and soon miners and settlers rushed in.

In 1869 Maxwell demanded an official survey but dropped the effort when the secretary of the interior ruled that the grant could encompass only 97,000 acres and any excess should be open to settlement. That left in doubt not only the grant's boundaries but also the validity of any sales or leases, to say nothing of the rights of the large number of squatters living and working on Maxwell's claim. In 1870 Maxwell decided to cash in and sold the land grant to a group of Coloradans who, in turn, sold it to European investors. Even at this late date, three decades after the original grant, no one knew exactly what they had purchased.[50]

FIGURE 3.II. The St. James Hotel in Cimarron, New Mexico, was the scene of violent episodes during the Colfax County War.

Clearly, the Maxwell Land Grant Company's foreign owners inherited a legal and political quagmire. The company's local representatives, who included a gang of New Mexico politicians and businessmen known as the Santa Fe Ring, were less tolerant of the squatters than Maxwell had been. With the Santa Fe Ring's backing, the company began efforts to evict the squatters, but many of them refused to budge. Tensions erupted into violence with the September 1875 murder of Franklin Tolby, a leader of the opposition to the company and the Santa Fe Ring. Settlers retaliated by lynching Cimarron's sheriff, whom they blamed for Tolby's death. For the next several years Cimarron and its environs was the scene of tit-for-tat murder, arson, vandalism, and cattle theft. Finally, in 1887 the US Supreme Court broke the back of the resistance by confirming the land grant's legitimacy. With no hope of support from either the territorial or federal government, squatters had little choice but to buy or lease land at whatever price the company dictated, or they just left. The company and its successors dominated the area until the 1960s. Oklahoma oilman Waite Phillips purchased 300,000 acres of the grant in 1922 and in succeeding years donated almost half of it, his Philmont Ranch, to the Boy Scouts of America. In Cimarron today,

FIGURE 3.12. Wagon Mound, New Mexico.

the town's most prominent building, the St. James Hotel, built in 1872 and witness to many scenes of the Colfax County War, still entertains visitors.[51]

When we left Cimarron, we also left the Mountain Branch of the Santa Fe Trail. We rode to the town of Springer, where we got back onto I-25 and joined the last leg of the Cimarron Cutoff. From the Springer interchange we could see very clearly, 25 miles away, one of the trail's most famous landmarks, Wagon Mound. It is easy to conjure up in the mind's eye this formation's resemblance to a Conestoga wagon with its canvas or animal hide cover, bench seat, and (with a little more imagination) a line of oxen or mules in front. When Wagon Mound came into view, travelers on the Mountain and Cimarron Cutoff branches knew the trail soon would merge into a single route for the final pull to Santa Fe.

The Mountain Branch and the Cimarron Cutoff meet near Fort Union and the town of Watrous. The army opened Fort Union in 1851 as a supply depot and garrison to protect the Santa Fe Trail against raids by Apache and Ute Indians. The red adobe ruins visible today at the Fort Union National Monument, 8 miles west of Watrous, are those of the third version of the fort built there.[52]

The small town of Watrous is another landmark of the convergence of the Mountain Branch and the Cimarron Cutoff. This was a favorite gathering place of Indians, hunters, and sheepherders long before Samuel Watrous

FIGURE 3.13. Fort Union, New Mexico, guarded the area where the Santa Fe Trail's Mountain Branch and Cimarron Cutoff merged, near Wagon Mound.

settled there. The Spanish called it La Junta de los Rios because two small rivers, the Mora and the Sapello, meet there. When the Santa Fe Trail opened, La Junta de los Rios became an important gathering and trading location, which is why Samuel Watrous chose the spot to open a store in 1849. Watrous's business eventually expanded into ranching and freighting. When the Santa Fe Railway arrived in the area, the company laid out a new town site and named it Watrous, in part to honor Samuel Watrous and in part to avoid confusion with another town on the line, La Junta, Colorado.[53] A grove of giant old cottonwood trees Watrous planted shields the village from the sight and noise of the interstate highway. When I pass through this part of New Mexico, I like to leave the interstate and drive through Watrous because I often see eagles in Samuel Watrous's trees.

In the 1860s Samuel Watrous developed a friendship with an ascetic hermit named Giovanni Agostini, a well-educated and well-traveled Italian émigré who had taken up residence on a nearby mountain now named Hermit's Peak. It is said that Watrous convinced Agostini to light a fire every three days to signal that he was well. When the hermit eventually failed to light the signal, Watrous found that he had disappeared. Agostini had set out on a trek south and in 1869 died a murder victim in the mountains near Las Cruces.[54]

Hermit's Peak also overlooks the town of Las Vegas, which dates to 1835 when the first Mexican settlers arrived. Santa Fe Trail diarist Josiah Gregg passed through Las Vegas in its first years and "found a large flock of sheep grazing upon the adjacent plain; while a little hovel at the foot of a cliff showed it to be a *rancho*." Gregg and his companions bought from the ranchero "a treat of goat's milk, with some dirty ewe's 'curdle cheese' to supply the place of bread." A decade or so later, Susan Magoffin found a well-established town, complete with "houses, pig sties, corn cribs, &c." Her dinner there, which included blue corn tortillas served with "chilly" verde, meat, and onions, was not to her liking.[55] Shortly before Magoffin passed through Las Vegas, General Kearny and his invading army made a dramatic visit there. Las Vegas was the first town of any size Kearny encountered in New Mexico, and he could not resist making a conqueror's declaration. Climbing to the roof of a building overlooking the plaza, the general told the townfolk that he had come to take possession of New Mexico for the United States and informed them that "henceforth, I absolve you of all allegiance to the Mexican government."[56] Thus, New Mexico began to learn that it no longer belonged to Mexico.

Just west of Las Vegas, I-25 passes through a large rock formation, a geological gateway between the New Mexico plains and the Sangre de Cristo Mountains. As it passes through this gateway the highway begins a steady 65-mile climb to Santa Fe. About 25 miles southeast of Santa Fe the road passes the Pecos National Historical Park, which includes the ruins of the ancient Pecos pueblo, an eighteenth-century Spanish mission, and the Glorieta battlefield.

Settlement at Pecos dates to about 800 CE, when pre-Puebloan people lived there. The first Puebloans arrived around 1100, and by the mid-fifteenth century they had constructed a five-story stone and adobe fortress housing a population of more than 2,000. They could field an army of 500 warriors, making the pueblo a formidable military and political presence. At its height, it was the most powerful of the pueblos. With its strategic position on the high ground between the other pueblos of the Rio Grande Valley and the Plains Indians tribes to the east, Pecos became a wealthy trading center.[57]

The arrival of the Spanish began a long decline for Pecos and all the other Puebloan societies. The Puebloans' first encounter with the Europeans occurred in 1541, when Francisco Vasquez de Coronado led an expedition north in search of the fabled wealth of Cibola. When Cibola turned out to be a cluster of pueblos near present-day Gallup, New Mexico, Coronado pushed on to Cicuye, the original name of Pecos. The Cicuyans welcomed the strange visitors but soon, in hopes of getting rid of them, sent them on a wild goose chase. A Plains Indian held captive there told Coronado of a fabulously wealthy kingdom, Quivira, far to the east. With the Indian as his guide, Coronado led his band into central Kansas in search of Quivira's gold. All he found were a few plains villages.[58]

Coronado retreated to Mexico, but in the late sixteenth century the Spanish returned to the Rio Grande Valley and the Sangre de Cristos with conquering armies and bands of priests to subjugate, exploit, and Christianize the Puebloans. After a century of abusive rule, in 1680 the pueblos rebelled and drove the Spanish out of New Mexico. Their freedom was short-lived, however, and in 1693 Spain re-conquered the province. The people of Picuris, where the rebellion began, fled to Kansas, where they settled briefly at El Cuartelejo.[59]

Spanish rule after the *reconquista* was more moderate than before the rebellion but still ultimately devastating to Pecos. The population found itself

FIGURE 3.14. The ruins of Our Lady of the Angels of Porciúncula loom over a restored kiva at Pecos, symbolizing the imposition of Spanish political and cultural authority over Puebloan society.

divided between traditionalists and those who cast their lot with the Spanish rulers. In addition, disease, Comanche raids, and drought battered the pueblo in the last decades of the eighteenth century. Finally, in 1838 the last residents abandoned Pecos and joined the Jemez Pueblo 80 miles to the west.[60] The red adobe ruin of the eighteenth-century Spanish mission at Pecos is one of the most recognizable artifacts of Spanish rule in New Mexico.

The Pecos National Historical Park also includes important sites of the Battle of Glorieta Pass. In 1861 and 1862 a Confederate force, composed largely of Texas volunteers, invaded New Mexico as part of a plan to sever much of the West from the Union. From New Mexico, the rebel army intended to invade Colorado and fatten the Confederacy's treasury with that territory's gold. The plan seemed to go well at first, and the Confederate force met little effective resistance as it swept north up the Rio Grande Valley to Santa Fe. During late February and early March 1862, a force of 950 Colorado volunteers marched from Denver to Fort Union, covering the nearly 400 miles in only 13 days. Among the Colorado regiment's officers was Major John

Chivington who, 2½ years later, disgraced himself as the butcher of Sand Creek. In a 4-day battle around Glorieta Pass (March 25–28, 1862) the Union force—composed largely of the Coloradans—caught the Confederate Army by surprise, inflicted heavy casualties, and sent the survivors retreating back to Texas. The Civil War in the West all but ended then and there.[61]

Phineas and I reached Santa Fe in the early afternoon. We found a convenient parking spot, walked to the plaza, and found the last of the Daughters of the American Revolution's trail markers, this one marking "the end of the Santa Fe Trail." Across the plaza, on the porch of the Palace of the Governors, artisans from nearby pueblos and from as far away as the Navajo Reservation sell silver and turquoise jewelry, pottery, and other artworks. For centuries the palace was the seat of government in New Mexico. Now, in addition to hosting the daily Indian market, it is a museum documenting its own, Santa Fe's, and New Mexico's history. One block east of the plaza is the Cathedral Basilica of Saint Francis. Built between 1869 and 1895, the cathedral's Romanesque architecture contrasts sharply with the town's dominant pueblo and Hispanic styles and represents the contempt of its builder, Archbishop Jean Baptiste Lamy, for New Mexico's native and Hispanic cultures. Two blocks west and one block north of the palace is the Georgia O'Keeffe Museum, with its collection of that great twentieth-century artist's works.

Santa Fe dates to 1610 when Spain's royal governor, Pedro de Peralta, built a new colonial capital there. Unlike the two previous capitals, San Juan and San Gabriel, located at the confluence of the Rio Grande and the Chama River near modern Española, the new site had no local population of bothersome Pueblo Indians. Located on a plateau overlooking the Rio Grande Valley to the west and backed up by the Sangre de Cristo Mountains, Santa Fe also offered a better strategic position for the small Spanish ruling elite. With the exception of thirteen years following the Pueblo Rebellion (1680–93), Santa Fe has been the seat of provincial, territorial, and state government in New Mexico and is the oldest capital in North America. From Santa Fe, Spanish rulers sent soldiers and missionaries to search for mineral wealth, exact tribute from the pueblos, and convert them to Christianity.[62]

Throughout the eighteenth and early nineteenth centuries, New Mexico's Spanish rulers tried to guard against encroachments from the north, but when Mexico broke free of Spain in 1821, the embargo on American trade ended. Over the next twenty-five years American traders, such as the

Magoffin brothers and the Bents, became financially and politically powerful players in New Mexico. As General Kearny's army approached Santa Fe in August 1846, those Americans persuaded Governor Manuel Armijo to yield the capital and the territory without a fight.[63]

By the 1840s Santa Fe had a population of about 2,000 but was not much of a town in American eyes. Entering the town for the first time, Josiah Gregg mistook its small adobe houses for "brick kilns scattered in every direction."[64] Soon after the American conquest, Santa Fe's new rulers added their own Americanizing architectural flourishes, crowning adobe walls with fired clay bricks and trimming doors and windows with neoclassic-style moldings in what came to be called the Territorial Style. Other forces also soon challenged pueblo and Hispanic culture and style.

Father Jean Baptiste Lamy arrived in New Mexico in 1851. Born and educated in France, Lamy came to the United States in 1839 and served in Ohio and Kentucky until the church sent him west to head the new Vicariate of New Mexico. In Santa Fe and Taos, local priests refused to acknowledge Lamy's authority until their former leader, the Bishop of Durango, instructed them to do so, and some continued to defy him even then. This set the stage for conflict between Lamy and the New Mexican priests. To Lamy, the New Mexican priests were too worldly, too Hispanic, and too independent. To counter them, the bishop imported new priests from Europe to displace the locals and even resorted to excommunicating one especially recalcitrant Taos cleric. For the remainder of his life that priest, Father Antonio José Martinez, celebrated mass and performed marriages, baptisms, and other sacraments for the many Taoseños who remained loyal to him. Lamy also battled another powerful local group, the Brotherhood of Our Father Jesus, or the Penitentes. Priests were spread thin in the Spanish and Mexican eras, and the Penitentes, an organization of deeply religious laymen, substituted for them in many communities. Lamy's efforts to disband the Penitentes succeeded only in driving them underground without breaking their popularity and influence.[65]

The Catholic Church rewarded Lamy's efforts in 1875 by elevating him to the rank of archbishop. In addition, his battle with the local priests inspired Willa Cather's 1927 novel, *Death Comes for the Archbishop*. But Lamy never fully succeeded in enforcing his will on the New Mexican priests, the Penitentes, or the Catholic population—one of the few instances in the history of the American West where the seemingly powerless at least held their own

FIGURE 3.15. Cathedral Basilica of Saint Francis of Assisi, Santa Fe. Buildings in the foreground represent the Puebloan and Hispanic influences in the town's architecture and culture.

against the institutionally powerful. Lamy did, however, manage to leave a permanent moral and aesthetic thumb in the eye of indigenous Hispanic New Mexican Catholicism with the construction of his cathedral in Santa Fe. An old adobe church had occupied the site east of the plaza since 1714. Instead of demolishing it, Lamy built the new cathedral around and over it, then had it dismantled and carried out the new building's door.[66]

The cathedral's Romanesque architecture may have supplanted the Hispanic style on the Santa Fe plaza, but the latter survives in nearby towns such as Chimayo and Las Trampas, where old adobe mission churches still stand and are decorated with small traditional wooden statues of saints (*santos*), religious paintings (*retablos*), and sculptures (*bustos*). Pilgrims visiting the Santuario de Chimayo often come to collect samples of soil from a hole in the stone floor in a room next to the sanctuary. The soil is said to have healing powers, and an adjoining room is filled with the discarded crutches and

FIGURE 3.16. San Jose de Garcia, Las Trampas, New Mexico.

wheelchairs of those who claim to have been healed by its touch. In nearby Las Trampas the mid-eighteenth-century church, San Jose de Garcia, is furnished with an old, worn, hand-carved altar and benches and is decorated with traditional retablos and bustos. The church does not have the glorious stained glass windows or other accoutrements of Lamy's cathedral, but it is the much-loved heart of this small community, which explains why it survived the archbishop's assaults against the Hispanic culture and the style of Catholicism it represents.

Except for the cathedral, the area around Santa Fe's plaza retains its mixture of traditional Pueblo, Hispanic, and Territorial styles. Since the 1920s, zoning laws have aimed to enforce a southwestern flavor in homes and commercial buildings (a style sometimes dismissed as "Santa Fake").[67] This traditionalism is exemplified in the state capitol building, the design of which is based on the Zia Indian sun symbol—a central ring with four oblong entry portals, one at each compass cardinal point. The building's doors and windows are trimmed in the Territorial Style.

Santa Fe's transformation from a market town to a tourist destination began when the railroad arrived in 1880. In addition to tourists, Santa Fe, along with Taos and other northern New Mexico towns, also began to attract artists and writers, drawn by the dramatic landscape and the romance of the West, including the Indian and Hispanic cultures. In the decades before World War II, the Santa Fe Railway employed a corps of artists to paint landscapes and scenes of the Pueblo and Hispanic cultures to decorate its ticket offices, calendars, and other advertising.[68]

Georgia O'Keeffe began visiting New Mexico in the 1920s and moved there in 1946, eventually settling on her Ghost Ranch home about 50 miles north of Santa Fe and in a second home in the nearby village of Abiquiu. O'Keeffe called New Mexico "her land" and Santa Fe and its environs "the Faraway." Her paintings of the desert, mesas, and sky capture the area's stark contrasts and subtle hues, perhaps as no other artist has. However, O'Keeffe was not especially interested in the people of New Mexico, and her art rarely includes a human presence. When she moved to Abiquiu, where all the villagers spoke Spanish, she refused to learn her neighbors' language.[69]

Many other white artists did take an interest in New Mexico's Pueblo and Hispanic cultures. In Taos, Mabel Dodge Luhan, an expatriate New York socialite and writer, presided over a colony of writers and artists who found inspiration in New Mexico's ethnic heritage. One of them was Joseph Henry Sharp, whose extraordinary painting *Sunset Dance, Ceremony to the Evening Sun* (1924) represents the crosscurrents in Pueblo culture in the early twentieth century. The setting is the Taos Pueblo, itself set against a background of mountains and sky. In the foreground, Taoseños pass through a gateway, crowned by the Christian cross, into the pueblo's plaza to participate in a traditional ceremony. Other Taos artists, such as Victor Higgins and Andrew Dasburg, painted in the modernist style, creating works influenced by cubism—a style that, despite its modernism, is well suited to evoke classical pueblo architecture. The Taos artists' works also pay homage to the native people, the textures and colors of their fabrics and handicrafts, and the landscape.[70]

Tourism and the fluorescence of art by transplanted whites also brought exposure for native Puebloan and Hispanic art. One measure of this is the enduring popularity of the Indian market at the Palace of the Governors. In addition, native artists have won critical acclaim for their works. For example, the black-on-black pottery works of Maria Martinez (1887–1980), of the San Ildefonso Pueblo, today are prized collectors items and are displayed in art museums. Contemporary Indian artists, such as painter and sculptor R. C.

Gorman, have also won a broad audience. Gorman, a Navajo who lived in Taos until his death in 2005, was known for his Picasso-like depictions of Indian women. "I draw beautiful women," he said, "who are sometimes fat and have calluses on their feet."[71]

The tourist trade drives the popularity of Puebloan and Hispanic art in the Santa Fe area. Tourist purchases account for 75 percent or more of the hundreds of millions of dollars of art sales there annually.[72] The experiences of Hispanic artists in this tourist-driven trade symbolize a larger social and political ambiguity. Santa Fe's hotels, restaurants, shops, and many homes are decorated with Spanish-style furniture, textiles, santos, and other Hispanic artworks. The city's official travel website devotes a page to Hispanic arts, noting that local artists' works are available in shops and galleries and at annual Spanish and Hispanic markets held on the plaza. Hispanic New Mexicans' art, the website declares, has "a well-deserved place in the world of fine art."[73]

Some Santa Fe artists, as well as some scholars, are less sanguine about the status of Hispanic art. As cultural historian Andrew Leo Lovato notes, by the early twentieth century white American tastes had defined Hispanic art as folk art rather than fine art. Lovato cites other scholars who argue that white tastes found Hispanic art neither as "pure" as Indian art nor as sophisticated as the works of white artists. By comparison, Hispanic art seemed crude or primitive.[74]

Lovato's study of contemporary Hispanic artists found that while they understand and value the cultural importance of traditional art forms such as santos, they feel pigeonholed by a market-driven notion of "authenticity," confining them to those art forms and discouraging experimentation with other forms and styles. Instead, to conform to the art market's demands, Hispanic artists often give their works an un-authentic aged look. Hispanic artists, Lovato notes, find themselves in a cultural, commercial, and artistic bind. If they remain bound to traditional art forms and styles, they risk being dismissed as only folk artisans. If they doctor traditional arts to meet market expectations, they are compromising their cultural heritage. And if they try to break away from both tradition and false "authenticity," they risk being accused of abandoning their heritage and suffering commercial and professional failure.[75]

The Hispanic artists' struggles are symptomatic of the almost two-century process of diminution of the Hispanic community's economic, political, and cultural status in Santa Fe. The town began as, and for most of its history remained, an essentially Hispanic community. Whether under Spanish or Mexican rule, Hispanics governed the city and the province, dominated its economic life, and defined its culture, including its religious life. That began to change when William Becknell arrived in 1821 and introduced American trade to Santa Fe. American goods meant American money, and dollars quickly altered power in the community. In a real sense, Americans already controlled Santa Fe, and with it New Mexico, before General Kearny and his army occupied the town. It was, after all, American businessmen who convinced Governor Armijo to yield Santa Fe and New Mexico without a fight. They could not have done so unless they were already dominant. Archbishop Lamy's battles with New Mexican priests and the Penitentes, as well as his cathedral, were an added assault against Hispanic culture.

So when Santa Fe's Hispanic population slipped below 50 percent at the end of the twentieth century, it was a demographic confirmation of a 150-year process of replacing Hispanic with white American power.[76] To be sure, Santa Fe's shops, restaurants, hotels, and homes are filled with Hispanic-style furnishings and art; women and men with Spanish names are still elected to public office; and building codes require deference to Hispanic (and Pueblo) styles, but the center of gravity of economic and political power, and with it cultural power, has long since shifted to whites. Hispanic culture certainly survives in outlying towns, but I wonder if the residue of it in Santa Fe persists because the tourists like it.

Phineas and I hung around Santa Fe for a few hours and then headed north on US 285 to our final destination for the day, the city of Española. From previous trips, I remembered the area between Santa Fe and Española as mainly undeveloped. The Tesuque, Nambé, and Pojoaque Pueblos were barely visible along the highway, and the Santa Fe Opera's outdoor theater was the most imposing architectural feature. There were desert views, a few landmarks such as Camel Rock, some chili stands selling decorative *ristras*, and the Santa Fe Flea Market, a redoubt of the 1960s counterculture. But Indian-owned casinos have transformed not only the scenery but also the economic and political landscape.

American Indian tribes began small-stakes gambling operations, such as bingo, during the 1970s and 1980s as a way to supplement meager reservation economies. When local and state governments, most notably in Florida and

California, tried to close their bingo halls, the Indians fought back with law-suits claiming the states had no authority to ban gambling on the reservations. The US Supreme Court in 1987 opened the way for reservation gambling in a ruling that affirmed that Indian tribes are sovereign entities and limited the authority of state governments to regulate or ban Indian gambling ventures. The following year the US Congress passed the Indian Gaming Regulatory Act to establish rules for reservation gambling operations, including requiring compacts between tribes and state governments.[77]

A decade of legal and political wrangling followed, but in 1997 the State of New Mexico and several Pueblo and Apache reservation governments finally agreed to gambling compacts. The casinos generate millions of dollars of income for the reservations and provide a tax revenue boost for the state. By 2003, gamblers were feeding about $1 million per day into New Mexico slot machines. Earnings from the casinos support reservation infrastructure improvements, schools, and other services. In addition, gambling money has given the Indian communities previously unimagined political influence. Indian contributions have helped to elect, and sometimes unseat, governors and legislators. Burgeoning bank accounts have enabled tribes to pursue other agendas, such as protecting or reasserting water rights. In New Mexico's pueblos and reservations, the weak have begun to become powerful.[78]

As we passed the casinos and their overflowing parking lots, we descended into the Rio Grande Valley and rode into Española. After a quick shower and a restorative nap on the low-end motel's lumpy bed, I was ready to have a look around. Four hundred years ago Española was the site of New Mexico's first capitals, San Juan and San Gabriel. Today the town claims to be the Lowrider Capital of the United States. Lowriders are lovingly customized cars boasting highly polished chrome, custom paint jobs and interiors, and booming sound systems. The term *lowrider* refers to the vehicles' lowered suspensions, which leave their bodies just inches above the pavement. Some of the cars are equipped with fast-acting hydraulic suspensions, which enable their drivers to make them bounce and even appear to hop.

Lowriders appeared in East Los Angeles, California, and in New Mexico after World War II. In contrast to the high-powered, jacked-up hotrods popular with white youths in the postwar era, Hispanic young people began to build lowriders. A *New York Times* article in 2000 noted the contrast between hotrod power and lowrider style: "Let the white kids race frenetically; Chicano youth defined cool by affecting a flamboyant, relaxed look." Where hotrods symbolized rebellion for white kids, "The lowriders were conspicuously reverent of their parents' generation. They embraced the zoot suits and drooping mustaches of the so-called *pachucos*, hipsters of a previous generation, as well as Roman Catholic imagery in the search for an identity with roots in [the] past." So lowriders are not about rebellion but about Hispanic identity. They were and remain, the *New York Times* article concludes, "symbols of ethnic defiance, in effect, giving young Chicanos a voice."[79] On weekend nights the lowriders cruise Española's two main drags, Riverside Drive and Paseo De Oñate. Unfortunately, Phineas and I were there on a Thursday and saw only a few of them. But the evening was far from lost.

Based on emphatic recommendations from the desk clerk, other motel guests, and some guys on the street, we headed for the El Paragua Restaurant for dinner. Given our experiences at the Dodge City steakhouse and a fast-food burger joint in Trinidad, we did not have especially high expectations; we were just hoping for some passable New Mexican food.

The El Paragua served a fine green chili–laden dinner and exemplified northern New Mexico's cultural eclecticism. The restaurant dates to 1958 when the Atencio family began selling tacos out of an old lemonade stand. They opened their first restaurant in 1966. Today's incarnation looks like an old stone Spanish hacienda. The first thing we noticed when we walked in was the 8-foot-wide cottonwood tree, the centerpiece of the entryway and bar. The restaurant is built around it, and we had parked our motorcycles under its branches outside. The tree stands over the restaurant like an enormous umbrella; hence the name El Paragua. Inside, a live singer performed a set of pop music standards, including a Spanish rendition of Kenny Rogers's country-western crossover "You Picked a Fine Time to Leave Me, Lucille." After the singer's set ended, the restaurant's sound system serenaded us with Luciano Pavarotti performing Italian opera selections (mostly Verdi, I think). So there we were, in the Lowrider Capital of the United States, eating wonderful New Mexican food and being entertained by country-western music and Italian opera.

Española is a cultural, geographic, and historic crossroads. Culturally, like Santa Fe, it connects Pueblo, Hispanic, and white cultures and populations, as our dinner at El Paragua demonstrated. From here, too, highways lead to important historic sites, both ancient and modern. Some roads head north-east to Taos, one following the Rio Grande into the mountains through steep, winding canyons. Pueblo settlement in the Taos Valley dates to about 1000 CE. Descendants of these early Puebloans built the Taos Pueblo sometime between 1300 and 1450, and their descendants have occupied it ever since, making the pueblo the oldest inhabited community in the United States. The pueblo's two main structures, *Hlaauma* (North House) and *Hlaukkwima* (South House), appear today much as they did when Spanish explorers/con-querors first came upon them in 1540. Hlaauma especially is one of the most photographed buildings in the world.[80]

Northwest of Española, on the other side of the Rio Grande Valley, are Abiquiu and Ghost Ranch, where Georgia O'Keeffe lived, painted, and refused to learn her neighbors' language. And high in the Jemez Mountains to the southwest is Los Alamos, where J. Robert Oppenheimer and his team of physicists and engineers built the first atomic bombs.

The nineteenth-century writer Charles Lummis called New Mexico the land of *"poco tiempo,"* where time moves slowly and little changes.[81] That may have *seemed* true in Lummis's day (if inaccurate even then), but the small area anchored by Española has witnessed a lot of change, albeit over a very long time. A line drawn on a map from Taos to Los Alamos passes almost directly through Española and represents only about 100 miles. However, that line connects a millennium of history, spanning the invention of adobe bricks to the unleashing of nuclear power. *Poco tiempo* indeed.

THE OLD SPANISH TRAIL

The last day of the trip promised to be a pretty easy ride north on US 285, which, with one 50-mile detour, would take us all the way home to Denver. From Española, the highway follows the northern branch of the Old Spanish Trail, a cluster of routes Spanish explorers and traders pioneered in the eighteenth century to link Santa Fe to California. The northern branch followed the Rio Grande Valley into southern Colorado and passed through the San Luis Valley before turning northwest to follow the Gunnison and Colorado Rivers to California. By the mid-nineteenth century, New Mexican settlers traveled north along the Rio Grande into Colorado to plant new set-tlements there.

As the highway climbs into the mountains just west of the Rio Grande, desert vistas give way to piñon forest. The air cooled rapidly as we climbed, and by the time we reached the little crossroads hamlet of Tres Piedras we were chilled to the bone and grateful to find the tiny café there open. We ordered breakfast, and the waitress brought us big mugs of coffee. I wrapped my cold, stiff hands around my mug for a few minutes until some feeling returned to my fingers.

Two other customers, local sheep ranchers, were seated a couple of tables away. One of the men was white and the other appeared to be of either Spanish or Mexican descent. They talked about how hard the winter had been on their stock, how much fencing they had to repair, and how the damned Forest Service was tightening restrictions on grazing. It was clear that they had been friends for longer than they probably cared to remember.

After a couple of minutes, the white fellow looked over to us and said, "Motorcycling, eh?" "Yep," I replied. "Where yuh headed?" he asked. "Home to Denver," I answered. "Hmmm—long ride then." "Yep," I agreed. The other fellow observed, "Bet it's cold on them things." Phineas and I both nodded.

I did not want the conversation to end and asked them how Tres Piedras got its name. "Oh, it's for the three big rock outcroppings around here, but there's really five of them," the white fellow replied. "Nope," said the other man, "there's seven of 'em, but two of 'em are small and hard to find." I had noticed one of the formations as we rode in and later saw the other two big ones as we rode away. The locale affords a spectacular vista of the Rio Grande Valley over to the Taos Mountains.

The two ranchers returned to their conversation. They agreed that George W. Bush was as dumb as sheep dung and that they would not soon again vote Republican. And even though the days of four-dollar gasoline were a year away, they worried about fuel prices. Then the white fellow, evidently forgetting about his old friend's ancestry, began to rail about illegal immigration and how all those Mexicans were coming into New Mexico, taking all the jobs, *and* going on welfare, and he just wished all the foreigners would go away. His friend stiffened visibly, worked his jaw around for a bit, and then said, "You know, that's how my ancestors felt about you *Americanos* coming here." The white fellow blanched a little as though embarrassed, then grinned and said, "Yeah, I guess so." They then turned back to talking about the joys of sheep ranching.

We had our breakfast and downed a couple more mugs of coffee, lingering in the warm little café for more than an hour. Finally, we stood up to leave and I observed optimistically that perhaps it was warmer outside. "Maybe," the Mexican/Spanish fellow said, "but you still got a thousand feet of climbing ahead of you up to the border. Got any warmer gear?" We followed his advice—wisely, as it turned out—and pulled on winter gloves and more layers of clothing.

By the time we reached the Colorado state line we were in the great San Luis Valley, the immense, 8,000-square-mile basin bounded on the east by the Sangre de Cristo Mountains and on the west by the San Juans and extending from the foot of Poncha Pass in the north into northern New Mexico. The valley's floor seems perfectly flat. It is one of those places in the West, like South Park or Wyoming's Sweetwater region, where you seemingly can see forever. In such a place, it is hard to imagine anything sneaking up on you, but the San Luis Valley is full of surprises.

Although Spain had established military control over the San Luis Valley by the late eighteenth century, colonial occupation grew slowly. The Utes, who remained the valley's dominant residents, maintained good relations with Spain and Mexico, largely because no significant Hispanic settlement occurred. In the 1830s and 1840s Mexico, concerned with strengthening its command of its northern frontier, deeded much of the valley in two major land grants, the Conejos Grant (1833) and the Sangre de Cristo Grant (1843), with the expectation that the grant holders would promote settlement. Hispanic settlement in the valley, however, did not begin until after the United States conquered New Mexico. In 1849 two brothers from El Rito, New Mexico, established Plaza de Manzanares, later renamed Garcia. Two years later fifty families from Taos founded the town of San Luis, about 15 miles north of the state line. San Luis and Garcia are the oldest non-Indian settlements in Colorado. Other Hispanic settlements took root in the valley in succeeding years. Significant white settlement in the valley began in the 1870s and 1880s as a result of gold and silver mining booms in the San Juan Mountains. Mormons settled in the southern part of the valley in this period, too, planting the towns of Romeo, Sanford, and Manassa (the latter the birthplace of the early-twentieth-century boxing great Jack Dempsey, the "Manassa Mauler"). Alamosa, the valley's largest town, appeared in 1878 and became the area's major railroad center. The influx of Hispanic and white settlers spelled doom for the Utes in the valley. Following the White River Uprising (1879) in northwestern Colorado, the government removed most of Colorado's Ute bands to reservations in Utah and southwestern Colorado.[82]

In the 1848 Treaty of Guadalupe Hidalgo, in which Mexico surrendered California, Arizona, and New Mexico (including parts of southern Colorado), the United States agreed to respect the property rights of Mexican citizens. Over succeeding decades, however, most of Colorado forgot about that commitment. Governments and investors divided the land and assigned property rights to others. Still, because the region remained fairly remote, the land grants and the rights they gave to the San Luis Valley's Hispanic communities remained a vital and largely undisturbed basis of economic and cultural life there until 1960. That year a North Carolina businessman, Jack Taylor, bought 80,000 acres in the Sangre de Cristo Mountains of southern Costilla County, intending to log the property's forests. Taylor knew local residents had held and exercised grazing and timber rights to this property for more than a century. His deed to the property even noted that the land was "subject to claims of the local people by prescription or otherwise to right to pasture, wood, and lumber and so-called settlements [sic] rights in, to and upon said land."[83] Taylor soon set out to extinguish the old land grant rights.

Taylor filed suit in federal court asking for exclusive property rights, and the court ruled in his favor in 1965. Meantime, Taylor fenced in the property and hired armed guards to keep the locals out. When his neighbors came onto the property, Taylor and his gunmen sometimes beat them before escorting them to the county sheriff. On one occasion Taylor's use of force against alleged trespassers landed him, not them, in court. Tensions grew in the valley, to the point that in 1975 assailants shot into Taylor's home and wounded him. Sometime after that, arsonists burned the house to the ground.[84]

As tensions boiled on the ground in the San Luis Valley, the battle shifted back to the courts in 1981. For more than two decades a team of attorneys, led by Denver's Jeff Goldstein, worked *pro bono* (for free) pressing the valley residents' legal and historical claims. For many years state courts continued to side with Taylor, basing their rulings on the 1965 federal decision. However, in 2003 the Colorado Supreme Court ruled that in his original federal suit, Taylor had not given proper notice to most of the potential claimants and that, therefore, San Luis Valley property owners who had not been notified of the suit and who could trace their property holdings back to the original Sangre de Cristo land grant still had grazing and timber rights on the Taylor Ranch. The US Supreme Court subsequently declined to review the Colorado ruling.[85]

The Taylor Ranch ruling was remarkable, not only because it sided with the weak against the powerful. Even though the Colorado Supreme Court's decision seemed based on a technical, procedural matter, it actually looked beyond the law books and deep into Colorado's history. It found in the old Mexican land grants, and in more than a century of custom and usage, precedents as powerful and compelling as statutes and court rulings. History, it seems, still matters in law and in life.

A few miles north of the state line we rolled through the town of Antonito, the northern terminus of the Cumbres and Toltec Scenic Railroad—a popular tourist attraction, especially for railroad buffs. A restored relic of the area's mining boom, the narrow-gauge line, originally built by the Denver and Rio Grande Railroad, runs through the southern San Juan Mountains to Chama, New Mexico. Along Antonito's Main Street, murals depicting the valley's Indian, Hispanic, and white heritage adorn buildings and four concrete silos.

Antonito's most striking artwork, however, is "Cano's Castle," the home of Donald "Cano" Espinoza. Located two blocks east of the highway, the house is hard to miss. The main structure's twin towers, "the King" and "the Queen," soar four stories high and are clad in hubcaps, strips of aluminum, and flattened aluminum cans; they shine like polished chrome in the noonday sun. Two smaller buildings are similarly decorated, and a stone and wrought-iron fence surrounds the entire compound. The buildings and fence are covered with signs honoring God, Jesus, and Jerusalem. Espinoza began the project as a religious gesture, to thank God for sparing his life in Vietnam. The first tower went up in the 1980s and the second after the 2001 attack on the World Trade Center. Cano takes no credit for his creation, claiming "it is not me building the towers, it is God." Outside the fence, two enormous arrows, with the messages "Alcohol + Tobacco Is Kills" [sic] and "Mary Jane Is Healing," protrude from the ground.

One writer has said of Cano, "His journey follows the lonely border between sanity and madness, a distinction that can often only be discerned in hindsight, the same edge that produces profound and visionary art—or work that is simply crazy." Not surprisingly, Cano is something of a local character.

FIGURE 3.17. Cano's Castle, Antonito, Colorado, is emblematic of the San Luis Valley's intriguing culture.

He is known on occasion to mount his horse and race the tourist train. Also, he is said to have once borrowed the sheriff's car only moments after he had been released from a stay in the local jail.[86] As I looked at Cano's Castle, I thought of John Nichols's novel *The Milagro Beanfield War*. Set in a small, fictional Hispanic town in northern New Mexico, the novel's central character, Joe Mondragon, along with a cast of delightful supporting characters, struggles against the entrenched, alien power of government and business.[87] Donald Espinoza's art may not be as "serious" as the murals on Antonito's Main Street, and his encounters with the powerful are not as serious as the fictional conflict in *The Milagro Beanfield War*, but he struck me as someone Nichols might recognize. And some might call Cano's Castle something of a miracle, too.

At Alamosa the Rio Grande turns west, toward its headwaters in the San Juan Mountains. We left both the river and US 285 there in favor of Colorado Highway 17, which runs through the middle of the San Luis Valley for 50 miles before rejoining US 285 at the foot of Poncha Pass. As we headed north through the towns of Mosca and Hooper and for many miles beyond, we could see to the east, at the base of the Sangre de Cristos, the Great Sand Dunes. The dunes cover 40 square miles, rise as high as 750 feet above the valley floor, and are the product of millennia of wind scouring the valley's alluvial sediments and depositing the sand at the foot of the mountain range.[88]

Just north of Hooper we passed a hand-painted sign by the road informing motorists that "This Is the Cosmic Highway." At first I thought the sign might refer to the field of photovoltaic panels we had just passed on the west side of the road between Mosca and Hooper (the 8.2-megawatt Alamosa Central Power Plant, which went online in September 2007). But that explanation soon proved too reasonable. A little farther up the road we discovered the sign's true meaning when we spotted Judy Messoline's UFO Watchtower.

The San Luis Valley has been a UFO "hotspot" for more than half a century. In the 1950s thousands of people in southern Colorado and northern New Mexico reported sightings of green fireballs in the night skies. In the 1960s motorists lined the highways at night to watch dancing lights over the Great Sand Dunes. Beginning in 1967, animal mutilations have occurred in the valley, which some folks attribute to extraterrestrial activity (though others are equally certain that the mutilations are a government conspiracy).[89]

Judy Messoline moved to the valley in 1995 and bought a ranch north of Hooper. By 2000 the cattle operation had failed and Messoline, looking for a new line of business, opened her 14-foot-high UFO Watchtower. She knew about the valley's UFO reputation but was not a believer. The watchtower was just a business venture. "I opened it as a tourist trap," she has said. The tower attracted the curious, the true believers, and some who claimed to be visitors from other planets. One guest complained that all of the pictures of aliens in Messoline's gift shop looked the same and that "the real space folks were annoyed that just 1 of the 157 races was represented." Another person asked if she had a guest register "for us." Messoline asked the man where he was from and he told her "Pluto." Though Messoline was not a UFO believer when she built her watchtower, a score of sightings changed her mind. "You will see dots moving real fast," she explained, "then one will stop and the other will catch up."[90] Unfortunately, by 2012 the vagaries of interplanetary economics had forced Messoline to close the watchtower.

Phineas and I saw no UFOs during our ride north through the valley. Indeed, the UFO Watchtower, along with Cano's Castle and the Colorado

Gators Reptile Park (home to hundreds of alligators, crocodiles, and other reptiles that thrive year-round in the farm's hot springs) are the strangest things we saw there.[91]

The rest of the ride through the valley went quickly, and we rejoined US 285. The ride over 9,000-foot Poncha Pass was a little exciting as fresh snow and ice lurked in shaded areas of the road, but we made it over without incident. Poncha Pass separates the Arkansas and Rio Grande watersheds. As we came off the north slope of the pass we found ourselves riding once again along the banks of the Arkansas River, which we had left in eastern Colorado two days before. It seemed as though our journey had come full circle. Soon we were in the familiar expanse of South Park, then over Kenosha Pass and home.

This journey covered 1,300 miles along four historic trails and two of the West's most important rivers. The Rio Grande and the Arkansas River, and the trails that paralleled them, were routes of conquest, commerce, and migration. Spanish conquistadors and settlers moved north from Mexico along the Rio Grande to Santa Fe and beyond. Later, American merchants and armies headed west, also bound for Santa Fe, along the Arkansas on the Santa Fe Trail. As avenues of conquest, commerce, and migration, those trails and rivers also defined one of the world's great meeting places. At Pecos, El Cuartelejo, Bent's Fort, Santa Fe, the San Luis Valley, the coal camps of Colorado and New Mexico, and Amache, indigenous peoples, Europeans, and Asians met, fought one another, changed one another's cultures, and learned to live together (if not always side by side, peaceably, or on equal terms). Some places—Sand Creek and Ludlow—became scenes of brutal violence by the powerful to control or destroy the weak. But other places—Santa Fe, Taos Pueblo, the remote Hispanic communities of northern New Mexico and southern Colorado, even Amache—represent resistance, persistence, and adaptation in the face of physical and cultural conquest. And sometimes, as in the Taylor Ranch case, the weak have prevailed over the powerful.

The archaeological, architectural, and artistic artifacts of the people in this small area, and their encounters with one another, tell very different stories. The fanciful tower of farm implements in Kit Carson, Dodge City's Front Street, the DAR's Santa Fe Trail markers, the scenic overlook at Garden City's feedlots, Bent's Fort, the *Madonna of the Trail* statue, and the Rio Grande

Railroad locomotive in Lamar, even Cano's Castle in Antonito, together tell the story of the march of American civilization, its cowboys, farmers, engineers, capitalists, and artists, across the continent. The story persists in popular culture—and not without justice—as a heroic tale of entrepreneurship, triumph over hardship, individualism and community, and democratic virtue.

Pecos and Sand Creek represent another side of that story, the experiences of the indigenous Pueblo and Plains Indians. It is no small irony that Pecos and Sand Creek today are places of sublime beauty. Standing on the ruins of Pecos's North Pueblo and gazing east down the valley toward the plains, the visitor senses the wealth and power Pecos once commanded. But a short walk to the south leads to the ruins of Our Lady of the Angels of Porciúncula, the early-eighteenth-century church and mission that looms over the site and represents Spanish conquest.

During a subsequent visit to Pecos, I had a long, sometimes heated conversation with two National Park Service employees, both descendants of the area's Spanish settlers whose families had lived and worked there since the eighteenth century. We greeted one another at the visitor's center and exchanged pleasantries about the beautiful day. Then the younger of the two men asked what I thought of the place. I said ruefully that the people of Pecos should have cut Coronado's throat when they had the chance. The young man, one of the monument's resident historians, was distressed by my comment. He made the argument that the Spanish had not come solely as conquerors and that they had done much to preserve and protect Pueblo civilization. To be sure, he conceded, Pecos had died away, but he went on to claim that the surviving Pueblos in New Mexico owed their survival to the Spanish. To say the least, I was unconvinced. I was much more taken with the older man's much wiser response. "If the people of Pecos had killed the Spanish when they first came, I would not be here," he said. He was a lovely, kind man, proud of his family's long history there and proud of his work in preserving both the Pueblo and Spanish heritage at Pecos. And yes, he agreed, Pecos was a place of conquest.

The Spanish conquistadors may not have gone to Pecos just to kill, but the same cannot be said of the Americans who went to Sand Creek. That encounter was not just conquest; it was murder. I am not a religious person, and I am not much impressed with ghost stories; but when I visited Sand Creek I was moved, almost shaken, by the sound of the wind rustling the leaves in the cottonwoods below the viewing site. I heard no voices and saw no specters, but I felt as though the dead of Sand Creek were saying, "We are still here; remember us."

Historians are professional rememberers. We are trained to gather information about events and people of the past, to ask questions about them, analyze the answers we get, and figure out what the past is trying to tell us. Most of the time, we collect our historical memories in libraries and archives. That is all well and good, but imagination and empathy are also important for us to have our conversations with the past. A sense of place is a vital part of imagining and empathizing with the past. I relearned this lesson on the Santa Fe Trail, at Amache and Pecos and Santa Fe and especially at Sand Creek.

Sand Creek is not a text in a library. It is a living place where the past speaks to anyone who will listen. So, too, are all the other places along the four trails and two rivers of this trip. It was a lesson well worth the journey.

NOTES

1. Thomas J. Noel, Paul F. Mahoney, and Richard E. Stevens, *Historical Atlas of Colorado* (Norman: University of Oklahoma Press, 1994), 25; A. Dudley Gardner, "The Cherokee Trail," part 1, at http://www.wwcc.wy.edu/wyo_hist/cherokee.htm, accessed August 3, 2014.

2. Carl Abbott, Stephen J. Leonard, and Thomas J. Noel, *Colorado: A History of the Centennial State,* 4th ed. (Boulder: University Press of Colorado, 2005), 43–59.

3. *Rocky Mountain News,* April 11, 1860, at http://www.forttours.com/pages/hmncco.asp#cherry, accessed June 4, 2008, July 31, 2014.

4. Elliott West, *The Contested Plains: Indians, Goldseekers, and the Rush to Colorado* (Lawrence: University Press of Kansas, 1998), 156–57; Calvin W. Gower, "The Pike's Peak Gold Rush and the Smoky Hill Route, 1," *Kansas Historical Quarterly* 25, no. 2 (Summer 1959): 158–71, at http://www.kshs.org/p/kansas-historical-quarterly-the-pike-s-peak-gold-rush-and-the-smoky-hill-route/13151, accessed August 3, 2014.

5. *Rocky Mountain News,* April 11, 1860, at http://www.forttours.com/pages/hmncco.asp#cherry, accessed June 4, 2008, July 31, 2014.

6. West, *Contested Plains,* 17–32.

7. City of Hugo, "History," at http://cityofhugoco.org/id16.html, accessed June 9, 2008; Roundhouse Preservation, Inc., at http://www.hugoroundhouse.com, accessed June 9, 2008.

8. Abbott, Leonard, and Noel, *Colorado*, 70–72; West, *Contested Plains*, 209–307; Jerome A. Greene and Douglas D. Scott, *Finding Sand Creek: History, Archeology, and the 1864 Massacre Site* (Norman: University of Oklahoma Press, 2004), 3–25; Dee Brown, *Bury My Heart at Wounded Knee: An Indian History of the American West*, 4th ed. (New York: Henry Holt, 2007), 83; National Park Service, Sand Creek National Historic Site, "History & Culture," at http://www.nps.gov/sand/historyculture/index.htm, accessed July 31, 2014; Stan Hoig, *The Sand Creek Massacre* (Norman: University of Oklahoma Press, 1961).

9. Stan Hoig's *The Sand Creek Massacre* (note 6) has been the standard work on the massacre for decades. However, West, *Contested Plains*, and Greene and Scott, *Finding Sand Creek*, are valuable recent additions shedding light on the historical context and the actual site and events of the massacre.

10. US Census Bureau, "State and County QuickFacts, Kiowa County, Colorado," at http://quickfacts.census.gov/qfd/states/08/08061.html, accessed July 31, 2014.

11. Abbott, Leonard, and Noel, *Colorado*, 69.

12. Quoted in ibid.

13. Ibid., 290–91; Brown, *Bury My Heart at Wounded Knee*, 74–75.

14. Quoted in Brown, *Bury My Heart at Wounded Knee*, 80.

15. Quotation in ibid., 83; West, *Contested Plains*, 294–95; Greene and Scott, *Finding Sand Creek*, 14–15.

16. Evans quoted in Greene and Scott, *Finding Sand Creek*, 15; Chivington quoted in Abbott, Leonard, and Noel, *Colorado*, 70.

17. Quoted in Brown, *Bury My Heart at Wounded Knee*, 85–86.

18. Ibid., 102.

19. Ibid., 166–69; West, *Contested Plains*, 312.

20. Greene and Scott, *Finding Sand Creek*, 98.

21. National Park Service, Survey of Historic Sites and Buildings, "El Cuartelejo (Scott County) Pueblo Site, Kansas," at http://www.nps.gov/history/history/online_books/explorers/site18.htm, accessed June 30, 2008; Kansas Historical Society, "El Cuartelejo, a Kansas Portrait," at http://www.kshs.org/kansaspedia/el-cuartelejo-scott-county/12026.htm, accessed August 3, 2014; Keystonegallery.com, "El Cuartelejo—the Home Far Away," at http://www.keystonegallery.com/area/history/el_cuartelejo.html, accessed May 20, 2008; Robert J. Hoard, "El Cuartelejo: Pueblo on the High Plains," *Kansas Heritage* 14, no. 1 (Spring 2006): 12.

22. Dodge City, Kansas, Convention and Visitors Bureau, "Dodge City History," at http://www.visitdodgecity.org/Index.aspx?NID=94, accessed July 31, 2014; RE *Rawhide*, at http://www.imdb.com/title/tt0052504/, accessed July 31, 2014; RE *Gunsmoke* (radio), "Gunsmoke: Radio's Last Great Dramatic Series," at http://www.imdb.com/title/tt0047736/?ref_=nv_sr_1, accessed July 31, 2014; RE *Gunsmoke* (TV

series), at http://www.imdb.com/title/tt0047736/?ref_=nv_sr_1, accessed July 31, 2014.

23. www.dodgecity.org/index.asp?NID=442, accessed July 26, 2008.

24. Richard White, *It's Your Misfortune and None of My Own: A New History of the American West* (Norman: University of Oklahoma Press, 1991), 330.

25. Ibid., 44; National Park Service, Santa Fe National Historic Trail, "Travel the Trail: Map Timeline, 1821–1845," at http://www.nps.gov/safe/historyculture /map-timeline.htm, accessed July 31, 2014; William H. Wroth, "1821 Santa Fe Trail Opens," New Mexico Office of the State Historian, at http://newmexicohistory. org/events/1821-santa-fe-trail-opens, accessed July 31, 2014.

26. Josiah Gregg, *Commerce of the Prairies: The Journal of a Santa Fe Trader* (Dallas: Southwest Press, 1933), 207.

27. Abbott, Leonard, and Noel, *Colorado*, 302–4; J. Burton, M. Farrell, F. Lord, and R. Lord, "A Brief History of Japanese American Relocation during World War II," in *Confinement and Ethnicity: An Overview of World War II Japanese American Reloca- tion Sites*, at http://www.cr.nps.gov/history/online_books/anthropology74/ce3 .htm, accessed July 31, 2014.

28. Kara Mariko Miyagishima, "Colorado's Nikkei Pioneers: Japanese Americans in Twentieth Century Colorado" (MA thesis, University of Colorado at Denver, 2007), 115; White, *It's Your Misfortune and None of My Own,* 511; *Denver Post* quotes in the *Durango Herald*, "Colorado Honors Gov. Carr's Courage," March 23, 2008, at http://www.fulcrum-books.com/productdetails.cfm?PC=5927&reviews=1, accessed August 3, 2014.

29. *Durango Herald*, "Colorado Honors Gov. Carr's Courage."

30. Ibid.; Miyagishima, "Colorado's Nikkei Pioneers," 116.

31. Miyagishima, "Colorado's Nikkei Pioneers," 128.

32. Go for Broke, National Education Center, "442nd Regimental Combat Team," at http://www.goforbroke.org/history/history_historical_veterans_442nd.php, accessed August 3, 2014.

33. Route40.net, "Madonna of the Trail Statues," at http://www.route40. net/page.asp?n=86, accessed August 3, 2014; Santa Fe Scenic and Historic Byway, "Madonna of the Trail," at http://www.santafetrailsscenicandhistoricbyway.org /madona[sic].html, accessed August 7, 2008.

34. Abbott, Leonard, and Noel, *Colorado,* 28–30.

35. National Park Service, "Bent's Old Fort National Historic Site" (pamphlet) (Washington, DC: Government Printing Office, 2005); "Bent's Old Fort on the Santa Fe Trail Mountain Branch," at http://www.santafetrailsscenicandhistoric byway.org/bentof.html, accessed August 8, 2008; George Rutledge Gibson, *Journal of a Soldier under Kearny and Doniphan, 1846–1847*, ed. Ralph P. Bieber (Glendale,

CA: Arthur H. Clark, 1935), 169; Stella M. Drumm, ed., *Down the Santa Fe Trail and into Mexico: The Diary of Susan Shelby Magoffin, 1846–1847* (Lincoln: University of Nebraska Press, 1982), 60.

36. Lewis H. Garrard, *Wah-to-yah and the Taos Trail, or Prairie Travel and Scalp Dances, with a Look at Los Rancheros from Muleback and the Rocky Mountain Campfire* (Norman: University of Oklahoma Press, 1955), 42.

37. White, *It's Your Misfortune and None of My Own*, 77–79, 157; William H. Wroth, "Taos Rebellion—1847," New Mexico Office of the State Historian, at http://dev .newmexicohistory.org/filedetails.php?fileID=515, accessed July 31, 2014.

38. Abbott, Leonard, and Noel, *Colorado*, 34, 69–70.

39. Garrard, *Wah-to-yah and the Taos Trail*, 42.

40. Tom Roeder, "Army Scales Back Piñon Canon Expansion," *The Gazette* (Colorado Springs), at http://gazette.com/army-scales-back-piñon-canyon-expansion /article/38338, accessed August 3, 2014; *Denver Post*, May 14, 2009, 1a, 13a; *Denver Post*, January 28, 2011, 2b.

41. Drumm, *Down the Santa Fe Trail and into Mexico*, 78; Garrard, *Wah-to-yah and the Taos Trail*, 140.

42. Abbott, Leonard, and Noel, *Colorado*, 36, 446; James Whiteside, *Regulating Danger: The Struggle for Mine Safety in the Rocky Mountain Coal Industry* (Lincoln: University of Nebraska Press, 1990), 7–9, 47–49.

43. On working conditions and labor relations in the western coal industry, see James Whiteside, *Regulating Danger: The Struggle for Mine Safety in the Rocky Mountain Coal Industry* (Lincoln: University of Nebraska Press, 1990).

44. Drumm, *Down the Santa Fe Trail and into Mexico*, 79–84.

45. Ibid., 397, 399, 401–2, 406.

46. Whiteside, *Regulating Danger*, 141, 144.

47. A record of the old historic marker is at http://www.historyquest.com /state/nm/radA2060_new_mexico_historic_site.html, accessed August 3, 2014. See also Legends of America, "Cimarron: Wild and Bawdy Boomtown," at http:// www.legendsofamerica.com/nm-cimarron.html, accessed August 3, 2014.

48. William H. Wroth, "Maxwell Land Grant," New Mexico Office of the State Historian, at http://newmexicohistory.org/places/maxwell-land-grant, accessed August 1, 2014.

49. Legends of America, "The Largest Land Grant in US History—the Maxwell Land Grant," at http://www.legendsofamerica.com/nm-maxwell6.html, accessed August 3, 2014.

50. Wroth, "Maxwell Land Grant"; Legends of America, "The Largest Land Grant in US History—the Maxwell Land Grant," at http://www.legendsofamerica .com/nm-maxwell3.html, accessed August 2, 2014.

51. Legends of America, "Largest Land Grant in US History—The Maxwell Land Grant," http://www.legendsofamerica.com/nm-maxwell6.html, accessed August 3, 2014.

52. US Department of the Interior, National Park Service, "Fort Union National Monument, History and Culture," at http://www.nps.gov/foun/historyculture/index.htm, accessed August 28, 2008.

53. National Historic Landmarks Program, "Watrous (La Junta)," at http://tps.cr.nps.gov/nhl/detail.cfm?ResourceId=340&ResourceType=District, accessed August 3, 2014; Marc Simmons, *Following the Santa Fe Trail: A Guide for Modern Travelers*, 3d rev. ed. (Santa Fe: Ancient City Press, 2004), 193.

54. Shirley Cushing Flint and Richard Flint, "Watrous," New Mexico Office of the State Historian, at http://www.newmexicohistory.org/places/watrous, accessed August 3, 2014.

55. Gregg, *Commerce of the Prairies*, 66; Drumm, *Down the Santa Fe Trail and into Mexico*, 92–94.

56. Sides, *Blood and Thunder*, 92.

57. National Park Service, Pecos National Historical Park, "People of Pecos," at http://www.nps.gov/peco/historyculture/peple-of-pecos.htm, accessed August 1, 2014.

58. National Park Service, Pecos National Historical Park, "Spanish Encounters," at http://www.nps.gov/peco/historyculture/spanish-encounters.htm, accessed August 1, 2014.

59. Ibid.; National Park Service, Survey of Historic Sites and Buildings, "El Cuartelejo (Scott County Pueblo Site), at http://www.nps.gov/history/history/online_books/explorers/sitec18.htm, accessed August 1, 2014; Robert J. Hoard, "El Cuartelejo: Pueblo on the High Plains, *Kansas Heritage* (vol. 14, no. 1, Spring 2006) 6–12.

60. National Park Service, Pecos National Historical Park, "The People of Cicuye/Pecos," at http://www.nps.gov/peco/historyculture/peple-of-pecos.htm, accessed August 3, 2014; National Park Service, Pecos National Historical Park, "Pecos National Historical Park: Spanish Encounters," at http://www.nps.gov/peco/historyculture/spanish-encounters.htm, accessed August 3, 2014; James Abarr, "Pecos Reigned over Early Pueblo World," at http://abqjournal.com/venue/day/heritage7.htm, accessed August 30, 2008.

61. Very good, brief accounts of the Battle of Glorieta Pass include Sides, *Blood and Thunder*, 362–79; US Department of the Interior, National Park Service, "Pecos National Historical Park: Battle of Glorieta," at http://www.nps.gov/peco/historyculture/spanish-encounters.htm, accessed August 3, 2014.

62. William H. Wroth, "Santa Fe," New Mexico Office of the State Historian, at http://newmexicohistory.org/places/santa-fe; accessed August 1, 2014.

63. Ibid.; National Park Service, Survey of Historic Sites and Buildings, "El Cuartelejo (Scott County Pueblo Site)," at http://www.nps.gov/history/history /online_books/explorers/sitec18.htm, accessed August 1, 2014; Robert J. Hoard, "El Cuartelejo: Pueblo on the High Plains," *Kansas Heritage* 14, no. 1 (Spring 2006): 6–12.

64. Gregg, *Commerce of the Prairies*, 66.

65. William H. Wroth, "Jean Baptiste Lamy," New Mexico Office of the State Historian, at http://newmexicohistory.org/people/jean-baptiste-lamy, accessed August 1, 2014.

66. Ibid.; Wroth, "Santa Fe"; Andrew Leo Lovato, *Santa Fe Hispanic Culture: Preserving Identity in a Tourist Town* (Albuquerque: University of New Mexico Press, 2004), 22–23.

67. Wroth, "Santa Fe"; Jori Finkel, "Welcome to New Mexico: Now Create," *New York Times*, January 27, 2008, at http://www.nytimes.com/2008/01/27/arts/design /27fink.html?pagewanted=all&module=Search&mabReward=relbias%3Ar&_r=0, accessed August 3, 2014; Candace Jackson, "Change Rolls into Santa Fe," *Wall Street Journal*, September 20, 2008, at http://online.wsj.com/news/articles/SB1221863929 23158615?mg=reno64-wsj&url=http%3A%2F%2Fonline.wsj.com%2Farticle%2FSB12 2186392923158615.html, accessed August 3, 2014.

68. Keith L. Bryant Jr., "The Atchison, Topeka and Santa Fe Railway and the Development of the Taos and Santa Fe Art Colonies," *Western Historical Quarterly* 9, no. 4 (October 1978): 446–53.

69. Michael Ann Sullivan, "Georgia O'Keeffe (1887–1986)," New Mexico Office of the State Historian, at http://www.newmexicohistory.org/people/georgia-okeeffe, accessed August 3, 2014; William H. Goetzmann and William N. Goetzmann, *The West of the Imagination* (New York: W. W. Norton, 1986), 427.

70. See Goetzmann and Goetzmann, *West of the Imagination*, 353–76.

71. *New York Times*, November 5, 2005, at http://query.nytimes.com/gst/fullpage .html?res=9A05E6D7173EF936A35752C1A9639C8B63&module=Search&mabReward =relbias%3Ar, accessed August 3, 2014.

72. Lovato, *Santa Fe Hispanic Culture*, 4.

73. Santa Fe Convention and Visitors Bureau, "Hispanic Arts," at http://santafe. org/Visiting_Santa_Fe/Art/Hispanic/index/html, accessed September 17, 2008.

74. Lovato, *Santa Fe Hispanic Culture*, 79.

75. Ibid., 85, 87–97.

76. US Census Bureau, "State and County Quick Facts: Santa Fe (city) New Mexico," at http://quickfacts.census.gov/qfd/states/35/3570500.html, accessed September 12, 2008.

77. W. Dale Mason, *Indian Gaming: Tribal Sovereignty and American Politics* (Norman: University of Oklahoma Press, 2000); Paul Krza, "Indian Power," *High Country News*, April 28, 2003, at http://www.hcn.org/issues/249/13904, accessed October 7, 2008; State of New Mexico, Gaming Control Board, "New Mexico Indian Gaming Historical Perspective," at http://www.nmgcb.org/tribal/history.htm, accessed October 7, 2008; *California et al. v. Cabazon Band of Mission Indians et al.*, 408 US 202 (1987), no. 85-1708, at http://scholar.google.com/scholar?q=california+v.+Cabazon+Band+supreme+court+case+citation&btnG=&hl=en&as_sdt=4006&as_vis=1, accessed August 1, 2014.

78. Mason, *Indian Gaming*; Krza, "Indian Power"; State of New Mexico, Gaming Control Board, "New Mexico Indian Gaming Historical Perspective."

79. James Sterngold, "How the Lowrider Evolved from Chicano Revolt to Art Form," *New York Times*, February 19, 2000, at http://www.nytimes.com/2000/02/19/arts/making-jalopy-ethnic-banner-lowrider-evolved-chicano-revolt-art-form.html?module=Search&mabReward=relbias%3Ar, accessed August 3, 2014. See also, Brenda Bright, "Heart Like a Car: Hispano/Chicano Culture in Northern New Mexico," *American Ethnologist* 25, no. 4 (November 1998): 583–609.

80. National Park Service, "Taos Pueblo, Taos, New Mexico," at http://www.nps.gov/nr/travel/American_Latino_Heritage/Taos_Pueblo.html, accessed August 3, 2014; Taos Pueblo, "About Taos Pueblo," at http://www.taospueblo.com/about, accessed August 3, 2014; Taos Pueblo, "Welcome to Taos Pueblo: The Place of the Red Willows" (Taos: Taos Pueblo, n.d.).

81. Charles F. Lummis, *The Land of Poco Tiempo* (Albuquerque: University of New Mexico Press, 1975 [1952]).

82. Virginia McConnell Simmons, *The San Luis Valley: Land of the Six-Armed Cross* (Niwot: University Press of Colorado, 1999), 84; Abbott, Leonard, and Noel, *Colorado*, 36, 113–19, 160; San Luis Valley Museum Association, "History of the San Luis Valley," at http://www.museumtrail.org/ValleyHistory.asp, accessed November 7, 2008.

83. *Lobato v. Taylor*, no. 00SC527 (Colorado Supreme Court, April 28, 2003).

84. Karl Hess Jr. and Tom Wolf, "Treasure of La Sierra," *Reason* 31, no. 5 (2008): 32; White, *It's Your Misfortune and None of My Own*, 596; Simon Romero, "'60s Latino Militant Now Pursues a Personal Quest," *New York Times*, May 5, 2006, at http://www.nytimes.com/2006/05/05/us/05tijerina.html?pagewanted=print&module=Search&mabReward=relbias%3Ar%2C%7B%222%22%3A%22RI%3A14%22%7D, accessed August 3, 2014.

85. *Lobato v. Taylor*. For a critique of the *Lobato* ruling, see Dick Johnston, *The Taylor Ranch War: Property Rights Die* (Bloomington, IN: Authorhouse, 2006).

86. Quotation in Susan J. Tweit, "Cano's Vision," *High Country News*, August 22, 2005, at http://www.hcn.org/issues/304/15735, accessed November 11, 2008; "Antonito, Colorado—Cano's Castle—Beer Can Folk Art," Roadside America.com, at http://www.roadsideamerica.com/tip/8936, accessed November 11, 2008; curiousexpeditions.org, "Cano's Vitamin-M Masterpiece, Antonio [*sic*], Colorado," at http://www.curiousexpeditions.org/?p=91, accessed November 11, 2008.

87. John Nichols, *The Milagro Beanfield War* (New York: Holt, Rinehart and Winston, 1974).

88. James S. Aber, "San Luis Valley, Colorado," at http://academic.emporia.edu/aberjame/field/rocky_mt/zapata.htm, accessed August 3, 2014.

89. David Kelly, "Things Are Looking up with UFO Watch Tower," *Los Angeles Times*, August 8, 2004, A-22, at http://articles.latimes.com/2004/aug/08/nation/na-ufo8, accessed August 3, 2014.

90. Ibid.

91. Colorado Gators Reptile Park, at http://www.coloradogators.com, accessed August 4, 2014.

4

Four Corners

Phineas and I were on the road again in the last week of June 2007, bound this time for the Four Corners region, where Colorado, New Mexico, Arizona, and Utah meet. Throughout the region, sandstone mesas and monoliths rise hundreds of feet from the desert floor. Some look like giant fingers pointing to the sky. It struck me that way up on top of them is where the surface of the earth used to be. Before that, in the late Cretaceous period about 80 million years ago, "way up there" had been the bottom of a sea that covered much of the Rocky Mountain region and the Southwest. I wondered where all that dirt and rock had gone. Wind, no doubt, had swept away much of it, but I guessed that more now lay on the bottom of the Gulf of Mexico and the Pacific Ocean, carried off by streams and rivers—some still flowing, most long dried up.

The law of the conservation of matter has it that matter can be changed but not destroyed. Everything that has ever been here is still here. So the landscape of the Four Corners region is dramatic evidence of how the Earth rearranges itself, that the world is both eternal and transient. "Geez,"

DOI: 10.5876/9781607323273.c004

I thought, "this is getting kinda deep for a motorcycle trip." Before and after that deep thought about geology and cosmology floated through my mind, however, this trip revealed other, more human-scale examples of timelessness and transience, especially in the relationship between humans and the West's fragile, arid environment.

MOUNTAINS AND VALLEYS

Clear blue skies spread over South Park as we descended Kenosha Pass. The valley was still green from the melted winter snows. Near the bottom of the pass, a small herd of pronghorns, unconcerned with the noise of our engines, grazed on the thick grass a few yards from the road. We raced across the valley unimpeded by traffic until we crested Trout Creek Pass, where we joined a long caravan of cars, trucks, and a few other motorcycles following a very old, very slow-moving motor home towing a large boat. I usually get irritated when I find myself trapped behind one of those behemoths, but that morning, on Old Blue, the slow descent into the Arkansas River Valley was pleasant. I especially enjoyed the spectacular view of the Collegiate Peaks rising abruptly from the valley floor, some of them over 14,000 feet. They loom like an impenetrable wall on the valley's western flank.

At the foot of Trout Creek Pass, US 285 meets US 24, which runs north through Buena Vista to Leadville. We detoured into Buena Vista (mispronounced "B-you-nuh" Vista in the local dialect) for gas and lunch, and then headed for our third mountain pass of the day. Just north of Poncha Springs and not far from a historical marker commemorating Zebulon Pike's Christmas 1806 encampment, we turned west onto US 50 and ascended Monarch Pass, which crests at 11,312 feet. The highway over the pass is winding and, though not especially dangerous, requires the rider's full attention.

At Gunnison, we turned off US 50 for a side trip to Crested Butte. Famous now as a ski resort, Crested Butte began as a coal mining town in the 1880s. Isolated as it was, the town also supplied fuel and other necessities for other, even more remote silver and gold mining camps in the area. When the coal mines closed in the early 1950s, Crested Butte withered away and was virtually a ghost town by the 1960s. Soon, however, Colorado's skiing boom resurrected the town and transformed it into a prosperous, if now overbuilt, resort community. The popularity of mountain biking in recent years has made

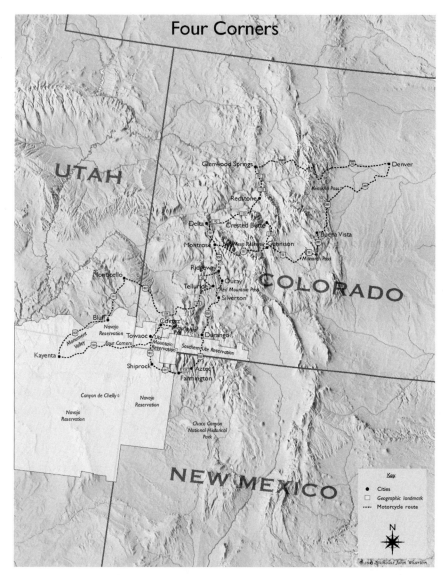

MAP 4.1. Map by Nicholas J. Wharton

Crested Butte a year-round tourist destination. What was once a small town of miners, merchants, and saloons today has an economy of restaurants, ski and bicycle shops, and chic boutiques doing business in restored Victorian-era buildings. Phineas and I lounged on benches in the afternoon sun, sipping overpriced iced tea, munching overpriced ice cream, and looking not quite de rigueur in our motorcycling leathers. It was sort of fun to be gawked at by the much more refined-looking tourists.

Back on US 50, we rolled through Gunnison bound for Montrose. Just west of Gunnison the highway skirts, and at one point crosses, the Blue Mesa Reservoir. This 20-mile-long lake is part of the Wayne N. Aspinall Storage Unit, named for a twelve-term Colorado congressman who never met a dam project he did not like. Colorado largely escaped the wave of dam building and water diversion that swept the American West in the first half of the twentieth century. But in 1956 the US Congress, with Representative Aspinall pushing hard, authorized the Blue Mesa Dam as part of the Colorado River Storage Project, a system of dams on the Colorado and its tributaries in Wyoming, Colorado, Utah, Arizona, and New Mexico. Aspinall saw expanding the West's infrastructure of dams and irrigation projects as vital to the region's and the nation's physical and economic health. Because irrigation would improve the nation's food supply, America's children would be "bigger, stronger, more alert, and healthier than their parents." With its economy strengthened, America, then in one of the darkest periods of the Cold War, would be better able to stand up to "increasingly severe challenges from abroad."[1]

The Colorado River Storage Project involved an important environmental tradeoff, one that soon looked to many to be a devil's bargain. One key element of the plan was a massive dam and reservoir in northwest Colorado, near the confluence of the Yampa and Green Rivers. This Echo Park site was right in the middle of Dinosaur National Monument, which included spectacularly scenic canyons and one of the world's most significant paleontological sites. Opponents of the Echo Park plan, led by the Sierra Club and noted western writers Bernard DeVoto and Wallace Stegner, mounted an effective campaign against it. The opposition's central concern was that the Echo Park project would open the door for others the Bureau of Reclamation aimed to build in national monuments and parks. Stopping Echo Park, they hoped, would set a precedent against other such plans. Eventually, as the Colorado River Storage Project made its way through Congress, Representative Aspinall and the opposition struck a deal. In exchange for the government dropping the Echo Park dam, the opposition agreed to support the rest of the Colorado River Storage Project, including the proposed Glen Canyon Dam on the Colorado River, near the Arizona-Utah border.[2]

At the time, trading Glen Canyon for Echo Park seemed to environmentalists to be a good deal. Glen Canyon was even more remote than Echo Park and very few people, including those who struck the deal, had seen it. Far more important was the precedent they believed they had set against water development projects in national monuments and parks. Over succeeding years they experienced buyer's remorse as they learned that Glen Canyon was a scenic, geological, and archaeological jewel even greater than Echo Park. By that time, though, the canyon's fate was sealed and the dam was already rising there.

Over the next decade, environmentalists also learned that the precedent against damming national monuments and parks was not as solid as they had hoped, forcing them to re-fight that battle. In 1963 Secretary of the Interior Stewart Udall announced plans to build two dams in the Grand Canyon that would inundate many miles of the great chasm. The dams' hydroelectric generators would power pumps to lift Colorado River water out of the canyon to irrigate lands of the Central Arizona Project. Udall and the Bureau of Reclamation immediately faced a buzzsaw of criticism, as environmentalists easily whipped up powerful public and editorial opposition. In the 1950s, only a small number of people knew anything about Echo Park and Glen Canyon. But in the 1960s, virtually every American knew of the Grand Canyon, and seemingly no one—except a few western politicians, Udall, and the Bureau of Reclamation—believed flooding even part of it was a good idea. When project supporters claimed that the dams would actually make the Grand Canyon and its scenery more accessible to visitors, the Sierra Club countered with an ad in major newspapers asking, "Should we also flood the Sistine Chapel so tourists can get nearer the ceiling?"[3]

Udall eventually found a way out of the hornet's nest of criticism over the Grand Canyon dam proposals. The solution, however, involved another devil's bargain. In 1967 Udall announced that the Department of the Interior had decided to abandon the planned dams. Instead, a massive new coal-fired power plant, the Navajo Generating Station near Page, Arizona, would produce the electricity needed for the Central Arizona Project's pumps. Once the Navajo Station was running at full power, visitors to the Grand Canyon began to notice that on many days they could not see across to the opposite side of the gorge because a haze of fly ash and gas from the power plant drifted over the canyon.[4]

Blue Mesa seems far removed from the battles surrounding Echo Park, Glen Canyon, and the Grand Canyon, but it is an important part of the hydrologic infrastructure supporting the West's agricultural, industrial, and urban development. Like Glen Canyon, Blue Mesa flooded a beautiful canyon, and the lake became a hub for outdoor recreation. Its waters irrigate thousands of acres of farmland and drive generators that send electric power to the region's homes, farms, cities, and factories. It is an artifact of a powerful dream—the dream of unlimited abundance to be wrested from the West's rivers and arid lands.

William Ellsworth Smythe, a nineteenth-century apostle of that dream, saw the Colorado River region as "a vast plain of opulent soil" that, because of aridity, "stood barred and padlocked against the approach of mankind." Irrigation, he prophesied, would unlock its treasures. "In no part of the wide world," he proclaimed, "is there a place where Nature has provided so perfectly for a stupendous achievement by means of irrigation." More than a century later, a Bureau of Reclamation document declared that even with all the dams, reservoirs, irrigation canals, and generating plants of the Colorado River Storage Project in place, the region's agricultural, industrial, and recreational potential had scarcely been tapped.[5] The dream, at least in some quarters, remained alive. But by the twenty-first century it had proven a fragile dream, one threatened by human hubris and environmental reality.

As the Bureau of Reclamation built its great dams, it also created for itself a reputation as a team of super-engineers who could tame the wildest rivers behind structures that would stand forever. That reputation took a severe beating in the spring of 1983 when a series of late-season storms dumped enormous amounts of wet snow on the mountains of Colorado, Utah, and Wyoming. Then, unseasonably high temperatures resulted in rapid snowmelt and unusually large runoff. Downstream, at Glen Canyon, dam managers had kept Lake Powell nearly full to maximize hydroelectric generating capacity for the approaching warm months when demand would be highest. That meant the lake and the dam could not contain all of the water coming down the Colorado River. If the lake crested the dam, water plunging more than 700 feet to the bottom would smash into the powerhouse, hitting it like a liquid bomb.

Glen Canyon's managers decided, reluctantly, to lower the lake by opening one of the dam's spillways, steeply descending tunnels that fall hundreds of

FIGURE 4.1. Blue Mesa Reservoir near Gunnison, Colorado. Dam builders saw irrigation and hydroelectric power as the best way to exploit the West's scarce water. Others wondered what would happen when the water ran out.

feet to intersect with the diversion tunnels that had rerouted the river away from the dam site during its construction. Soon after they opened the spillway, dam officials saw that the water blasting from the discharge outlet was red, the color of the surrounding sandstone. And it contained large chunks of concrete. The discharged water had scoured away the tunnel's thick concrete lining and eaten away at the rock around it. In the worst case, the rushing water might undermine the dam's foundations, causing a catastrophic breach that could send downstream a wave of water almost 600 feet high, inundating everything along the way to the Gulf of California. Engineers closed the damaged spillway and decided not to open the other one, since it had the same design and ran even closer to the dam. The water kept rising. Finally, the engineers came up with a solution. They rigged a wall of plywood atop the spillways (replaced several days later with steel panels), temporarily adding 4 feet of capacity to the lake. Then they waited. Finally, on July 15, Lake Powell began slowly to recede and the crisis passed. In the aftermath, construction crews repaired the damaged spillway and engineers devised ways to prevent damage if it ever had to be opened again.[6]

By the first years of the twenty-first century, nature had created a completely different sort of crisis for Lake Powell and the irrigated West: drought.

During 2005 the lake's water level fell more than 150 feet below the flood level of 1983. In early 2009 it was still 97 feet below the 1983 high. The decline at Blue Mesa was less dramatic, but in late 2008 that lake stood 34 feet below capacity. Four years later, despite heavy winter and spring snows in the central Rocky Mountains, both lakes remained well below full pool. In June 2013, when they reached their maximum elevation for the year, Lake Powell remained 98 feet and Blue Mesa 48 feet below capacity.[7]

Flood and drought proved that nature, not man, controlled the Colorado River and its tributaries. More than the threat of flood, however, drought challenged the irrigation dream because while too much water for the system was aberrant, too little was proving to be the norm. In 1922 the seven states along the Colorado River agreed to a compact dividing up the river's water. The Colorado River Storage Project and Hoover Dam were built to maximize and ensure the river's orderly division. But the Colorado River Compact and the storage project were based on river flow estimates taken in the early twentieth century, years that were extraordinarily wet. In recent years, tree-ring studies have yielded climate estimates dating back to the twelfth century, showing that much lower river volume has been the norm. So the economic and demographic growth of much of the West, insofar as it has been built on the foundation of exploiting the Colorado River system, is based on bad data. There is barely enough water to sustain what has already been built, if that. In 2009, University of California at San Diego researchers Tim Barnett and David Pierce concluded that if current climate conditions persist, as seems likely, the Colorado River system would be unable to deliver water at scheduled rates 60 percent to 90 percent of the time by the mid-twenty-first century. In a previous study, in 2008, Barnett and Pierce predicted a 50 percent chance that by 2017 water levels in Lake Mead could fall below the level required for Hoover Dam's turbines to generate electric power.[8]

But this is really not new information. In 1893—four decades before Hoover Dam, seven decades before Glen Canyon Dam, and seventy-four years before Blue Mesa Dam—John Wesley Powell, the American adventurer who first surveyed the Colorado River and himself an advocate of limited irrigation, warned a congress of irrigation apostles: "When all the rivers are used, when all the creeks in the ravines, when all the brooks, when all the springs are used, when all the reservoirs along the streams are used, when all the canyon waters are taken up, when all the artesian waters are taken up, when all the wells are sunk or dug that can be dug in all this arid region, there is still not sufficient water to irrigate all this arid region." The audience practically booed Powell off the stage, and William Ellsworth Smythe dismissed him as "in no sense a man of practical commercial instincts."[9]

But Powell was the better prophet. The irrigation dream is over. Some people today would drain Lake Powell and tear down Glen Canyon Dam. Even Floyd Dominy, the Bureau of Reclamation director who presided over the dam's construction, once sketched a way to empty the lake. But if a millennium of climate data is correct, the day may come when man and nature together will simply dry up the rivers and all the manmade lakes. If that should ever happen, we will all be in a fine fix.[10]

INTO THE DESERT

US Highway 550 runs south from Montrose along the Uncompahgre River. It eventually ends at Interstate 25 just north of Albuquerque. In that distance, the road passes through mountain valleys, the alpine majesty of San Juan Mountain passes, piñon forest, and desert. Along the way, the traveler also passes through thousands of years of human history.

The Four Corners region is one of the richest archaeological zones in the world. From the Canyon of the Ancients and Hovenweep National Monuments, northwest of Cortez, Colorado, to Canyon de Chelly in Arizona and Chaco Canyon in New Mexico are the remains of the civilization of the Anasazi, or Ancestral Puebloans, who populated the region from approximately the beginning of the common era until around 1300. (Archaeologists in the early twentieth century used the Navajo word *Anasazi* to identify these ancient people. The term can be translated as "ancient enemy," a characterization the Ancestral Puebloans' modern descendants dislike.) In the middle of this complex of archaeological treasures is Mesa Verde. The Four Corners area today remains the home of indigenous cultures—the Navajos, Hopis, Utes, and Pueblo Indians.[11]

More recent is the history of the San Juan Mountains mining booms of the nineteenth and twentieth centuries. Ouray, Silverton, Durango, Telluride, and scores of other lesser-known towns and camps are rich in highly romanticized Wild West stories of gold and silver mining. Many towns have disappeared. Those that remain have survived by tapping new mother lodes such as skiing and mountain biking.

At Ridgway, 25 miles south of Montrose, the Uncompahgre Valley rises into the San Juan Mountains and narrows until, a few miles north of Ouray, it becomes a canyon with near-vertical deep red and purple sandstone walls. Soon, that defile opens into a great natural amphitheater containing the town of Ouray, a mining town turned resort. The 13-mile ascent up Red Mountain Pass begins at the south end of town. This is not a road for the faint of heart. A memorial along the roadway pays tribute to snowplow drivers who have died working to keep the pass open in the winter months. Another marker memorializes a family swept away by a snow slide. The road is narrow, and the southbound lane runs perilously close to precipitous falls varying from hundreds to thousands of feet more or less straight down. There are long stretches with no guardrails. Phineas hugged the centerline all the way up the pass.

The payoff for challenging Red Mountain Pass comes a few miles before the final climb to the summit. The road levels and passes through an alpine meadow that affords a view of the pass's namesake, Red Mountain. The mountain's three peaks are vivid red from iron oxide on the surface. The mountain is, in effect, rusted. The descent down the south side of the pass and on into Silverton is less exciting than the ascent, especially after the first few miles as steep switchbacks give way to longer, sweeping curves. Nevertheless, the occasional marmot—a small, furry, football-shaped critter with a rattail—sunning itself in the roadway adds a minor thrill, especially in a hairpin curve.

After the chill of riding up and down Red Mountain Pass, a breakfast of biscuits and gravy at Silverton's Brown Bear Café was a welcome warmup. Compared with Ouray and Crested Butte, Silverton is still a little frayed at the edges. Many buildings apparently have not felt the caress of a paintbrush for some time. Unlike the other, better-restored towns, Silverton retains the feel of a real working town, with more pickup trucks than BMWs parked on the street. Like Ouray, however, Silverton makes its living these days by mining the pockets of skiers, mountain bicyclists, and other tourists. Especially important is the Durango and Silverton Narrow Gauge Railroad. The Denver and Rio Grande Railroad put down narrow-gauge tracks between Silverton and Durango in 1882 to haul ore out of the San Juans. Word of the route's scenic beauty spread quickly, and the railroad soon added passenger runs. Now, only the tourist traffic keeps the line running.

Fifty spectacular miles and two more passes separate Silverton and Durango, where we stopped just long enough to shed a layer of leather in the parking lot of a city recreation center. A group of seniors standing about the doorway eyed us suspiciously until I flashed my biggest, most disarming grin and waved to them, signaling that we had come in peace and intended no harm. They smiled and waved back, signaling that they probably would not summon the police. Then, still rolling south on Highway 550, we crossed the Animas River, climbed over a broad mesa, crossed the Southern Ute Reservation, and descended into the desert.

Fourteen miles south of the New Mexico line we reached the town of Aztec and the Aztec Ruins National Monument, a remarkable Ancestral Puebloan site constructed in the early twelfth century. Archaeologists believe colonists sent out from Chaco Canyon, 55 miles to the south, built and settled Aztec. Chaco had been the dominant political, religious, and economic site of the Ancestral Puebloan world, but by the beginning of the twelfth century it fell into decline, possibly as the result of drought and overpopulation. Its great houses, most notably Pueblo Bonito and Chetro Ketl, were not primarily residential structures but were public buildings used for administrative, religious, and trade purposes. They were, in essence, expressions of Chaco's power. Aztec's West Ruin, the most thoroughly excavated part of the site, is similar to Chaco's Chetro Ketl great house. The bracket-shaped structure stood three stories high and included more than 400 rooms and kivas (circular pits used for ritual and other community activities). The great house is built of yellow sandstone with two decorative bands of green stone, one at the base and another about 3 feet up the walls. In front of the great house, between its two wings, is the Great Kiva, the community's spiritual center. In the 1930s Earl H. Morris, who did the first systematic archaeological work at Aztec, restored the Great Kiva to look as it did a thousand years ago. Four pillars support massive wooden roof beams 30 feet overhead. Light filters in from ground-level windows, illuminating a stone bench running around the perimeter. In the floor is the *sipapu*, representing the portal through which the Ancestral Puebloans believed humans migrated from the spirit world below to the surface of the earth.[12]

When we arrived at the Aztec Ruins National Monument, the park service officer on duty inside the combined office, museum, and store seemed

FIGURE 4.2. Aztec Ruins National Monument, New Mexico. A portion of the West Ruin's exterior wall shows the structure's decorative bands of green stone.

FIGURE 4.3. Aztec's West Ruin and Great Kiva.

more interested, insistent really, in selling us season passes to the national park system than in telling us anything about the ruins. I took this as evidence of the financial pressure the national parks have been under in recent years. Finally, with one-day tickets bought and guidebooks in hand, we stepped out the door and into the twelfth century. I was more than a little

FIGURE 4.4. Interior of the reconstructed Great Kiva, Aztec Ruins National Monument. Note the *sipapu* in the center.

surprised that visitors pretty much have free run of the place. The pathways lead to all the key features, including interior areas of the great house and the Great Kiva, which visitors are allowed to enter. I was struck most by the architectural and construction prowess of the "primitive" people who built the Aztec Ruins using only stone tools. They also dug irrigation ditches connecting their fields to the nearby Animas River. They completed the West Ruin by about 1130 and continued building the community's twelve other structures over the next 150 years. Then they left. I wondered where they had gone, and I wondered why.

From Aztec we headed west, through Farmington and into the Navajo Indian Reservation. The most taxing part of this stretch was the ride through Farmington. The city's traffic engineers have very carefully timed the traffic lights along the entire length of West Main Street to ensure that motorists have ample opportunity to admire the town's car dealerships, fast-food restaurants, service stations, and strip malls while stopped at each and every light. After what seemed like hours of idling in the midday heat at Farmington's intersections, we finally cleared the city limits and headed toward Shiprock.

FIGURE 4.5. Shiprock dominates the landscape of much of the Four Corners region. Photographer: Dana Rae Echohawk.

In the shimmering desert heat, Shiprock looks like a three-masted schooner. The Navajos call the rock Tse' Bit'a'i, "the Winged Rock," and it is linked to several of their legends. The eroding volcanic rock formation dominates the landscape for scores of miles in all directions.[13]

Back in Colorado, we rode across the Mountain Ute Indian Reservation, where the Weeminuche band resides. The treaty of 1880, forced on Chief Ouray after the White River Uprising against the Indian agent Nathan Meeker, consigned the Weeminuche and the neighboring Mouache and Capote bands to this remote and seemingly desolate corner of Colorado (see chapter 2). Long a desperately poor place, the Ute Mountain Ute reservation's economy has grown rapidly in recent years as a result of oil and gas development and because the Mountain Utes, like many other Indian groups, have opened a large gambling casino at Towaoc.

We stopped for the night in Cortez, a relatively young settlement in this area that has been home to human occupants for millennia. Early the next

FIGURE 4.6. Spruce Tree House, Mesa Verde National Park, Colorado.

morning we rode to Mesa Verde National Park, a few miles east of Cortez. We arrived at the gate at 8:00 a.m. in hopes of getting in ahead of the crowds that fill the park daily during the summer months and to see the major cliff dwellings while leaving plenty of time for the rest of the day's agenda, riding to Kayenta, Arizona. We decided to focus on the two most famous and accessible of the cliff dwellings: Spruce Tree House and Cliff Palace.

Spruce Tree House is my favorite site at Mesa Verde, and only a few visitors were there when we arrived. It was profoundly quiet. From a bench across the narrow canyon you can look at the ruins and, if other people are not around and no airplanes are flying overhead, you can hear nothing. Then, one of the area's big ravens may call, or a breeze might rustle tree leaves. As I sat there, I imagined the ancient cliff dwellers working, playing, and praying in the cool shade of the cliff. A short, steep trail of perhaps one-third of a mile leads down into and across the canyon to Spruce Tree House. The temperature at the ruins was easily 20 degrees cooler than at the top of the mesa. The cliff dwellers may have been "primitive," but they were not dumb. They had figured out how to live comfortably in a climate that is hot and dry in the summer and at times numbingly cold in the winter. This was clearly a sophisticated society capable of creating buildings that have stood for more than 700 years. I wondered what would be left of Denver after 700 years if the city's population disappeared suddenly.

As I walked around Spruce Tree House, the same questions, and others, came to mind that I had wondered about the day before at Aztec. Why did the Ancestral Puebloans of Mesa Verde build in the caves and overhangs of the mesa's canyons? How did they live? And why did they leave?

The Ancestral Puebloans began building Mesa Verde's spectacular cliff dwellings during the twelfth century, and they represent only the final phase of ancient settlement there. Centuries earlier, beginning in the late sixth century, their ancestors lived on top of the mesa. The earliest Mesa Verdeans lived in small communities of pit houses dug several feet into the ground and roofed with latticework of branches and brush, covered with soil and supported by interior posts and timbers. The interiors, sometimes divided into living and work areas, featured a fire pit, ventilation openings, storage niches, and a *sipapu*. Occupants entered and left the pit houses through openings in the side walls or the roof. They supported themselves by hunting and gathering and by growing small crops of corn, beans, and squash.[14]

The Mesa Verdeans began to move out of the pit houses and into surface buildings during the eighth century. As the surface structures took shape, the pit houses evolved into ceremonial kivas. Over time, the surface buildings became large and more complex, reflecting the culture's growing population and sophistication. During the twelfth century they constructed major buildings similar to the great houses of Chaco and Aztec, including Far View House, Pipe Shrine House, and Coyote Village. In addition, they built extensive water storage and irrigation systems to water their fields.[15]

The shift from surface structures on top of the mesa to Mesa Verde's famous cliff dwellings began during the mid-twelfth century. Archaeologists have no definitive explanation for the shift to the cliff dwellings. One popular writer suggests that growing violence throughout the region prompted the move to the more readily defensible cliff sites. "The archaeological record from the thirteenth century around the Four Corners," Craig Childs claims, "reads like a war crimes indictment." Archaeologists Arthur H. Rohn and William M. Ferguson agree that the Ancestral Puebloans undoubtedly experienced raiding, probably by Apachean and Ute peoples, and they characterize the move to the cliffs as "a passive response to the threat of warfare." They note, however, that the Ancestral Puebloans did not depict war and war heroes in their artworks, suggesting that they were not a warrior culture. The fact that the Mesa Verde cliff houses have yielded no evidence of large-scale violence may suggest that the move to the cliffs was, in fact, a successful defensive strategy. A possibly related explanation notes that the cliff dwellings are often located next to, or even built around, reliable water sources. A population fearing attack would certainly want to be able to ensure access to water. Spruce Tree House's proximity to one of Mesa Verde's most reliable springs is a case in point.[16]

Another explanation is connected to the cliff dwellers' ultimate fate. Archaeologist Susan Ryan notes that significant population growth occurred at Mesa Verde during the late thirteenth century, coinciding with the height of cliff dwelling construction. This growth, she suggests, may have been a gathering of the population in preparation for departure from the area. That is, they may have gathered in the cliff dwellings to prepare to leave Mesa Verde and resettle elsewhere as a cohesive community.[17]

Mesa Verde's cliff dwellers built and lived in a sophisticated and, apparently, a successful society, as demonstrated by the buildings and other artifacts they left behind. Especially significant was their diverse diet, which included foods from hunting, gathering, and agriculture. Important staples were berries, yucca and cactus fruit, and piñon nuts; deer, rabbit, and squirrel meat; and domesticated turkeys. They raised the turkeys not only for meat but also for feathers, which they used for clothing, and bones, used for tools. The cliff dwellers also cultivated large fields of corn, beans, and squash on top of the mesa and in terraced plots in the canyons. To irrigate their crops they built an extensive system of reservoirs and ditches. Excavation of the cliff dwellings uncovered exotic artifacts such as seashells, copper bells, macaw feathers, and cotton textiles, linking Mesa Verde to an extensive trading network that reached to the Pacific Ocean and far south into Mexico.[18]

Why, then, did this successful and prosperous people pack up and leave in the last years of the thirteenth century? Violence, which may help explain their gathering together in the cliff dwellings, does not account for their departure. Archaeologists have found no evidence of violence on a scale large enough to cause the Mesa Verdeans' flight. And there is no evidence of a successor population occupying the cliff dwellings.

A powerful migratory impulse, such as that suggested by Ryan, is perhaps a better explanation. Rohn and Ferguson look to modern Puebloan people and their folklore for guidance. After coming from the spirit world to the physical world, each Puebloan group wandered for long periods until they found their "central place," where they settled permanently. Every modern pueblo, Rohn and Ferguson say, "recognizes its present location as the central place for that pueblo, reached after long wanderings guided by supernatural powers." The Ancestral Puebloans' sudden abandonment of Mesa Verde and the rest of the Four Corners region may have been the result of their concluding that the area was not their central place.[19] Why they made that decision is less clear, though Rohn and Ferguson suggest disease or environmental change as causes. Certainly, if Mesa Verde's Ancestral Puebloans left to search for their central place, it would have made sense for them to do so at a time when they were thriving and thus could depart at a moment of their choosing and with plenty of food and other necessities to sustain them on their journey.

My Immutable Second Law of History (revised edition) states that the simplest and most obvious explanation for a historical problem is usually a pretty good one. The Second Law of History also states, however, that simple and obvious explanations are rarely sufficient. Between 1276 and 1299 the Four Corners region experienced a dry spell known as the Great Drought. This period of drought coincided with the cessation of construction of the cliff dwellings and their abandonment. By 1300 the Ancestral Puebloans had abandoned all of the settlements in Mesa Verde and the Four Corners area. So the simple and obvious explanation would be that the rains ceased, the streams went dry, the fields dried up, and the people left. However, climate studies, based on tree-ring data, suggest that despite the protracted drought, enough groundwater was available during the last two decades of the thirteenth century to support a significant population.[20] These data complicate, but do not discount, the role of the Great Drought in the abandonment of Mesa Verde.

The rise and abandonment of the Ancestral Puebloan settlements are consistent with the history of boom and bust that characterizes the experience of the modern American West. Like the gold and silver camps of the nineteenth century or of Jeffrey City, Wyoming, in the late twentieth century, the story of the Ancestral Puebloans fits the historical pattern of settlements appearing and organizing themselves on the basis of resource exploitation.

Again, the equation seems obvious and simple. The resource that drew people to a place—gold, silver, uranium, water—runs out, and the people leave.

But in the case of the Ancestral Puebloans, the tree-ring data suggest that their key resource—water—did not run out, so the Great Drought seemingly does not explain their abandonment of the Four Corners area. In fact, however, it does. By the late thirteenth century the Ancestral Puebloans had built a complex society characterized by increasing population density in their settlements, supported largely by intensive, irrigated crop production. In short, they created a hydraulic society. That society was smaller and less complex than that of the modern American West, but it, too, was built on the dream of irrigation. When the Great Drought struck, it undermined the whole structure of their society. It was not that there was not enough water to support the population per se. The problem was that there was not enough water to support their society as they had organized it. And so, while they still had the material resources and social organization to do so, the Ancestral Puebloans packed up and left Mesa Verde and the Four Corners area for places more suited to their way of life. Today, their descendants are found among the modern Pueblo peoples of the Rio Grande Valley in New Mexico and the Hopi of Arizona.

The Ancestral Puebloans' story is instructive for the contemporary American West and its hydraulic society. The West's highly urbanized population, its industries and its agriculture, depend on a complex infrastructure of dams, reservoirs, hydroelectric generators, and irrigation systems, just as the Mesa Verdeans depended on their system of reservoirs, ditches, and irrigated fields. We know that the modern West's irrigation dream was built on bad data, the assumption that the exceptionally wet years of the early twentieth century were normal. We also know that normal precipitation in the Colorado River Basin is historically much lower. So the modern West's hydraulic system, and the society it supports, is very fragile, probably more fragile than that of the Ancestral Puebloans. Almost eight centuries separate the Ancestral Puebloans of Mesa Verde from the Glen Canyon, Hoover, and Blue Mesa Dams and the society that built them, but the environmental reality of the American Southwest connects them in ways that today are all too apparent. The Colorado River will not dry up completely, just as the rivers and streams of the San Juan Basin did not dry up completely in the late thirteenth century. But if river and reservoir levels continue to decline as

FIGURE 4.7. A small herd of tourists inspecting one of the many kivas at Cliff Palace, Mesa Verde National Park, Colorado.

climatologists predict, then we in the contemporary West may someday face the same problems and decisions the Ancestral Puebloans confronted.

From Spruce Tree House, we made the short ride to Cliff Palace. We stayed there only long enough to take a few pictures from the observation platform. The place was crawling with noisy school kids and small herds of *tourist Americanus, tourist Japonica,* and *tourist Europeanus.* I had to give one kid my best pissed-off professor stare to get him to stop placing himself between my camera lens and the scene of Cliff House. Finally, though, the photo taken, we got back on the motorcycles and headed out of the park, bound for the Four Corners and, beyond that, Kayenta, Arizona.

We stopped for gas at a truck plaza in Towaoc, the headquarters of the Ute Mountain Ute Reservation. Right next door is the Ute Mountain Casino. The truck plaza, with its acres of concrete, and the brightly painted, perpetually illuminated casino appeared strikingly incongruous in the surrounding desert environment. Phineas observed that, based on what he had seen of this country, it seemed clear to him that the Utes had been screwed. I could not disagree with him, though the neighboring Navajos had made their

home in this area for many centuries and in the nineteenth century, having
been forced out, begged the government to let them return (discussed later).
Nevertheless, the United States had seemingly confined the Utes to a place
white people would never covet. That, of course, was long before anyone
found oil, gas, and coal there. When that happened, fossil fuel companies
became very interested in the reservations. Like other Indian nations around
the country, the Utes developed another extractive industry—gambling—
to enhance their tribal economy by separating tourists from their money.
Carbon and vice: two surefire moneymakers.

From Towaoc it was a short ride to the Four Corners Monument, which is
operated by the Navajo Nation. A three-dollar fee admits you to a small compound, at the center of which is a concrete platform supporting a large granite disk encircling a smaller bronze disk marking the spot where Colorado,
Utah, New Mexico, and Arizona meet. According to my GPS device, that
point is 36.59.937 north and 109.02.717 west (plus or minus 16 feet). In 2009
the National Geodectic Survey (NGS), evidently having nothing better to
do, announced that the monument is actually 1,807 feet east of where it
should be. The late western writer Ed Quillen, the Sage of Salida, responded
to the NGS claim by challenging its assumptions and methods; he insisted
that the marker was off by, at most, a few hundred feet. As Quillen notes,
Colorado's constitution locates the state's southwest corner at the intersection of the 37th parallel north and the "32nd meridian of longitude west from
Washington." The NGS, he says, made the mistake of equating 32 degrees
west of Washington, DC, with 109 degrees west of the prime meridian in
Greenwich, England. Depending on the spot in the District of Columbia
used as a survey starting point, Colorado's western boundary would be in the
vicinity of 109.2.sparechange west, right about where my GPS device had it.[21]

Regardless of whether the monument is precisely where it should be, since
1912 tourists have come here to make fools of themselves, assuming sundry
preposterous postures to place parts of their bodies in all four states simul-
taneously, all recorded photographically by family or friends. When Phineas
and I arrived, we joined about 200 other visitors and had a fine time watching the show. We stood by the monument for several minutes watching a
German tourist standing on his hands. He began with one hand and one foot
in each of the four states. Then he kicked up into a handstand with his right
hand planted firmly in New Mexico and pivoted to place his left hand in each

FIGURE 4.8. Four Corners Monument, which may or may not mark the juncture of Colorado, New Mexico, Utah, and Arizona.

of the other three states. After a while, Phineas wandered off to browse the jewelry, pottery, and art for sale in the surrounding vendors' stalls as I waited in line for what seemed like hours to mount the observation platform next to the monument. After a few more minutes waiting atop the platform, I finally secured a photo of the monument sans acrobats. That mission accomplished, we headed off into the Arizona desert and the Navajo Indian Reservation.

THE *DINÉ*

Compared with the Puebloans and their ancestors, the Navajos are recent migrants to the Four Corners region. They and another southwestern people, the Apaches, speak an Athapaskan language, placing their origins in northwest Canada or Alaska. Their long migration south brought them to present-day northern New Mexico by the twelfth or thirteenth century and perhaps as early as the eleventh century.[22]

The *Diné*, as the Navajos call themselves, quickly adapted to life in the Southwest, so much so that anthropologist David Brugge has concluded that "remarkably little" in their culture "can be traced to their Northern Athapaskan ancestors aside from language and basic cultural themes such as individualism, fear of the dead, high status for women, [a] pragmatic and optimistic outlook and, as a corollary to the last, flexibility in adapting to new situations."[23] Without taking issue with Brugge, those basic cultural themes are crucial in the development of Navajo culture.

Sheep and horses, brought to North America by Spanish conquistadors and settlers, were especially important. The acquisition of sheep ended forever the Navajos' nomadic ways, substituting more limited pastoral migrations. Sheep became the foundation of Navajo social, cultural, and economic life. Holdings of the animal determined an individual's wealth and status. Wool became an item of trade with other Indians, the Spanish, and the New Mexicans, especially after Navajos mastered the use of the Spanish broad loom to weave blankets. Culturally, sheep came to symbolize the Mother, a reflection of the Navajos' matrilineal culture and the status of women. Horses facilitated management of sheep flocks. They also enhanced another important element of Navajo culture: raiding. Raiding was acquisitive, defensive, and retaliatory. Navajos raided other Indians, as well as Spanish and New Mexican settlements, to acquire more sheep and horses. However, the Navajos also raided to defend themselves against, or to retaliate for, depredations by Comanches and the Spanish who stole Navajo women and children for a slave trade in Mexico and the Southwest that flourished well into the nineteenth century, even beyond the era of the American Civil War. With the transition to pastoralism, the Navajos also learned to raise crops— primarily corn—and planted orchards of fruit-bearing trees, most notably their richly productive peach orchards in Canyon de Chelly (pronounced "de shay").[24]

With growing flocks of sheep and herds of horses, the Navajos needed more land. The *Dinétah*, the region east of Farmington, New Mexico, where they first settled, was not only too small but also became more vulnerable to Spanish, Comanche, and Ute raids. So by the late eighteenth century the Navajos moved to the west. Canyon de Chelly became the spiritual and economic center of a vast Navajo territory, the *Diné Bikéyah*. In Navajo tradition the *Diné Bikéyah* is a vast territory defined by four sacred mountains: Blanca Peak, near Fort Garland, Colorado; Mount Hesperus, near Durango, Colorado; Mount Taylor, near Grants, New Mexico; and the San Francisco

Peaks, near Flagstaff, Arizona. To be safe and content, the *Diné* must live within the *Diné Bikéyah*.[25]

The portion of Navajo country we rode through along US 160 is desert land straight out of a Hollywood western. For long stretches the surface is covered with enormous slabs of flat, deep-red sandstone. Great mesas of the same red sandstone rise abruptly from the desert floor and stand in vivid contrast to the brilliant blue sky. Small clumps of desert grasses and cactus were the only vegetation. This, I thought, is what the moon would look like if it were red. The area seems sparsely settled, though as we rode by the town of Teec Nos Pos, a large regional medical center suggested otherwise. Occasionally, we rode by a small farm or sheep ranch. Most had modern homes, many with big satellite dishes. But several yards away from each modern house stood a hogan, the traditional earth-covered dome structure used for dwellings, ceremonies, and meetings. Hogans next to satellite dishes. Despite all they have been through or perhaps because of it, the Navajos have clung to basic elements of their culture, even as they have had to adapt to changed conditions.

Neither Spain nor Mexico ever conquered the Navajos. In the *Diné Bikéyah* they prospered as sheepherders, farmers of corn and peaches, and artisan-traders. And their young men continued to exchange raids with the Spanish, New Mexicans, and other Indians. Tit-for-tat raiding remained a basic fact of life in New Mexico in the late 1840s when the United States seized the territory from Mexico. The new rulers immediately set themselves to the task of suppressing the raids and within twenty years achieved what Spain and Mexico could not accomplish in three-and-a-half centuries: the conquest and subjugation of the Navajos.

The Navajos were divided among themselves about how to deal with the Americans. Some, especially the wealthy, wanted to curtail raiding and conflict and come to terms with the new rulers. Others were determined to resist. Among the latter was Manuelito, who watched his father-in-law, Narbona, sign a peace treaty with the Americans in 1848. In 1849 he watched as US troops killed Narbona in a conflict over a stolen horse. Manuelito figured in several key episodes of the Navajo-American war and was the last Navajo leader to surrender.[26]

In August 1862 General James Henry Carleton assumed command of American forces in New Mexico. Carleton was determined to end the long conflict with the Navajos. He intended not only to subdue and confine them but also to remove them from their territory entirely, to a place far away where they would "acquire new habits, new values, new modes of life," including Christianity and "the art of peace." There might be some resistance, but eventually, as the old died off, a new generation would come of age not burdened by their parents' "longings for murder and robbing."[27]

Carleton knew exactly where he would take the Navajos to reform and civilize them. On a previous posting in New Mexico in the 1850s, he had surveyed the course of the Pecos River in search of a site for a fort. He found it at a place called Bosque Redondo (round woods), a bit south of the intersection of US Highways 84 and 60 in southeastern New Mexico. There, at a bend in the Pecos, stood a large grove of cottonwood trees. Carleton saw it as a kind of pastoral Eden, with lumber, water, and fertile soil—an ideal spot for a fort and a reservation. Unfortunately, Carleton was the only person who saw Bosque Redondo that way. Others who took a closer look found the resources scarce, the soil infertile, and the water unfit for human use.[28]

Carleton put Christopher "Kit" Carson—the famous explorer, trapper, trader, and soldier—in charge of his war on the Navajos. By the 1860s Carson was a larger-than-life character whose exploits, grossly exaggerated in so-called blood and thunder novellas, made him a national hero, especially as an Indian killer—a reputation Carson did not especially appreciate.[29] In July 1863 Carson assembled a large force of American soldiers and Ute mercenaries and headed for Navajo territory. Carleton ordered Carson to "prosecute a vigorous war" against the Navajos.[30] Carson complied, but not as Carleton intended. Rather than fight the Navajos in their own country, Carson set out to starve them into submission by sending his troops to find and destroy their sheep, cattle, and horse herds and their crops. In a decisive foray into the Navajos' stronghold, Canyon de Chelly, Carson's men even destroyed their treasured peach trees. By early 1864, starving Navajos began to stream into army posts to surrender. They did not all come in at once and some small groups never surrendered, preferring to live starving and on the run rather than face deportation. Manuelito, the last major leader to give up, came into Fort Wingate, starving and wounded, in September 1866.

After surrender, there followed the Long Walk. For three years, soldiers escorted groups of Navajos on an arduous trek to Bosque Redondo. In all seasons of the year, ill-fed and poorly clothed Navajos tramped the more than 250 miles to Carleton's Eden in the desert. Hundreds died along the way, usually because of hunger or disease or exposure but sometimes also at the hands of their soldier-escorts. For Carleton and for the United States, the Long Walk and its aftermath were necessary chapters in the fulfillment of America's Manifest Destiny. From the comfort of his headquarters in Santa Fe, the general characterized "the exodus of this whole people from the land of their fathers" as a "touching sight." But the Navajos understood, he said, that it was "their destiny . . . to give way to the insatiable progress of our race."[31]

Once settled at Bosque Redondo, things went from bad to worse for the Navajos. The army provided insufficient rations, and the few that arrived often included tainted flour and rancid bacon. The water from the Pecos made them sick, so dehydration complemented malnutrition. For the first three years they planted fields of corn, but none made it to harvest, as insects devoured the immature ears. In addition, the disarmed Navajos became helpless victims of raids by Comanches, who stole their few remaining sheep and horses and sometimes abducted their children. The *Diné* remember Bosque Redondo as *hwéeldi*, the place of suffering. About one-third of the Navajos who survived the Long Walk, as many as 3,000, died there. The Mescalero Apaches, who shared Bosque Redondo's miseries with the Navajos, proved less tolerant of the place than their fellow prisoners. In November 1865 they stole 200 Navajo horses and left in the dead of night, never to return.[32]

General Carleton refused to acknowledge the catastrophe he had created at Bosque Redondo, insisting that the Navajos had been cared for "with great kindness."[33] Another general, however, saw for himself the horror at Bosque Redondo, and he did something about it. General William Tecumseh Sherman, the scourge of the Confederacy, traveled to the West in the spring of 1868 as part of a peace commission charged with ending the Indian wars that had raged from the Northern Plains to the Mexican border since 1862. The commission's task was to negotiate treaties to move Indian tribes to reservations and open most of the West to white settlement. Their work on the Northern Plains, most notably the Fort Laramie Treaty of 1868, set the stage for another war that erupted in 1876. Sherman's efforts in New Mexico were much more successful.

Sherman arrived at Bosque Redondo in May 1868 and, after inspecting the place, acknowledged to a gathering of Navajo leaders what they knew all too well: "You have no farms, no herds, and are now as poor as you were when the government brought you here." Sherman also made it clear to the Navajos that they would not be staying at Bosque Redondo. He briefly broached he possibility of moving to Indian Territory but quickly added, "If you don't want that we will discuss the other proposition of going back to your own country." Barboncito, the Navajos' spokesman, replied, "I hope to God you will not ask me to go to any other country than my own. It might turn out [to be] another Bosque Redondo. They told us this was a good place when we came, but it is not."[34]

That settled the matter. On June 1, 1868, Sherman and the Navajos signed a treaty to restore the *Diné* to their homeland. The new reservation was only a small part of the *Diné Bikéyah*, but it included Canyon de Chelly. For their part, the Navajos agreed never again to make war on the United States or other Indians. Most of the Navajos had to walk back home, but the journey was better provisioned than the Long Walk and, most important, it led them home.

Memories of the Carson campaign, the Long Walk, and Bosque Redondo are fundamental elements of Navajo identity. Historian Richard White calls them "a lasting reminder of the power and ruthlessness of the federal government." To be sure, the Navajos were the victims of a ruthless and powerful government, one driven by visions of empire and racial superiority. But to leave it at that seems inadequate because the Navajos' experience in the 1860s was also one of survival, adaptation, and triumph. Another historian, Peter Iverson, states it well: "They had defended their mountains. They had begun to see themselves as a great people, destined to do great things."[35]

Compared with many Indian people, the Navajos' experience since 1868 has been a story of triumph over adversity. Between 1878 and 1933, a series of executive orders and congressional acts more than doubled the size of the reservation. One order by President Chester Alan Arthur in 1882 also carved out a reservation within the Navajos' reservation for the Hopis and "other Indians." The order's lack of specificity as to occupation rights in that tract became a cause of conflict between Navajos and Hopis that persists today.[36]

Certainly, poverty, health problems, and illiteracy plagued the *Diné* and still do, but as a people they had two powerful things going for them. One was the sense of unity and purpose they brought home with them from Bosque Redondo. The second was their control of their land. Unlike most Indian people, the Navajos escaped the depredations of the Dawes General

Allotment Act of 1887. Sold as a reform measure intended to accelerate the process of turning American Indians into farmers, the act was the biggest land steal in American history. Reservations were surveyed and divided into family farms of up to 160 acres. The government then sold the surplus land—and there was a lot of it—to white settlers. By 1900 American Indians had lost half of their reservation lands to allotment, and by 1934 more than half of their remaining lands, including two-thirds of allotted property, had been lost as a result of sales and fraud.[37]

Because the Navajo Reservation was not allotted, the *Diné* retained both communal and individual rights to their lands. That enabled them, over the first six decades after 1868, to rebuild their sheep, cattle, and horse herds. They also developed new farms and expanded their weaving, pottery, and silver arts industries. But in the 1930s a government-imposed program inflicted upon the Navajos another period of great personal, cultural, and economic pain.

By the 1930s, sheep herding was once again central to *Diné* economic and cultural life. Unfortunately, the federal government decided that they had succeeded too well. Navajo herds had grown so large that they were overgrazing reservation lands, the government concluded. That would not only harm the long-term health of the animals and the land but might also cause silting in the Colorado River drainage system, which could damage the newly constructed Hoover Dam. And so, with Bureau of Indian Affairs chief John Collier—a professed friend and respecter of Indian culture—leading the charge, government agents imposed livestock quotas on Navajo families and impounded and slaughtered tens of thousands of animals. The government did not consult the Navajos in any meaningful way. It simply imposed its will.[38]

The livestock reduction program was enormously harmful, both economically and culturally. Historian Richard White notes that it "helped destroy one of the last functioning Indian economies in the United States." In doing so, it forced many Navajos into wage work in extractive industries on the reservation or forced them to leave the reservation entirely. Between 1942 and 1979, many Navajos worked in uranium mines on the reservation. They worked in poorly ventilated mines and mills without adequate respirators. The result was an epidemic of illness and death. Of 150 men who worked at a mine in Shiprock before 1970, 133 died of lung diseases. Mines and tailings continue to pollute groundwater, wells, and the land.[39]

Culturally, livestock reduction brought back painful memories of the Carson campaign, the Long Walk, and *hwéeldi*. The Navajos had a deep, personal relationship with their animals. Anthropologist Edward T. Hall noted, "Sheep were not a commodity . . . Each sheep was known individually. Any Navajo with a herd could tell you how many lambs each ewe had dropped and could identify every lamb's mother." The wholesale slaughter of their animals seemed like an attack on the *Diné* themselves. One Navajo woman recalled her husband telling federal agents, "You have now killed me. You have cut off my arms. You have cut off my legs. You have taken my head off. There is nothing left for me. This is the end of the trail."[40] He died a few months later, sick and heartbroken.

The livestock reduction program also embodied an important historical irony. The *Diné* had created an economy and culture, based on sheep cultivation, that was very well adapted to the Southwest's arid climate. However, federal government experts decided in the 1930s that the sheep might become a threat to Hoover Dam and therefore to the irrigation dream. So at least in part to protect the West's irrigation dream, that well-adapted economy and culture had to be altered. The sustainable was sacrificed for the unsustainable.

The ride from Four Corners to Kayenta was hot and dry, so we stopped at a little café at a wide spot in the road called Mexican Water and downed several cold drinks. A sign inside promised that unruly kids would be added to the day's beef stew, and all the youngsters there were indeed well behaved. Refreshed, we stepped back out into the 100-degree heat and set out on the final hour of the day's ride. As we approached Kayenta, we began to see more sandstone monoliths to the north, a foretaste of the scenery we expected to ride through the next day in Monument Valley.

Kayenta is a small but interesting place that demonstrates the Navajos' pride in their history and culture, as well as their accommodation with modernity. We stayed in a brand-new, very nice mid-price-range hotel. Next door was a large, brand-new fast-food restaurant. Between them was a display of traditional hogans and sweat lodges, with informative placards explaining the structures' designs and uses. Inside the restaurant was a display commemorating the Navajo Code Talkers of World War II, a group of Marines who volunteered to be battlefield radio operators in the Pacific theater. The Code Talkers, who were vital to operations at Guadalcanal, Tarawa, Peleliu, and Iwo Jima, developed a dictionary of Navajo words used as substitutes for

FIGURE 4.9. A hogan displayed next to a modern hotel illustrates the persistence of tradition among the Navajos as they accommodate modernity.

English letters. A string of unrelated Navajo words would spell out a single English word. The Japanese never broke the code, though they seemed to realize that it was based on the Navajo language. They had a Navajo prisoner of war listen to Code Talker transmissions, but even he could not understand them. After the war, that POW told a Code Talker, "I never figured out what you guys who got me into all that trouble were saying."[41]

We had a pleasant dinner at the hotel's restaurant. Phineas, however, was disappointed to find that he could not order one of his expensive-sounding European beers, or any other beer, there. The restaurant served no alcohol, a reflection of one of the unfortunate social realities of reservation life. After dinner, we took our cold nonalcoholic drinks out to the restaurant's pleasant patio. Within a couple of minutes, several dogs that hang around the hotel and the fast-food restaurant next door began to approach us. One very pregnant female made the rounds, evidently as starved for human attention as for food. Another dog was wearing a collar that was so tight it had begun to cut into his neck. He would not let me try to loosen it. In the morning, as we rode out of town, I was pretty sure I saw one of the dogs lying dead on the highway.

FIGURE 4.10. Monument Valley, on the Navajo Reservation in northeastern Arizona and southeastern Utah.

Despite that unpleasant start, I had a sense that the day's ride would be special. Early in the morning I had looked out my room window and seen the still bright, nearly full moon hanging low over the red mesa across the road. I ran to the parking lot with my camera to get a picture of the scene. A good omen for the day, I hoped.

The ride from Kayenta to Mexican Hat, Utah, is one of the classic, must-do motorcycling trips in the United States. Monument Valley with its sandstone monoliths is probably one of the most recognizable places in the world, made famous as the setting for any number of Hollywood westerns. We pulled out early, hoping both to beat the desert heat and to see the Monument Valley formations before the sun rose high enough to wash out the colors. It turned out at first, however, that many of the rocks were backlit and looked kind of gray in the early morning light. But as we progressed northeastward, the rocks glowed intensely red with a vivid blue sky as backdrop.

Monument Valley is actually a broad plateau. At its north end is the town of Mexican Hat, Utah, on the banks of the San Juan River, the northern boundary of the Navajo Reservation. The town, named for a prominent sandstone feature that does, in fact, resemble a sombrero, sits at the foot of a long, steep, brake-squealing hill. The sandstone scenery does not end at

Mexican Hat. Red sandstone canyons, especially the Valley of the Gods, and yellow sandstone mesas dominate the climb up from the San Juan River to the town of Bluff.

Bluff was an interesting surprise. Set in a narrow valley of yellow sandstone, it is an old farming town turned artist colony. We pulled into the parking lot of Comb Ridge Coffee. This was not Starbucks. The parking lot had a number of artworks by local artists, including what appeared to be some sort of shrine to travel in the Southwest. Customers are invited to buy sticks of incense to burn in the shrine's wire fence. Inside the building, a restored trading post, are more paintings and jewelry. The owner, with her husband, came to Bluff as a VISTA (Volunteers in Service to America) volunteer. They stayed on and opened the coffee house/art gallery as a community service project, giving local artists a venue for their works and donating a percentage of art sale proceeds to charity. It was here that a Mormon patron informed me that the Oregon Trail is misnamed, that it should be called the Mormon Trail.

BACK TO THE MOUNTAINS

A yellow sandstone formation called the Navajo Twins looms over the road on the way out of Bluff, a final example of the region's monumental scenery. From Bluff, we rode northeast to Monticello (pronounced mon-ti-sell-o) and then headed southeast along the edge of the Canyon of the Ancients National Monument to the town of Dolores, Colorado. From there, Colorado 145 follows the Dolores River through a lush valley of farms and ranches and then ascends to the river's headwaters on Lizard Head Pass in the San Juan Mountains.

The descent down the other side of the pass to the old mining town of Telluride is fast and winding. As we approached Telluride, traffic increased, with Lexus, Cadillac, and Lincoln SUVs outnumbering ranch pickup trucks. Telluride and its environs have become a playground for the rich. At a place called "Mountain Village," 5,000-square-foot "cabins" surround a private golf course. Telluride itself has been transformed from a virtual ghost town into a gentrified resort with pricey boutiques, five-star restaurants, art galleries, and a surfboard shop. Little of its historic mining town past remains.

On a visit there at least three decades ago, when Telluride's gentrification was just beginning, I visited the town museum, located in an old building off the main street, Colorado Avenue. On the ground by the front steps were the decaying armature and brush of mine owner Lucien Lucius Nunn's alternating-current hydroelectric generator. Nunn's generator, designed in part by the physicist and engineer Nikola Tesla for George Westinghouse, represented a major step in the development of America's industrial technology. Westinghouse had been in competition with Thomas Edison and his direct-current system, and Nunn's request to install an alternating-current system for his mine in the mountains above Telluride was an opportunity for him to demonstrate his technology's ability to generate and transmit electric power over long distances in even the most remote places. The closest generating site, at the confluence of the Lake and Howard's Fork branches of the San Miguel River, was 3 miles from Nunn's mine. When the generator went into service in 1891, it produced so much power that Nunn was able to sell current to other mines in the district and to electrify the entire town of Telluride, making it the first city in the country lit completely by alternating-current electricity.[42]

I wanted to ride into Telluride to see if the museum and armature were still there, but at a gas stop on the way other motorcyclists warned us that some sort of art festival was going on and the town was clogged with beautiful people. As we approached the town, we could see that the highway was backed up and at a standstill. We did not have to discuss the matter; we hung a left and continued down Colorado 145, following the San Miguel River through a narrow canyon of purple sandstone to the town of Placerville. From there we rode out of the San Juan Mountains and made our way to Montrose.

Heading north out of Montrose the following morning, we saw much of the rest of the Uncompahgre Valley, one of Colorado's great fruit-growing regions. At Delta, we turned onto Colorado 92 and, after a few miles, onto Colorado 133, which follow the Gunnison River and its north branch for about 45 miles. Ten miles north of McClure Pass we rode into Redstone, a significant site in the history of Colorado's coal industry and labor relations. Here, in 1902, the founder of the Colorado Fuel and Iron Company, John Cleveland Osgood, built brick beehive ovens to make coke for his steel mill at Pueblo. But Osgood had something else in mind, too. He intended to build Redstone as a new model of industrial relations in the troubled times of the late nineteenth century. He built a modern boardinghouse for single men and nice Craftsman-style cottages for managers and workers with families.

FIGURE 4.11. Beehive coke ovens are remnants of John C. Osgood's industrial paradise at Redstone, Colorado.

The boardinghouse and cottages had electric lights and indoor plumbing. Osgood also provided recreation facilities, a school, and medical care. Nearby, Osgood built a forty-two-room home for himself. Called Cleveholm, the house loomed over Redstone like a feudal-era baronial manse.[43]

Redstone, like George Pullman's industrial suburb of Chicago, seemed to be a fine place to work and live. However, as at Pullman, where the great railroad strike of 1894 erupted in protest against Pullman's wage cutting and dictatorial control of all aspects of life in the town, Osgood expected his employees to surrender to him virtually all authority over their lives. To be sure, no industrial violence occurred while Osgood ran the place, and the workers generally seemed satisfied with their lot. Redstone residents especially liked Osgood's wife, Alma, who earned the nickname "Lady Bountiful" for her annual holiday gifts to workers and their families.[44]

Osgood lost control of Colorado Fuel and Iron in 1903 to John D. Rockefeller Jr., but he stayed in the coal industry as president of the Victor-American Fuel Company and in 1913–14 became a major leader in the coal companies' campaign to crush the United Mine Workers–led strike in Las Animas and Huerfano Counties. That struggle culminated in the Ludlow Massacre in April 1914. Obviously, by then Osgood had abandoned his paternalistic idealism toward industrial workers.[45]

From Redstone it was only about a 40-mile ride to Glenwood Springs, where we rolled onto Interstate 70. The scenery along the interstate is beautiful, but the highway was clogged with traffic and we spent a hot half-hour sitting at a construction stop west of Vail. Once clear of that, we raced non-stop home to Denver.

While we waited in that construction jam, I started thinking about the trip now coming to its end and especially about the distance separating Mesa Verde and the Blue Mesa Reservoir, about 100 miles and 800 years. Despite the centuries that separate them and vast differences in technology and material wealth, the people of thirteenth-century Mesa Verde and the people of the twenty-first-century American West have much in common. Like us, the Mesa Verdeans lived in organized communities. Also like us, they built their lives and communities on an infrastructure based on managing scarce water resources. It occurred to me, however, that there is one key difference: they could pack up and leave when they had to. Could we do that? Where would we go? How would we live?

NOTES

1. Donald Worster, *Rivers of Empire: Water, Aridity and the Growth of the American West* (New York: Pantheon Books, 1985), 265 (second quotation), 277–78 (first quotation); Carl Abbott, Stephen J. Leonard, and Thomas J. Noel, *Colorado: A History of the Centennial State*, 4th ed. (Boulder: University Press of Colorado, 2005), 383–84; US Bureau of Reclamation, "Colorado River Storage Project," at http://www.usbr .gov/uc/rm/crsp/index.html, accessed August 6, 2014; US Bureau of Reclamation, "Colorado River Storage Project, Aspinall Unit," at http://www.usbr.gov/uc/rm /crsp/aspinall/index.html, accessed August 6, 2014.

2. Worster, *Rivers of Empire*, 273–74; Abbott, Leonard, and Noel, *Colorado*, 384–85.

3. Russell Martin, *A Story That Stands Like a Dam: Glen Canyon and the Struggle for the Soul of the West* (Salt Lake City: University of Utah Press, 1989), 273–82. On the Echo Park and Grand Canyon battles, see James Lawrence Powell, *Dead Pool: Lake Powell, Global Warming, and the Future of Water in the West* (Berkeley: University of California Press, 2008), 3–142; Worster, *Rivers of Empire*, 273–74, 276.

4. Powell, *Dead Pool*, 145; Martin, *Story That Stands Like a Dam*, 308.

5. Smythe quoted in Powell, *Dead Pool*, 62; US Bureau of Reclamation, "Colorado River Storage Project."

6. Powell, *Dead Pool*, 1–17.

7. Summit Technologies, Inc., "Lake Powell Water Database," at http://lake powell.water-data.com/index2.php, accessed March 12, 2009; US Bureau of Reclamation, "Upper Colorado Region Historic Data: Upper Colorado Region Reservoir Operation," http://usbr.gov/uc/crsp/charts/displaysites.jsp, accessed March 12, 2009; http://lakepowell.water-data.com, accessed August 6, 2014; http://bluemesa .water-data.com, accessed August 17, 2013.

8. Powell, *Dead Pool*, 166–68; studies by Barnett and Pierce summarized in Robert Monroe, "Climate Change Means Shortfalls in Colorado River Water Deliveries," April 21, 2009, at http://ucsdnews.ucsd.edu/archive/newsrel/general/04-09ColoradoRiver.asp, accessed August 4, 2014; Robert Monroe, "Lake Mead Could Be Dry by 2021," at http://ucsdnews.ucsd.edu/newsrel/science/02-08 LakeMead.asp, accessed April 26, 2009.

9. Powell, *Dead Pool*, 46; Patricia Nelson Limerick, *Desert Passages: Encounters with the American Deserts* (Albuquerque: University of New Mexico Press, 1985), 171 (quotation), 203.

10. Powell, *Dead Pool*, 146–47.

11. Arthur H. Rohn and William M. Ferguson, *Puebloan Ruins of the Southwest* (Albuquerque: University of New Mexico Press, 2006), 8; Craig Childs, *House of Rain: Tracking a Vanished Civilization across the American Southwest* (New York: Little, Brown, 2007), 263–66; US Department of the Interior, Bureau of Land Management, "Who Were the Anasazi?" at http://www.blm.gov/co/st/en/fo/ahc/who_were_the_anasazi.html#who, accessed August 2, 2011.

12. Paul F. Reed, *The Puebloan Society of Chaco Canyon* (Westport, CT: Greenwood, 2004), 36–37; US Department of the Interior, National Park Service, "Chaco Culture National Historic Park: History and Culture," at http://www.nps.gov /chcu/historyculture/index.htm, accessed March 24, 2009; Rohn and Ferguson, *Puebloan Ruins of the Southwest*, 64, 177–79.

13. New Mexico Bureau of Geology and Mineral Resources, "The Ship Rock Formation," at https://geoinfo.nmt.edu/tour/landmarks/shiprock/home.html, accessed August 8, 2014.

14. Rohn and Ferguson, *Puebloan Ruins of the Southwest*, 84–86; Stephen Plog, *Ancient Peoples of the American Southwest*, 2nd ed. (London: Thames and Hudson, 2008), 58; Abbott, Leonard, and Noel, *Colorado*, 12.

15. Rohn and Ferguson, *Puebloan Ruins of the Southwest*, 92–98.

16. Ibid., 101–2; Childs, *House of Rain*, 156; Mark D. Varien, William D. Lipe, Michael A. Adler, Ian M. Thompson, and Bruce A. Bradley, "Southwestern Colorado and Southeastern Utah Settlement Patterns: A.D. 1100 to 1300," in Michael A. Adler, ed., *The Prehistoric Pueblo World: A.D. 1150–1350* (Tucson: University of Arizona Press, 1996), 98–99.

17. Susan Ryan's work is discussed in Childs, *House of Rain*, 123. See also Craig Childs, "Out of the Four Corners," *High Country News*, October 3, 2005, at https://www.hcn.org/issues/307/15806, accessed August 4, 2014.

18. Rohn and Ferguson, *Puebloan Ruins of the Southwest*, 61–62, 73–74.

19. Ibid., 80.

20. Childs, *House of Rain*, 172–73; Plog, *Ancient Peoples of the American Southwest*, 153.

21. Associated Press, "Correction: Four Corners Marker Story," April 22, 2009, at http://www.highbeam.com/doc/1A1-D97NODCG3.html, accessed August 4, 2014; Ed Quillen, "Where Is Four Corners?" at http://www.denverpost.com/search/ci_12213262, accessed May 1, 2009. The National Geodetic Survey quickly blamed the media for inaccurately reporting that the agency had claimed the marker is as much as 2.5 miles from the true Four Corners location and asserted that it meant only to claim that it is about 1,800 feet off. National Geodetic Survey, "Why the Four Corners Monument Is in Exactly the Right Place," May 15, 2009, at http://www.ngs.noaa.gov/INFO/fourcorners.shtml, accessed August 8, 2014.

22. Peter Iverson, *Diné: A History of the Navajos* (Albuquerque: University of New Mexico Press, 2002) 16, 19.

23. Ibid., 19.

24. Ibid., 23–24; Hampton Sides, *Blood and Thunder: The Epic Story of Kit Carson and the Conquest of the American West* (New York: Anchor Books, 2006), 25–27.

25. Iverson, *Diné*, 8–11.

26. Ibid., 39–41.

27. Ibid., 49.

28. Ibid., 50.

29. See Sides, *Blood and Thunder*, 311–13, 320–21, 351–52.

30. Ibid., 420.

31. Iverson, *Diné*, 50.

32. On conditions at Bosque Redondo, see ibid., 57–63; Sides, *Blood and Thunder*, 445–58, 475–82.

33. Sides, *Blood and Thunder*, 480.

34. Iverson, *Diné*, 63–64.

35. Ibid., 72–73; Richard White, *It's Your Misfortune and None of My Own: A New History of the American West* (Norman: University of Oklahoma Press, 1991), 100.

36. Iverson, *Diné*, 72–73.

37. Robert M. Utley, *The Indian Frontier of the American West, 1846–1890* (Albuquerque: University of New Mexico Press, 1984), 213–15; White, *It's Your Misfortune and None of My Own*, 115.

38. Iverson, *Diné*, 136–66; White, *It's Your Misfortune and None of My Own,* 493; Ronald Takaki, *A Different Mirror: A History of Multicultural America* (Boston: Little, Brown, 1993), 238–45.

39. White, *It's Your Misfortune and None of My Own,* 493; Erin Klauk, "Human Health Impacts on the Navajo Nation from Uranium Mining," at http://serc.carle ton.edu/research_education/nativelands/Navajo/humanhealth.html, accessed June 25, 2009; Shelley Smithson, "Radioactive Revival in New Mexico," *The Nation* 288, no. 25 (June 29, 2009): 16–20; Associated Press, "EPA to Rebuild Uranium-Polluted Navajo Homes," June 14, 2009, at http://www.nbcnews.com/id/31355123 /ns/us_news-environment/#.U-K8wVbxVGM, accessed August 6, 2014.

40. White, *It's Your Misfortune and None of My Own,* 493; Hall quoted in Iverson, *Diné,* 153; "Blind Man's Daughter (Navajo) Discusses Navajo Stock Reduction," excerpt from *Navajo Historical Selections,* Department of the Interior, ed. Robert W. Young and William Morgan (Phoenix: Phoenix Indian School Print Shop, 1954), final quote in Peter Nabokov, ed., *Native American Testimony: A Chronicle of Indian-White Relations from Prophecy to the Present, 1492–2000* (New York: Penguin Books, 1999), 330–31.

41. Iverson, *Diné,* 182–86; quotation in Alexander Molnar Jr., "Navajo Code Talk-ers: World War II Fact Sheet," US Department of the Navy, Naval Historical Center, at http://www.history.navy.mil/faqs/faq61-2.htm, accessed June 25, 2009.

42. Caitlin Switzer, "Let There Be Light . . . L. L. Nunn and the Ames Power Plant," *Montrose Mirror,* January 15, 2013, at http://montrosemirror.com/uncategorized /let-there-be-light-l-l-nunn-and-the-ames-power-plant/, accessed August 5, 2014; Alan E. Drew, "Telluride Power Co.: Pioneering A.C. in the Rocky Mountains," *IEEE Power and Energy Magazine* (January-February 2014), at http://magazine.ieee-pes.org/janu-aryfebruary-2014/history-11/, accessed August 5, 2014.

43. James Whiteside, *Regulating Danger: The Struggle for Mine Safety in the Rocky Mountain Coal Industry* (Lincoln: University of Nebraska Press, 1990), 23.

44. Ibid.; Martie Sterling, "American Castle Was Built by Iron, Coal Baron," *Los Angeles Times,* November 1, 1987, at http://articles.latimes.com/1987-11-01/travel /tr-17597_1_redstone-castle, accessed August 5, 2014; Barbara Rowley, "Colorado's Redstone Castle," *Snow Country,* August, 1989, 92–93, at http://books.google.com /books?id=yzj71xbQ9VMC&pg=PA92&lpg=PA92&dq=alma+osgood+lady+boun tiful&source=bl&ots=0RUC5U8M8x&sig=AEEvbwB9AEHiwX3F_LkVGiDew44&hl =en&sa=X&ei=KGvhU9mHLI_soATqxICoDQ&ved=0CDoQ6AEwBQ#v=one page&q=alma%20osgood%20lady, accessed A%20bountiful&f=false, accessed August 5, 2014.

45. Whiteside, *Regulating Danger,* 9, 27–28, 117–18; Abbott, Leonard, and Noel, *Colorado,* 133, 147–51.

5

The Warrior Trail
TRIUMPH

When I was a young boy, my dad dragged me to the neighborhood barber-shop every other Saturday morning. He had his thick, wavy hair trimmed to proper business executive length and then had the barber zip his clippers over my thin, straight hair to form it into a sort of buzz cut. The shop smelled of hair tonic, shaving cream, and aftershave lotion. Side tables had stacks of sports, hunting and fishing, and car magazines; on a shelf in the back, a covered box contained magazines kids were not allowed to look at.

On one of the shop's walls hung a print of artist Cassilly Adams's *Custer's Last Fight* (1884), depicting the final moments of the Battle of the Little Bighorn (1876). The brightly colored print shows the doomed Colonel George Armstrong Custer and a few soldiers of the Seventh Cavalry atop Last Stand Hill, overlooking the Little Bighorn River in southeast Montana, surrounded by, and about to die at the hands of, attacking Indians. The fearless Custer has just shot an Indian attacker, who is shown falling backward. But scores of other Indians have their weapons aimed at Custer, and the outcome of his heroic last stand cannot be doubted.[1]

DOI: 10.5876/9781607323273.c005

As a young boy I had no idea who George Armstrong Custer was and had never heard of the Battle of the Little Bighorn. But I knew darned good and well what *Custer's Last Fight* was about. After all, I had watched hundreds of hours of westerns on television and at the movies. I knew the soldiers were good men, probably protecting helpless travelers on some wagon train, and that the Indians were nefarious troublemakers who, in this case, were obviously killing the soldiers for no good reason in what equally obviously was not a fair fight. *Custer's Last Fight* simply depicted what most American boys in the 1950s knew to be a core truth about the history of the American West: heroic white men fought and sometimes died in the struggle against the Indians who for some reason, or for no reason at all, wanted to rob and kill white people.

You can see Last Stand Hill and most of the Little Bighorn National Battlefield from the highway. The hill, capped by a stone obelisk honoring Custer and his troopers, is only about half a mile from the junction of Interstate 90 and US Highway 212. Around 350 miles to the southeast is a place called Wounded Knee. The two sites are tragic bookends in the history of the Plains Indians and their confrontation with the expanding United States. The segment of US 212 from the Little Bighorn to the Montana-Wyoming border is called the Warrior Trail.

When I told Phineas of my plan to ride to the Little Bighorn and from there to follow the Warrior Trail and the other highways leading to Wounded Knee, he quickly signed on for the trip. He had recently purchased yet another new, high-end touring motorcycle and was anxious to break it in with a road trip. Phineas recalled reading Dee Brown's now classic book on the history of American Indians, *Bury My Heart at Wounded Knee* (1970), and so was also interested in seeing the Little Bighorn battlefield and Wounded Knee. As we discussed the trip, Phineas noted that he had never been to Yellowstone or the Grand Tetons, so we figured that, since we had to go through Wyoming anyway, we might as well add a couple of days to the trip and ride through the two national parks first. That addition to our itinerary led to interesting encounters with the tourist West, one very private and elite and the others in the public domain, before we reached the Warrior Trail. We set out right after the July Fourth holiday, 2009.

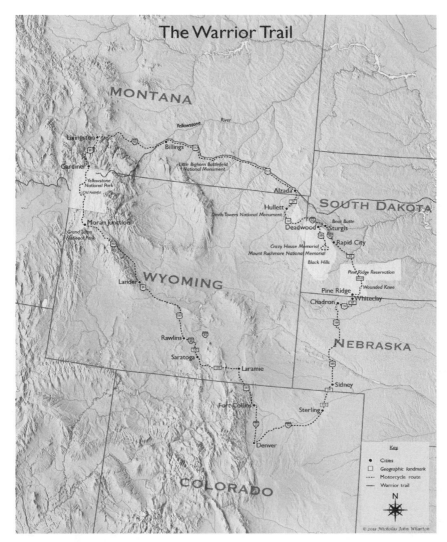

MAP 5.1. Map by Nicholas J. Wharton

SARATOGA

We left early to beat the morning rush hour traffic out of Denver, heading north through Fort Collins and on to Laramie. There, instead of getting onto Interstate 80, we headed west into the Medicine Bow Mountains on the Snowy Range Road (Wyoming 130). In the distance we could see the still snowcapped top of 12,000-foot Medicine Bow Peak. The first 20 miles or so cross the immense basin of the Laramie Plains before the road ascends into the mountains. After about an hour we came to the top of Snowy Range Pass. This is one of those spots where you feel as though you are standing atop the world. Like the view into South Park from Kenosha Pass, the first sight of it sucks your breath away. North of the road, the rugged, silvery rocks at the top of Medicine Bow Peak seemed close enough to touch. Lush grasses and yellow and blue wildflowers carpeted the alpine meadow below the peak. From a fortress-like viewing structure, we looked south to Long's Peak—80 miles away in Colorado—west to the Sierra Madre Range, and east to Laramie.

From the summit of Snowy Range Pass, the terrain along Wyoming 130 changes rapidly as the road descends past the picture postcard scenery of Lake Marie, through mountain forests, and finally into the sagebrush plain of the North Platte River Valley. After 25 miles we rolled into the town of Saratoga, looking for lunch. Saratoga has a population of about 1,700, and I expected to find a typical agricultural town. On the way into town, however, I noticed to the east, along the river, what appeared to be a mega-mansion. Then, on the southern edge of town, we rolled by a small airport where two gleaming white private jets sat on the tarmac. The mega-mansion and the jets were unexpected sights in a place that would meet most people's notion of remote.

Saratoga is known (though not widely) for its hot springs and has long attracted a small tourist trade. For the most part, the town remains pretty conventional and unpretentious. But, I learned, Saratoga is also the home of a very exclusive fishing and golf resort; hence the private jets and the mega-mansion by the river.

Jet-setters and other glitterati occupying and transforming scenic areas into their private playgrounds is a well-established fact of cultural and economic life in the West, usually associated with high-profile recreational venues such as Sun Valley, Aspen, Vail, or Telluride. Saratoga is different. I saw no limousines or expensive personal cars parked on the streets and no chic boutiques, bistros, or "fusion" restaurants offering fashion and food that people who actually live there could not afford. Indeed, Phineas and I had an inexpensive lunch at a quiet little café called Stumpy's.

Comfortable exclusivity is a staid tradition of elite tourism in the American West. Historians of western tourism tell of the wealthy and their role in opening once remote places to travel. In the late nineteenth century George Pullman built his Palace Cars to convey the rich in comfort to resorts, national parks, and dude ranches, where hosts saw to it that guests enjoyed high standards of luxury while guides and cowboys squired them through sightseeing and hunting excursions.[2] Saratoga's upscale resort fits that pattern, but I was struck that I had never heard of it. Neither had Phineas or any of my colleagues and other acquaintances, including Wyoming natives. The resort there seems determined to keep a low profile as a place where the Really Rich go to get away from the Run-of-Mill Rich and, of course, the rest of us.

I began to wonder, however, if Saratoga might not represent something a bit more complex than an out-of-the-way resort for the über-elite. The American West has always been a zone of consumption, whether of its mineral, water, and animal resources or its scenery. In the latter sense, the elite traveler seeking a western experience is not fundamentally different from the working- or middle-class family in their motor home seeing the roadside sights. They arrive, admire the scenery, glance at some history, take some photos, chase a bear, hook some fish, and then go home.

However, the rich sometimes consume the West in ways that are qualitatively and quantitatively different from the experiences of ordinary people. A magazine titled *Cowboys and Indians* (yes, in the twenty-first century!) provides plenty of illustrations. *Cowboys and Indians* is devoted to travel, the arts, and fine dining in the West. Its target audience is the wealthy. The magazine's June 2009 cover article is about businessman Ted Turner, the cable television pioneer who founded CNN (Cable News Network). Turner owns 2 million acres of ranchland (some of it in Argentina) and is one of the largest individual landowners in the United States. In the article, which features photos of him on horseback, Turner characterizes himself as a steward of the land. "I don't feel like I'm the owner of this place," he says of his Montana properties; "I feel like I'm the custodian of it." A major part of his custodianship, however, is strictly business as Turner raises bison—45,000 in all—to supply his chain of western-theme restaurants.[3]

Elsewhere in the same issue of *Cowboys and Indians*, advertisements offer numerous ranches for sale. For prices ranging from only $1.3 million all the way up to $100 million, anyone can join Ted Turner as a custodian of the

West. The magazine also includes ads for upscale western wear (the type no bovine management specialist, male or female, would actually wear). Western-style belts, with silver and gold buckles and tips, go for $750, while prices are not specified for silver and turquoise jewelry, handcrafted cowboy boots with brightly colored inlays, and designer dresses and jeans.[4]

Saratoga's private jets, Ted Turner's ranches, and cowboy haute couture represent an American West remote and very different from the West most of us see and experience. That is not to say that the wealthy elite's West is any less or more authentic than the West we "lesser" beings see, smell, and touch from our cars, motor homes, and motorcycles. Indeed, one is hard-pressed to come up with a one-size-fits-all definition of an "authentic" West. There is the scenic West, the cowboy West, the mining West, the American Indian West, and the Hispanic West, to name a few authentic Wests. All are more or less accessible to anyone who can visit a national park or pull on jeans and a pair of boots. So what is it that sets apart the elite's West? One important difference is ownership. Most of us, even those of us who live in the West, are visitor-consumers. We get into our cars and motor homes or ride our motorcycles and visit the scenic and historic places and try on the different cultures, usually by sampling foods and taking home inexpensive souvenir art or jewelry. The very wealthy, however, buy their West. Celebrities' mansions in Aspen, golf course "cabins" in Telluride, Ted Turner's ranches, and a private jet strip in a remote river valley in Wyoming are zones of privilege. We ordinary folks can sometimes drive or ride by and even peer in through the fence lines, but otherwise that West is off-limits to us.

After lunch we rode north to Interstate 80. As soon as we rolled onto the interstate, Wyoming reminded us that we were in, well, Wyoming. Powerful, swirling winds buffeted us all the way to Rawlins and continued after we turned onto US 287, finally letting up just a few miles from Lander, where we stopped for the day.

We rolled out of Lander at 7:30 a.m., made good time through the Wind River Reservation, and climbed Togwotee ("toe-go-tee") Pass into the Absaroka Mountains. The pass is named for a Shoshone man who in 1873 guided a US Army Corps of Engineers expedition into northwest Wyoming, leading the group over the pass then known as the Big Gap.[5] Once we crested the pass, we began to see in the distance the tops of the Grand Teton peaks.

THE GRAND TETONS AND YELLOWSTONE

In 1872, when the US Congress took up legislation to create Yellowstone National Park, the measure passed with barely a murmur of debate. In contrast, it took decades of robust controversy and bureaucratic infighting to establish Grand Teton National Park in its present form. At first glance, the Tetons and the adjoining valley of Jackson Hole seem to meet all of the criteria historian Richard White identifies for a national park; namely, an area of great scenic beauty with few readily exploitable natural resources.[6] The Teton peaks are essentially inaccessible, and Jackson Hole has little in the way of mineral resources and is not especially good farming or livestock country. In fact, Jackson Hole dude ranchers, who made their living by herding summer tourists rather than cattle, were among the first proponents of conservation and preservation of the area, though many resisted the idea of a national park.

The first step toward preserving the Tetons and Jackson Hole came in February 1897, when President Grover Cleveland used his authority under the Forest Reserves Act (1891) to set aside an area approximating today's national park as the Teton Forest Reserve. That same year poachers were damaging Yellowstone's elk herd, which prompted park superintendent Colonel S.B.M. Young (the park was under military supervision) to propose extending his authority south into Jackson Hole. Nothing came of that proposal. Instead, in 1908 President Theodore Roosevelt expanded the Teton Forest Reserve to almost 2 million acres, rechristened it the Teton National Forest, and put it under the control of the US Forest Service. Colonel Young's proposal to expand Yellowstone, and President Roosevelt's decision to give control of the Tetons and Jackson Hole to the Forest Service, were auguries of a half-century struggle between competing visions for the region: one was the multiuse concept of conservation, emphasizing managed development and economic exploitation; the other was the ideal of preservation, to maintain unspoiled the area's scenic beauty as an environmental and national heritage.[7]

The first legislative attempt to preserve the Tetons occurred in 1918–19 when the US House of Representatives passed a bill, sponsored by Wyoming congressman Frank Mondell, to extend Yellowstone's southern boundary to include the Tetons and Jackson Lake. The bill died in the US Senate, however, because of opposition by sheep growers, who feared losing grazing permits;

the Forest Service, which worried about losing its authority over the region; and dude ranchers concerned about the possibility that their activities might be regulated.[8]

While Congress debated and ultimately killed Representative Mondell's bill, President Woodrow Wilson took executive action to advance the cause of preservation in the Teton region. In July 1918 Wilson withdrew from development 600,000 acres of the Teton National Forest and assigned control of the land to the National Park Service (NPS). That enabled the NPS in subsequent years to block several Forest Service–backed dam and irrigation projects aimed at Teton lakes.[9]

During the 1920s a loose and at times uneasy alliance of dude ranchers, cattlemen, and business interests formed in the Jackson Hole area in support of preserving the area's scenic beauty, not only as a national treasure but as the best long-term economic option for the region. They did not initially support creating a national park but hoped instead to drum up private capital to buy vulnerable lands that could be preserved for recreational activities and grazing. However, the group represented an important break in the solid support the Forest Service had enjoyed in the area and ultimately helped pave the way for a park, even as private capital began to buy up large tracts of land around Jackson Lake.[10]

By 1929 support had jelled for at least a small park, and Congress that year passed legislation creating Grand Teton National Park. The law and the park, however, represented only a partial victory for preservation. The new park was confined to a 96,000-acre tract encompassing the Teton peaks and six lakes at their base. Excluded from the park were Jackson Lake and adjoining lands to the north, east, and south. Historian Robert W. Righter describes it as "only half a park."[11]

As the political system worked its way toward creating the park's first incarnation, another powerful player, John D. Rockefeller Jr., entered the picture. Rockefeller visited Jackson Hole in the mid-1920s and was taken not only by the spectacular scenery but also by what writer Jackie Skaggs characterizes as the "shabby developments" already littering the area. Rockefeller's guide, Yellowstone National Park superintendent Horace M. Albright, was one of the leaders of the area alliance in favor of preservation. Albright explained to Rockefeller his group's hope that private capital might save the valley from further development.[12]

As successor to command of his father's oil, financial, and philanthropic empire, John D. Rockefeller Jr. made philanthropy his major life interest, taking over and expanding investments in education, scientific research, the arts, social welfare, and conservation. Philanthropy became particularly important to Rockefeller as he worked to repair the damage the 1913–14 Colorado coal strike and the Ludlow Massacre had caused to his and his family's reputation.

During the late 1920s and much of the 1930s Rockefeller, operating behind a front organization, the Snake River Land Company, acquired 35,000 acres of land surrounding Jackson Lake. Rockefeller's intention was to give the land to the federal government to enlarge the national park. However, continued opposition by the Forest Service, suspicion about Rockefeller's motives and tactics for acquiring the land, concerns about lost tax revenue for Teton County, and renewed anxiety about the growing federal role in the area were enough to thwart efforts to enlarge the park. Rockefeller seemingly had acquired something of a philanthropic tar baby.[13]

In November 1942 Rockefeller and Secretary of the Interior Harold Ickes engaged in a bit of political theater to force the government to accept the philanthropist's gift of the Jackson Hole land. In a letter to Ickes, Rockefeller stated that if the government did not act soon to take the land off his hands, he would have to "make some other disposition of it or sell it in the market to any satisfactory buyers." Rockefeller's letter gave Ickes an opening to press President Franklin Roosevelt to accept the Rockefeller land and make it part of a new national monument. Roosevelt acted in March 1943, creating by executive order a new 221,000-acre Jackson Hole National Monument controlled by the NPS. The new monument included Rockefeller's land.[14]

The president's fiat provoked outrage in Wyoming and throughout the West and met with lawsuits and congressional efforts to nullify it. Wyoming governor Lester Hunt made bellicose threats to use force to block NPS officials from taking control of the monument. Jackson Hole–area ranchers joined with politicians to stage their own bit of political theater by organizing an illegal cattle drive across the new monument. A star of the show was the past-his-prime actor Wallace Beery, whom publicists characterized as a Jackson Hole rancher (he had a Forest Service use permit for half an acre of land on which he grazed one cow).[15]

Anger over Roosevelt's action lingered into the postwar years, but rapidly growing tourism in the Teton region eventually overcame it, and the idea of expanding the national park gained new strength. Creation of the national monument marginalized the Forest Service's role as an opponent of expansion, and business interests realized that the area's economic future was in tourism. In September 1950 all the pieces came together in legislation merging the original park and the national monument. The expanded park preserved one of America's greatest scenic treasures and so was a victory for the preservation ideal over the more traditional conservation ethic, with its emphasis on resource exploitation.

Historian Robert Righter characterizes the creation and expansion of Grand Teton National Park as "one of the most notable conservation victories of the twentieth century."[16] While that is correct, the struggles over the park also represent other important historical themes. Certainly, they illustrated the long-standing tension between western political and business interests and the West's largest landowner, the federal government. From the mid-nineteenth century to the present, a staple of western politics has been resentment among business interests and political leaders regarding the supposedly heavy-handed exercise of federal authority over federal lands, preventing stock growers, mining companies, timber interests, and water developers from using those lands and resources as though they, not the American people, owned them.

Righter also characterizes the park as "a victory for the democratic process."[17] However, the Teton saga actually illustrates another political theme that transcends regional politics and resentments and goes to the very core of the American political system: the shift of power from Congress to the president. While the most visible, and arguably the most significant, manifestation of this political and constitutional reordering has been in the realm of foreign policy, this shift in the political center of gravity can also be seen in domestic politics.

Creating a national park requires an act of Congress. But in establishing and then enlarging Grand Teton National Park, Congress actually only lent its sanction to what various presidents had already done in practice. Theodore Roosevelt's enlargement of the Teton National Forest, Woodrow Wilson's transfer of 600,000 acres of the national forest to NPS control, and Franklin Roosevelt's creation of the Jackson Hole National Monument were

FIGURE 5.1. The Teton Peaks look like colossal uncut diamonds.

executive actions that proved beyond the power of Congress and the courts to challenge. The 1950 law enlarging the national park merely confirmed what President Roosevelt had done in practice.

Presidential park making in the West has continued in recent times. President Bill Clinton's order in 1996 establishing the 1.9-million-acre Grand Staircase–Escalante National Monument in southern Utah carved out an area more than six times larger than Grand Teton National Park. Clinton's action provoked the sort of angry response that Franklin Roosevelt's creation of the Jackson Hole National Monument met in Wyoming fifty-three years earlier.

Phineas and I entered Grand Teton National Park at Moran Junction and rode in a few miles to a small scenic viewpoint. We got off our bikes and just stood there, staring in slack-jawed wonder at the scene before us. The Teton peaks seemed to rise out of Jackson Lake like colossal uncut blue diamonds. As we stood there gazing at the peaks, it seemed crazy to me that there had ever been any question of preserving them and Jackson Hole.

Back on our bikes, we continued north along the shore of Jackson Lake to the park's northeast boundary and crossed into the John D. Rockefeller Jr. Memorial Parkway, a 24,000-acre reserve between the Grand Tetons and

Yellowstone parks, and on to Yellowstone's south entrance. We had planned to stop at a number of scenic spots in Yellowstone, following the southwestern loop of the park's central figure-eight roadway through the Upper, Lower, and Norris Geyser Basins and then east, north, and west over Dunraven Pass to the park's north entrance. Our bicycling friend Gandhi, who spends several weeks each year fly fishing in Yellowstone, wrote detailed directions to various waterfalls, canyons, geysers, and hot springs along our route. We made it to only one spot, Tower Falls on Dunraven Pass in the northern part of the park. All of the other sites were either too packed with tourists or inaccessible because of road construction.

We even tried, foolishly as it turned out, to see Old Faithful, the park's most famous and heavily visited site. Photos of Old Faithful, which erupts about every 90 minutes, shooting boiling water and steam well over 100 feet into the air, almost always show the geyser's setting as an open field with forested mountains in the background. Those photos are taken from a paved and developed complex of parking lots, gift shops, restaurants, and a hotel.

Every one of the several hundred parking spots in the main lot was occupied when we arrived. In the lanes between the rows we found ourselves in a seemingly endless line of SUVs, cars, and vans filled with bored-looking kids, driven by parents who affected looks ranging from grim determination to angry frustration, with a few cases of benign resignation mixed in. We quickly recognized the futility and possible danger of trying to find a parking spot and decided to leave. That is when the trap snapped shut.

It took us almost a half hour to get out of the parking lot. At one critical choke point, five lanes of traffic came together. The converging vehicles, their occupants all equally desperate to escape, had to form themselves into two new lanes without the benefit of traffic signals or a cop. Yellowstone's traffic engineers must have designed this vehicular mousetrap either to punish those who visited Old Faithful or as a devilish test of humanity's ability to behave civilly under stress.

As we crept along, our engines began to protest the July heat rising from the surrounding asphalt and concrete, so we shut them down and foot-paddled our way along until we were within one or two car lengths of making our escape. At that point we fired the engines again and gunned them noisily to alert those around us that we were about to enter the merging zone. Sure enough, a guy in a pickup truck with Texas license plates plowed into the intersection out of turn. We exchanged horn blasts and manual greetings, but I quickly reckoned that his truck outweighed Old Blue and so let him have his little victory. When at last I got clear of the prison that was the Old Faithful parking lot, I hoped the worst was behind us and we could look forward to clear roads and unobstructed enjoyment of Yellowstone's scenic wonders for the rest of the day. Silly me. We were, after all, in Yellowstone in early July, the height of two conflicting seasons in the park, the tourist and construction seasons. Six more construction stops kept us standing still for lengthy periods during the rest of the day.

Almost as annoying were additional traffic delays caused by Yellowstone's two-legged wildlife. As I had noticed in my 2006 foray through the park, Yellowstone tourists believe it is appropriate behavior, upon spotting a four-legged critter, to stop in the middle of the narrow, two-lane roadway and jump out, cameras in hand, to photograph their quarry—leaving their vehicles idling so air-conditioned interiors do not heat up. We experienced four of these critter stops. Two of them evidently involved snipes, the legendary creatures no sober person has ever actually seen. The other two were less disappointing. At one, we watched a mangy-looking grizzly bear root around in the grass about 50 feet from the road. At the other, we saw a large bull moose foraging in a roadside pond. After idling for several minutes, I decided to get off Old Blue and dig out my camera and join the herd taking pictures of the moose. With exquisite timing, a park ranger came along at that moment and made everyone get back into, or on, their vehicles and move along.

After the moose stop, we had clear sailing the rest of the way through the park. Tired, hot, and hungry, we looked forward to the short ride to Gardiner, Montana, where our hotel, a warm shower, and a large dinner of grilled cow awaited. As the park's iconic Roosevelt Gate and the town beyond came into sight, I could practically feel the shower's warm spray and taste medium-rare New York strip. Then, as we crossed the bridge over the river at the edge of town, traffic ground to a halt in one final, mood-shattering construction delay. After ten motionless minutes we began a long, slow crawl along Gardiner's main thoroughfare. Traffic moved at less than walking speed and, because the road was level, we cut our engines and foot-paddled most of the quarter of a mile from the bridge to our hotel. At one point in the 45-minute ordeal, with the hotel in sight and yet still so far away, I considered jumping the curb and riding the last stretch on the sidewalk. But my rapidly fading sense of civilized behavior, reinforced by the presence of a police car not far behind, led me to decide against that option. At last, at 6:30 p.m., 11 hours after we left Lander, we pulled into the hotel parking lot. The shower ran warm and soon we set out in search of dinner. We learned later that the road construction that had caused the penultimate misery of our day was north of town on US 89, where we were going the next morning.

With the road construction north of Gardiner in mind, we decided to make an early start the next morning and were on the road by 6:30 a.m., early enough to avoid any serious delay. US 89 follows the Yellowstone River north from Gardiner to Livingston, Montana, through the Paradise Valley, a narrow defile between the Gallatin and Absaroka Mountain ranges. Low, gray clouds hovered over us the entire 52 miles up the valley. It was cold and damp. About halfway along we pulled over and changed into winter gloves, pulled balaclavas over our heads, and slipped on rain jackets.

As we approached Livingston, the cloud cover began to break, but a cold chill still gripped us. Even with winter gloves and a balaclava on, my fingertips and chin had gone numb. We stopped at the first café we came across, in part to get breakfast but mainly just to get warm. As I wrapped my hands around my coffee mug, I thought about the cold morning in Tres Piedras, New Mexico, when we stopped at a rural café. Unfortunately, while our breakfast was tasty, the café in Livingston had no interesting characters on a par with the two New Mexican sheep ranchers we met at Tres Piedras. In fact, Phineas and I were probably the only real characters in the place.

Looking out the window at the café's sign, I noted that it was called the Café at Clark's Crossing. Captain William Clark, of the Lewis and Clark expedition, made camp nearby on July 15, 1806.[18] It took Captain Clark about ten days to travel the stretch from Livingston to Billings; we made the journey in about two hours. From Livingston, the highway descends gently and steadily from the mountains, and by the time we reached Billings the mountains gave way to the rolling, somewhat hilly plains of southeastern Montana, a historically rich and hotly contested geopolitical region.

THE LITTLE BIGHORN

The Yellowstone River bisects a region of plains and mountains that Crows, Shoshones, Cheyennes, Arapahos, Lakotas, and others claimed as homeland, hunting grounds, and sacred territory long before William Clark passed through. In fact, the entire territory between the Missouri and Platte Rivers was a Northern Plains Indian empire. Here the Plains Indians followed the bison herds and built their hunting and raiding culture around that iconic American animal. By the mid-nineteenth century the expansive Lakotas had become the strongest power on the Northern Plains as they pushed their territory west from the Dakotas. Lakota territory eventually extended west to the Bighorn Mountains and the Musselshell River and north to the Missouri River.[19]

At the heart of this Northern Plains empire were the Black Hills—*Paha Sapa* or *Hesapa* in the Lakota language. Nineteenth-century Lakotas valued the Black Hills as a source of spiritual and physical sustenance. The Lakota chief Sitting Bull called the Black Hills their "food pack," and Black Elk, the Oglala Lakota holy man whose memoirs are related in John G. Neihardt's *Black Elk Speaks*, characterized them in the same terms. There the Lakotas found abundant game and tall trees ideal for making poles for tepees and travois. Bear Butte, on the northern perimeter of the Black Hills, a few miles east of the town of Sturgis, and Devils Tower, on the western edge in Wyoming, were important gathering places for ceremonies and inter-band councils.[20] Perhaps even more than their ancestors, modern Lakotas revere the Black Hills as a sacred place, claiming them as the spiritual center of their culture.

Phineas and I reached Billings by late morning. We found our motel, dropped off our bags, and headed for the Little Bighorn Battlefield National Monument, about 65 miles southeast of Billings. The June 25, 1876, Battle of the Little Bighorn was the most important victory of Indian forces against the invading *wasicus*—white Americans—in the post–Civil War struggles on the Great Plains. For the Lakotas, however, it was a pyrrhic victory. Only a year later, American military might, bent on vengeance and determined to crush Indian power forever, forced most Lakota bands onto reservations or into exile in Canada.

The Fort Laramie Treaty of 1851 had established a fragile peace on the Great Plains. Indians agreed to permit migrants safe passage across the plains along the Oregon Trail corridor, and in exchange the United States recognized Indian territories north and south of the corridor that were to remain off-limits to white settlement. That arrangement, and the peace, collapsed in the 1860s as white migration and settlement undermined the treaty. War erupted on the Northern Plains in 1864 with the opening of the Bozeman Trail, linking Fort Laramie with goldfields in western Montana. Lakotas, especially the bands led by the Oglala war chief Red Cloud and the Miniconjou war chief High Backbone, set out to block the trail, attacking migrants and a chain of army posts set up along the route to protect them. The largest of the army posts, Fort Phil Kearny (about 20 miles south of Sheridan, Wyoming), became an especially important target after its construction in July 1866. Indian forces did not attempt to assault the fort directly but instead waged a campaign of harassment against scout parties, work teams foraying out to cut wood and hay, and the fort's cattle herd.[21]

Throughout the siege, the Lakotas hoped to lure a large army force out onto the open plains, where they would be vulnerable to a major attack. That moment came on December 21, 1866, when a war party of Oglalas and Miniconjous led by High Backbone set upon a wood-cutting party. As the Indians hoped, an army force commanded by Captain William J. Fetterman came out of the fort to rescue the woodcutters. Fetterman disregarded orders not to pursue the attackers beyond sight of the fort and soon found himself enveloped by the far larger Indian force. The fight lasted just over an hour, and when it was done Fetterman and his entire command—eighty-one men in all—lay dead. The Oglalas and Miniconjous lost only eleven warriors.[22]

The Fetterman battle stopped traffic on the Bozeman Trail, but it did not force the army to abandon Fort Phil Kearny and the other posts along the route. Indeed, the army was anxious to avenge the loss of Fetterman and his troops. However, in Washington, DC, the mounting costs of the multi-front war against the western Indians raging through Wyoming, Nebraska, Kansas, Colorado, and New Mexico, combined with backlash against the atrocity at Sand Creek, undermined the federal government's will to press the conflicts. So instead of turning the army loose, President Andrew Johnson sent west a peace commission led by General William Tecumseh Sherman and Nathaniel G. Taylor, the head of the Indian Bureau. The commission's first success was the October 1867 Treaty of Medicine Lodge Creek, by which the Southern Plains tribes—including the Cheyennes, Arapahos, Comanches, and Kiowas—agreed to move to reservations in the Indian Territory south of the Arkansas River. The following June, General Sherman signed a treaty with the Navajos permitting their return to their homeland in the *Diné Bikéyah* (see chapter 4). Bringing the Lakotas to terms proved much more difficult.[23]

The proposed treaty for the Northern Plains promised to remove the war's *casus bellus* by closing the Bozeman Trail and abandoning the hated army forts. It also set aside the area of South Dakota west of the Missouri River, including the Black Hills, as a Great Sioux Reservation. Lakotas who agreed to move to the reservation would receive annuities of clothing and food for 30 years, as well as tools and schools to help transform themselves into farmers. The treaty also designated western Nebraska and the Powder River region of northeast Wyoming and southeast Montana as unceded Indian territory where Lakotas who so chose could continue to live as hunting nomads "so long as the buffalo may range thereon in such numbers as to justify the chase."[24] Beyond the unceded territory in Montana, west of the Tongue River, the commission also established a reservation for the Crows. The peace commission summoned Lakotas to come to Fort Laramie in the spring of 1868 to hear the treaty.

The treaty was a mixed bag for the Lakotas. By agreeing to close the Bozeman Trail and to abandon the forts built along it, the government conceded defeat on the issue that had started the war. The unceded territories in Nebraska, Wyoming, and Montana seemed to promise that the Lakotas could continue their traditional way of life. Yet the establishment of the Great Sioux Reservation envisioned the end of that traditional life in favor of a life of dependency and pastoralization. Some bands, most notably the Brulés, quickly agreed to the treaty, but the Oglala war chief Red Cloud was in no hurry to accept the *wasicus'* settlement without a demonstration of good faith. When messengers came to his camp in the Black Hills in May 1868 to invite him to join the peace conference at Fort Laramie, Red Cloud sent them away with a message of his own: "We are on the mountains looking down on the soldiers and the forts. When we see the soldiers moving away and the forts abandoned, then I will come down and talk."[25] Only after the army had withdrawn from the forts and his warriors had burned them to the ground did Red Cloud agree to the new treaty.

By the time Red Cloud agreed to the 1868 Fort Laramie Treaty, another key figure in the history of the Plains Indian wars had made his presence felt. The Lakotas referred to George Armstrong Custer as *Pehin Hanska*, Long Hair. A Civil War hero, Custer intended to make an even more glorious reputation for himself by conquering the Plains Indians.[26] Custer had graduated last in his class at West Point, and his poorest grades were in cavalry tactics. Despite that inauspicious start to his career, Custer made a big name for himself during the Civil War as an aggressive and fearless cavalry officer. At age twenty-three Custer became a brevet brigadier general, but he held that rank only until the Civil War ended, when he reverted to being a mere captain.[27]

In 1866 Custer, now a lieutenant colonel, joined the newly formed Seventh Cavalry at Fort Riley, Kansas, with orders to suppress Cheyenne Indian raids in Kansas and the Indian Territory. In November 1868 he attacked the essentially defenseless camp of the Southern Cheyenne chief Black Kettle, who four years earlier had survived the Sand Creek Massacre. Black Kettle and his wife were among those gunned down in this "battle" of the Washita River. In killing the Southern Cheyennes' peace chief, Custer thus accomplished what John Chivington had failed to do in 1864.[28]

Five years later, in 1873, the army transferred Custer and the Seventh Cavalry to Fort Abraham Lincoln, located on the banks of the Missouri River near Bismarck, North Dakota. Their mission was to protect the expansion of white settlement across the Northern Plains. During the summers of 1872 and 1873, survey parties working for the Northern Pacific Railroad entered the Yellowstone River Valley in Montana to blaze a route for the railroad. Some of Custer's Seventh Cavalry went into the Yellowstone country with the surveyors during the summer of 1873.[29]

The Northern Pacific and the US government believed their activity was legal since the 1868 treaty permitted the construction of roads through the Great Sioux Reservation and the unceded territory. However, the Lakota bands that claimed the lands south of the Yellowstone as theirs were not parties to the treaty and were ready to resist any American intrusion. This was especially true of the Hunkpapas and their leader, Sitting Bull, and a large band of Oglalas led by the war chief Crazy Horse, who harassed the survey parties during the two summers they worked in the area. Custer and Crazy Horse met in battle for the first time in August 1873 in an indecisive engagement.[30] The Northern Pacific went bankrupt later that year and abandoned the survey project. Though the Lakotas' resistance did not stop the railroad, it did signal their willingness to band together to resist *wasicu* encroachments into their territory.

The conflict over the Northern Pacific was a prelude to the outbreak of all-out war on the Northern Plains. The flash point was an area in the heart of the Great Sioux Reservation that was supposed to be uncontested, the Lakotas' *Paha Sapa* (Black Hills). In July 1874 Colonel Custer led a 1,200-man expedition into the Black Hills, supposedly to scout a location for a new fort, which was permitted under the 1868 treaty. However, Custer reported finding gold, triggering a rush of prospectors into the hills. The government did nothing over the next two years to stop the invasion. Instead, it tried to buy or lease the Black Hills from the Lakotas. Even peace chiefs like Red Cloud refused to go along with such a deal. As Lakota attacks against miners grew, the army moved in to protect them and their illegal operations. Finally, in late 1875 the Ulysses Grant administration declared war. An order went out directing all non-reservation Indians to turn themselves in at a reservation agency by January 31, 1876. When the deadline passed, the government declared those who did not report to be hostiles and sent the army to deal with them.[31]

The army planned to envelop the Indians in a three-armed offensive. From the west, Colonel John Gibbon was to lead a force out of Fort Ellis, Montana (near Bozeman); from the south, General George Crook and his troops were to march out of Fort Fetterman (near Douglas, Wyoming); and from the east, General Alfred Terry would come from Fort Abraham Lincoln. Terry's forces included Custer and the Seventh Cavalry. The plan envisioned a winter and early spring campaign in which Gibbon, Crook, and Terry would trap Indian bands in the Yellowstone basin, crush them in battle, and force them onto the reservation. The plan, however, fell apart almost immediately.[32]

Crook set out from Fort Fetterman in March and on the seventeenth attacked a camp of Northern Cheyennes, Miniconjous, and Oglalas on the Powder River. The soldiers managed to burn the Indian camp but inflicted only light casualties before withdrawing to the fort. The damage to the Indians' camp was serious, but the attack's major consequence was to alert the non-reservation bands to the impending offensive.[33]

Gibbon's Montana column reached the mouth of Rosebud Creek in mid-May, just as Terry departed from Fort Abraham Lincoln. Crook did not set out again from Fort Fetterman until late May. The delayed campaign gave the Lakotas ample time to gather their bands into a single large fighting force and to prepare for the oncoming assault. By the end of May, Hunkpapas, Oglalas, Miniconjous, Sans Arcs, Brulés, and Northern Cheyennes, with the

Hunkpapa chief Sitting Bull as their leader, had gathered along Rosebud Creek in south-central Montana, forming a village of about 450 lodges. Of the 3,000 or so people in the village, about 800 were warriors. More were on the way.[34]

In mid-June, scouts brought word that General Crook's army, including more than 1,000 troops and about 260 Crow and Shoshone scouts, was approaching from the south. Crazy Horse set out with a force of 750 Lakotas and Cheyennes to meet Crook's advance. On the morning of June 17, Crazy Horse's warriors found Crook's troopers bivouacked on the banks of the Rosebud about 25 miles north of the Montana-Wyoming border. The initial attack caught the soldiers by surprise, but they rallied quickly and the two sides fought fiercely until early afternoon, when the Indians disengaged. Crazy Horse's outnumbered warriors fought Crook's cavalry and infantry to a draw, losing 20 men to the soldiers' 10 dead. In his official report on the fight, Crook claimed victory since the Indians had disengaged. But the Battle of the Rosebud was really a major victory for the Indians. Crook was shocked by the ferocity of the battle and the Indians' ability to fight off his counterattacks. Short on rations and needing to care for his wounded, Crook withdrew to his base camp on Goose Creek in northern Wyoming the next day. He did not venture north again for six weeks, removing his force from the campaign just as its most critical moment approached.[35]

One week later the Lakota and Cheyenne village, now numbering about 6,000 to 8,000 people, including 1,500–2,000 warriors, camped along the Little Bighorn River. The Lakotas called the river the Greasy Grass. The village extended for more than 2 miles along the river's west bank. As was the custom in multi-band gatherings, the Northern Cheyennes made their camp circle at the northern end of the village and Sitting Bull and the Hunkpapas set theirs at the southern end. In between were Lakota Blackfeet, Sans Arcs, Miniconjous, Oglalas, and Brulés.[36]

Early on the morning of June 25, scouts for Custer's Seventh Cavalry column spotted the village from the mountains 15 miles to the south. Custer had been on the Indians' trail for three days, since leaving Terry and Gibbon at the junction of the Yellowstone and the Rosebud. Custer's job was to locate the Indian village, while Terry and Gibbon followed with the main force. Terry and Gibbon planned to arrive at the Little Bighorn on June 26. The original plan was for Custer to strike the village and drive the Indians north

FIGURE 5.2. The Seventh Cavalry Monument atop Last Stand Hill, Little Bighorn National Battlefield. The white stones mark the locations where Custer and his soldiers fell.

Memorial on the north slope of Last Stand Hill lists the names of fifty-four warriors who fell in the battle and pays tribute to unknown women and children who died that day, too.

An early newspaper report of the Battle of the Little Bighorn declared, "Not a man had escaped to tell the tale."[47] That was not only untrue but also downright silly. Thousands of Lakotas and Cheyennes lived to tell the tale and their recollections, along with modern battlefield archaeology, are the best sources available to historians to reconstruct the battle. In addition, the surviving soldiers of the Seventh Cavalry under Reno and Benteen—most of the Seventh Cavalry, in fact—watched the last phases of the fight from their distant hilltop position.

From the time of the battle until the present, the mainstream cultural memory of Custer and his troopers, especially in art and cinema, is one of great heroism. (An exception was actor Richard Mulligan's portrayal of Custer as a lunatic in the 1970 film *Little Big Man*.)[48] Custer and his men did fight bravely, but emphasizing him and his doomed troopers ignores the people impacted most directly by the battle and its consequences: the Lakotas and Cheyennes who actually won the day.

Unfortunately, winning the battle ensured that the Indians would lose the war. They never had a chance of prevailing anyway, but after the Little Bighorn the *wasicus* were determined to exact a bloody vengeance and end the Indians' challenge to white expansion across the Northern Plains. Within days of the battle the great Lakota and Cheyenne village broke up, as individual bands and family groups dispersed both to flee the expected counterattack and to go on the hunt for bison.[49]

The reservation Indians were among the first to pay a heavy price for the Little Bighorn. Congress in 1877 abrogated the 1868 Fort Laramie Treaty with a law that seized the Black Hills from the Lakotas, opening to unlimited white occupation the lands Sitting Bull and Crazy Horse had fought for so desperately. Worse, the Black Hills confiscation was the first step in the eventual breakup of the rest of the Great Sioux Reservation.[50]

Through the summer and fall of 1876, the non-reservation Indians generally evaded army expeditions and held their own when they did have to fight. But the army's relentless pursuit, winter's bitter cold, and hunger doomed the Indians' effort to evade capture and confinement. Throughout the winter and early spring, individuals, families, and bands began to surrender. Even Crazy Horse finally gave up and, with about 900 followers, surrendered at Camp Robinson in Nebraska. Four months later army and reservation officials, fearing he was about to bolt from the reservation, tried to arrest him; when he resisted, a soldier thrust a bayonet into his back and killed him. Many years later the Oglala holy man Black Elk said of the great war chief's death, "Crazy Horse is the last big chief, and then it's all over."[51]

Sitting Bull and his dwindling band held out the longest. At about the same time Crazy Horse rode into Camp Robinson, Sitting Bull led his people to safety across the Canadian border. The Canadians offered protection from the pursuing American army but little else. For a time, bison and other game were sufficient, but they seemed to disappear in the winter of 1881. Starvation led to dissention and finally to resignation. In July 1881 Sitting Bull rode into Fort Buford, in North Dakota, and surrendered. After a two-year confinement at Fort Randall, South Dakota, the government settled him in a house on the Standing Rock Reservation, where he lived until his death in December 1890. Like Crazy Horse, Sitting Bull met a violent end (see chapter 6).[52]

Phineas and I arrived at the Little Bighorn Battlefield National Monument early in the afternoon. It was crowded, and we had to circle the small parking lot a few times until a spot we could get both bikes into opened. We stripped off our leathers and helmets, downed some water, and walked to the visitors' center. A park ranger was just beginning a lecture on the battle. He very ably described the context of the war on the Northern Plains and the major phases of the battle, pointing out key locations on the field. He spoke movingly of how bravely everyone, Indians and soldiers, fought that day. As the ranger spoke, I was struck by a double irony. He was a member of the Crow Nation, and the battlefield sits within the boundaries of the Crow Reservation. The Crows and the Lakotas were bitter enemies in the nineteenth century, and by 1876 the Lakotas had occupied much of the Crows' traditional territory in eastern Montana. Partly for that reason, the Crows had made peace with the United States, and many of the scouts who led Custer to the Little Bighorn were Crows. In fact, the sole survivor of Custer's immediate command was a Crow scout called Curly, whom Custer sent away shortly before the final moments of the battle. In his lecture, the park ranger conveyed no sense of historical triumph over his people's old enemies. Instead, he emphasized a shared Indian experience of conquest and loss in the face of relentless *wasicu* expansion.

After the lecture, we walked up the path to the top of Last Stand Hill, stood in front of the obelisk commemorating the Seventh Cavalry's dead, and surveyed the battlefield and the site of the Lakota and Cheyenne village below. Another ranger was there and, hoping to get the battle's complicated geography clear in my mind, I had several questions for him. However, I had to wait for several minutes before I could approach him. An older gentleman had buttonholed him and was railing about how "them injuns didn't need to kill all them soldiers. They had 'em whipped and shoulda let 'em surrender and go home." It occurred to me that "them injuns" would have much preferred that Custer and his men, and all the *wasicus*, had stayed home in the first place.

When I was finally able to talk with the ranger, he quickly answered my questions about the battle and its key incidents. He pointed out where the

Hunkpapa camp circle had been and where Reno had started the fight; the hilltop where Reno retreated, visible 4 miles to the south; and Medicine Tail Coulee, Deep Coulee, and Deep Ravine. As he pointed out these places, he traced the major cavalry and Indian movements around the field. I did somewhat stump him with one question, however. Why did the Lakotas call the area and the river the Greasy Grass? Did the name refer to a specific species of grass? He confessed that he did not know for certain but hypothesized, credibly, that Greasy Grass referred to the general lushness of the grasses and their high nutritional value. The Indians liked to camp there in the early summer and fatten their horses.

White marble markers in the shape of military gravestones are scattered down the slope from Last Stand Hill toward the river, marking the spots where individual soldiers fell. A few red granite markers have been placed where Indian warriors died.

The Seventh Cavalry memorial dominates the hilltop, but a short distance away the Indian Memorial also commands attention. Congress authorized the memorial in 1991, at the same time it changed the monument's name from the Custer Battlefield to the Little Bighorn National Battlefield. After an open competition, an advisory committee, including Indian representatives, selected the memorial's design; because of funding delays, it did not open until 2003.

On the advice of Lakota and Northern Cheyenne elders, the park service chose as the memorial's theme the ideal of "Peace through Unity." The memorial is a circular plaza built into the hillside. Its shape, with entries on the east and west sides, evokes the sacred medicine wheel. On the south side a "spirit gate" frames the view up the hill to the cavalry monument. According to the designers, the gate is "a visible landmark and counterpoint" to the Custer monument and also serves to welcome the Seventh Cavalry's dead into the memorial itself. Atop the north wall, bronze wire sculptures depict three horse-mounted warriors riding to battle. An Indian woman is shown handing one warrior his battle shield.[53]

The decision to build the Indian Memorial provoked criticism and opposition. Some Lakotas and Cheyennes objected to memorializing the Crow and Arikara scouts who had ridden with Custer. Others argued that the memorial's design, especially the "spirit window," did not accurately reflect Indian beliefs.[54]

FIGURE 5.3. Red granite stones mark the locations where Indian warriors fell in the Battle of the Little Bighorn.

FIGURE 5.4. The Indian Memorial, Little Bighorn National Battlefield, represents an inclusive understanding of the battle and its historical significance.

Much more strident was white opposition to memorializing the Indian experience at the Little Bighorn. One Custer enthusiast likened it to "handing the Vietnam War memorial over to the Vietnamese." Another critic, a history professor, implied that the memorial would desecrate the memory and the grave of the soldiers who fell in the battle. "If you want to emphasize the Indian victory," he said, "please don't do it at the mass grave of 200 U.S. soldiers." (I wonder what these critics think of the statue of Robert E. Lee at Gettysburg.) A battlefield visitor huffed, "They're trying to make this over into an Indian battleground." Imagine that! Custer led about 750 men into the Little Bighorn Valley. He tried to attack a Cheyenne and Lakota village with a population of about 6,000 to 8,000 people. In the battle, Indian warriors outnumbered his force by more than two to one, and they won the battle. Why wouldn't one think of this place as an Indian battleground? Referring to the Indian warriors, the same man declared, "These people were savages!"[55]

A *New York Times* article about the memorial and the surrounding controversy noted rather shrewdly that "part of the anger of the white traditionalists stems from a sense that they are losing control of history."[56] Opposition to the Indian Memorial reflects a persistent, intellectually immature, and historically inaccurate notion that the Battle of the Little Bighorn was something that happened to heroic white Americans and that to the extent that an Indian role must be acknowledged, that role was one of savagery versus advancing civilization.

The debate over the Indian Memorial is also symptomatic of a deeper intellectual and ideological struggle over the contested terrain that is the history of both the American West and the United States. In the last quarter of the twentieth century, historians began to reexamine and to challenge the generally triumphalist historiography that, from the earliest days of the republic, portrayed American history as a story of the progress of democratic civilization under the leadership of an enlightened, always white, usually male elite who represented the values and aspirations of the people. In contrast to that narrative, recent generations of historians have written into American history the lives and experiences of minorities, immigrants, women, the working class, and the poor. In doing so, they have written a genre of history that seems to some to threaten a historical consensus, the old triumphalist narrative, that supposedly bound together the social, cultural, and political fabric of American society. Conservative ideologues derisively dismiss this history as "revisionist."

In a sense, they are correct. Recent historiography does revise American history and it does challenge the old triumphalism. But that is not a bad thing. Slavery, the Ludlow Massacre, the internment of Japanese Americans during World War II, and the real story of the Little Bighorn are no less true and no less important in a mature and accurate understanding of American history than are Valley Forge, the Gettysburg Address, and Lewis and Clark's epic journey. I do not object to being called a revisionist; in fact, I embrace it. However, I think *inclusionist* is a better term. Renaming the Little Bighorn Battlefield and building the Indian Memorial there does not erase Custer and his men from the scene or from history. Instead, it includes all the other people who were there. And that more truly respects America's history and democratic values.

NOTES

1. Adams specialized in western landscape and historical topics. He painted the original version on a wagon canvas. Adolphus Busch bought the Adams painting

in 1888 and had it lithographed by F. Otto Becker of the Milwaukee Lithographing Company. Ed Kimmick, "Custer's Last Fight Sales to Benefit Battle Memorials," *Billings Gazette*, June 22, 2002, at http://billingsgazette.com/news/local/article_f5c84656-0506-5617-b7c5-dcaceobf95da.html, accessed August 10, 2014.

2. Earl Pomeroy, *In Search of the Golden West: The Tourist in Western America* (Lincoln: University of Nebraska Press, 1957); Lawrence R. Borne, *Dude Ranching: A Complete History* (Albuquerque: University of New Mexico Press, 1983); Hal K. Rothman, *Devil's Bargains: Tourism in the Twentieth-Century American West* (Lawrence: University of Kansas Press, 1998); David M. Wrobel and Patrick T. Long, eds., *Seeing and Being Seen: Tourism in the American West* (Lawrence: University of Kansas Press, 2001, published for the Center of the American West, University of Colorado at Boulder).

3. *Cowboys and Indians* 17, no. 4 (June 2009): 81.

4. Ibid., 11, 13, 16, 23, 159.

5. Peter Nabokov and Lawrence Loendorf, *Restoring a Presence: American Indians and Yellowstone National Park* (Norman: University of Oklahoma Press, 2004), 135, 138, 294–95; Thomas H. Johnson, *Also Called Sacajawea: Chief Woman's Stolen Identity* (Long Grove, IL: Waveland, 2007), 38.

6. Richard White, *It's Your Misfortune and None of My Own: A New History of the American West* (Norman: University of Oklahoma Press, 1991), 410.

7. Robert W. Righter, *Crucible for Conservation: The Creation of Grand Teton National Park* (Boulder: Colorado Associated University Press, 1982), 13–21.

8. Ibid., 28–31; Jackie Skaggs, "Creation of Grand Teton National Park," at http://www.nps.gov/grte/planyourvisit/upload/creation.pdf, accessed December 18, 2009.

9. Righter, *Crucible for Conservation*, 32.

10. Ibid., 32–40.

11. Ibid., 40; Skaggs, "Creation of Grand Teton National Park."

12. Skaggs, "Creation of Grand Teton National Park"; Righter, *Crucible for Conservation*, 43–65.

13. Skaggs, "Creation of Grand Teton National Park"; Righter, *Crucible for Conservation*, 66–102.

14. Rockefeller quoted in Skaggs, "Creation of Grand Teton National Park"; Righter, *Crucible for Conservation*, 104, 107, 110.

15. Skaggs, "Creation of Grand Teton National Park"; Righter, *Crucible for Conservation*, 111–25.

16. Righter, *Crucible for Conservation*, viii (quotation), 140.

17. Ibid. (quotation on p. 140).

18. Thomas Schmidt, *National Geographic Guide to the Lewis and Clark Trail* (Washington, DC: National Geographic Society, 2002 [1998]), 179–84; William Clark, July

15, 1806, entry in *The Journals of the Lewis and Clark Expedition*, ed. Gary Moulton (Lincoln: University of Nebraska Press / University of Nebraska–Lincoln Libraries–Electronic Text Center, 2005), at http://lewisandclarkjournals.unl.edu/namesindex /journals.php?id=lc.1806-07-15&key=Livingston,%20Mont., accessed August 10, 2014.

19. Kingsley M. Bray, *Crazy Horse: A Lakota Life* (Norman: University of Oklahoma Press, 2006), 64; Robert M. Utley, *Sitting Bull: The Life and Times of an American Patriot* (New York: Henry Holt, 1993), 16, 91.

20. Utley, *Sitting Bull*, 115; John G. Neihardt, *Black Elk Speaks: Being the Life Story of a Holy Man of the Oglala Sioux*, Premier Edition (Albany: State University of New York Press, 2008), 50; Bray, *Crazy Horse*, 53–54.

21. Clyde A. Milner II, "National Initiatives," in Clyde A. Milner II, Carol A. O'Connor, and Martha Sandweiss, *The Oxford History of the American West* (New York: Oxford University Press, 1994), 176; Richard White, *It's Your Misfortune and None of My Own: A New History of the American West* (Norman: University of Oklahoma Press, 1991), 90, 97; Robert M. Utley, *The Indian Frontier of the American West, 1846–1890* (Albuquerque: University of New Mexico Press, 1984), 103–4; John Monnett, *Where a Hundred Soldiers Were Killed: The Struggle for the Powder River Country in 1866 and the Making of the Fetterman Myth* (Albuquerque: University of New Mexico Press, 2008), 53.

22. Bray, *Crazy Horse*, 95–102. According to Bray, Crazy Horse played a major role in the Fetterman fight. However, a more recent book by John Monnett, *Where a Hundred Soldiers Were Killed*, 210–19, discusses the possibility that Crazy Horse may not have been involved in the battle.

23. Utley, *Indian Frontier of the American West*, 105–16.

24. Bray, *Crazy Horse*, 117.

25. *Omaha Weekly Herald*, June 10, 1868, quoted in ibid., 118.

26. Bray, *Crazy Horse*, 165–66.

27. James Donovan, *A Terrible Glory: Custer and the Little Bighorn—the Last Great Battle of the American West* (New York: Little, Brown, 2008), 44, 47, 54; Public Broadcasting System, *New Perspectives on the West*, "George Armstrong Custer," at http:// www.pbs.org/weta/thewest/people/a_c/custer.htm, accessed August 10, 2014.

28. Utley, *Indian Frontier*, 125–27; National Park Service, "Washita Battlefield National Historic Site, Cheyenne, Oklahoma," at http://www.nps.gov/nr/travel /cultural_diversity/Washita_Battlefield.html, accessed August 10, 2014.

29. Donovan, *Terrible Glory*, 31, 80–82; Nathaniel Philbrick, *The Last Stand: Custer, Sitting Bull, and the Battle of the Little Bighorn* (New York: Viking, 2010) 14.

30. Bray, *Crazy Horse*, 165–67.

31. Philbrick, *Last Stand*, 62–65; Donovan, *Terrible Glory*, 31–35.

32. Philbrick, *Last Stand*, 44; Donovan, *Terrible Glory*, 97–98; Utley, *Indian Frontier*, 183–84.

33. Donovan, *Terrible Glory*, 131–32; Philbrick, *Last Stand*, 65–66; Utley, *Indian Frontier*, 183.

34. Utley, *Sitting Bull*, 134–35.

35. Ibid., 140–42; Bray, *Crazy Horse*, 204–12; Crook quoted in Neil Mangum, "A Big Prelude to the Little Bighorn," *Montana Outdoors* (November-December 2004), at http://fwp.mt.gov/mtoutdoors/HTML/articles/2004/RosebudSP.htm, accessed January 25, 2010.

36. Bray, *Crazy Horse*, 212–213; Philbrick, *The Last Stand*, 123–125, 167; Utley, *The Indian Frontier*, 183; Joseph M. Marshall III, *The Day the World Ended at Little Bighorn: A Lakota History* (New York: Penguin Books, 2007), 25–26; National Park Service, Little Bighorn Battlefield National Monument, "Battle of the Little Bighorn," at http://www.nps.gov/libi/historyculture/battle-of-the-little-bighorn.htm, accessed August 9, 2014.

37. Philbrick, *The Last Stand*, 139–142; Marshall, *The Day the World Ended at Little Bighorn*, 132–133; Donovan, *A Terrible Glory*, 204–209.

38. Donovan, *Terrible Glory*, 212–16; Philbrick, *Last Stand*, 153, 159; National Park Service, Little Bighorn Battlefield National Monument, "Battle of the Little Bighorn."

39. Donovan, *Terrible Glory*, 225–30; Philbrick, *Last Stand*, 168–75; Marshall, *Day the World Ended*, 1–4; National Park Service, Little Bighorn Battlefield National Monument, "Battle of the Little Bighorn."

40. Philbrick, *Last Stand*, 183–201; Donovan, *Terrible Glory*, 236–49; Marshall, *Day the World Ended*, 50–51; National Park Service, Little Bighorn Battlefield National Monument, "Battle of the Little Bighorn."

41. Philbrick, *Last Stand*, 181–82, 203–5, 220–30; Donovan, *Terrible Glory*, 250, 256–57, 281–82, 285–99; Marshall, *Day the World Ended*, 92.

42. Bray, *Crazy Horse*, 219, 222–26; Donovan, *Terrible Glory*, 252, 266; Philbrick, *Last Stand*, 216.

43. Bray, *Crazy Horse*, 226–30; Donovan, *Terrible Glory*, 267.

44. Donovan, *Terrible Glory*, 268–78; Bray, *Crazy Horse*, 227–33; Philbrick, *Last Stand*, 264–75.

45. Philbrick, *Last Stand*, 237–51, 286; Bray, *Crazy Horse*, 233–34; Donovan, *Terrible Glory*, 279–99.

46. Utley, *Sitting Bull*, 160–61.

47. *New York Tribune*, July 8, 1876, quoted in Brian W. Dippie, *Custer's Last Stand: The Anatomy of an American Myth* (Missoula: University of Montana Publications in History, 1976), ix.

48. *Little Big Man*, directed by Arthur Penn, Cinema Center Films, 1970.

49. Donovan, *Terrible Glory*, 327; Philbrick, *Last Stand*, 287–88; Bray, *Crazy Horse*, 235–42; Utley, *Indian Frontier*, 184; National Park Service, Little Bighorn Battlefield National Monument, "Battle of the Little Bighorn."

50. Donovan, *Terrible Glory*, 327; Bray, *Crazy Horse*, 246; North Dakota Studies, "The History and Culture of the Standing Rock Oyate: The Taking of the Black Hills," at http://www.ndstudies.org/resources/IndianStudies/standingrock/historical_blackhills.html, accessed August 9, 2014; *An Act to Ratify an Agreement with Certain Bands of the Sioux Nation and Also with the Northern Arapaho and Cheyenne Indians*, Fortieth Congress, Second Session (1877), 19 Stat. 254, at http://www.littlebighorn.info/Articles/agree76.htm, accessed August 9, 2014.

51. Bray, *Crazy Horse*, 360–90; Raymond J. DeMallie, ed., *The Sixth Grandfather: Black Elk's Teachings Given to John G. Neihardt* (Lincoln: University of Nebraska Press, 1984), 322. Thomas Powers, *The Killing of Crazy Horse* (New York: Alfred A. Knopf, 2010), is the most recent study of the Oglala war chief's death. Powers finds no specific, overt conspiracy to murder Crazy Horse, though rival chiefs, especially Red Cloud, and military authorities who viewed him as a destabilizing force were not sorry for his death.

52. Utley, *Sitting Bull*, 182–301.

53. National Park Service, Little Bighorn Battlefield National Monument, "The Indian Memorial Peace through Unity," at http://www.nps.gov/libi/the-indian-memorial-peace-through-unity.htm, accessed January 30, 2010; National Park Service, Little Bighorn Battlefield National Monument, "Winning Design Entry," at http://www.nps.gov/libi/winning-design-entry.htm, accessed August 10, 2014.

54. Todd Wilkinson, "At Custer's Last Stand, a First Stand for Indians," *Christian Science Monitor*, June 24, 2003, at http://www.csmonitor.com/2003/0624/p01s01-ussc.html, accessed August 10, 2014; Ron Fire Crow and Russell Brooks, "Little Bighorn Memorial Offends Some Indians," *People's Voice*, November 27, 1999, at http://www.yvwiiusdinvnohii.net/News99/1199/Commentary991127Memorial.htm, accessed January 30, 2010.

55. James Brooke, "Controversy over Memorial to Winners at Little Bighorn," *New York Times*, August 24, 1997, at http://www.nytimes.com/1997/08/24/us/controversy-over-memorial-to-winners-at-little-bighorn.html?pagewanted=1, accessed January 30, 2010 (first two quotatiohns); http://www.nytimes.com/1997/08/24/us/controversy-over-memorial-to-winners-at-little-bighorn.html?pagewanted=2, accessed January 30, 2010; Frederick Turner, "No Surrender," *Outside Magazine* (August 1997), at http://www.outside.away.com/magazine/0897/9708custer.html, accessed January 31, 2010 (third quotation).

56. Brooke, "Controversy over Memorial to Winners at Little Bighorn."

6

The Warrior Trail
CATASTROPHE

Montana's Warrior Trail, US 212, extends 160 miles from the Little Bighorn southeast to the Wyoming border. Along the way it passes through the Crow and Northern Cheyenne Reservations. Many of the Northern Cheyennes who had been with the Lakotas at the Little Bighorn surrendered with Crazy Horse in May 1877. They had hoped they would be allowed to live with the Lakotas on the Great Sioux Reservation, but the government instead shipped them to Oklahoma to live among the Southern Cheyennes. Their stay there was a time of misery, privation, and death. The Indian Bureau did not provide adequate rations for the Southern Cheyennes, much less for the added population from the north. In addition, malaria swept through the northerners' camps, killing scores of people.

Finally, in the fall of 1878 two Northern Cheyenne chiefs, Dull Knife and Little Wolf, led 297 of the survivors in a daring escape in hopes of returning to southeast Montana. They managed to evade pursuing troops all the way across Kansas and well into Nebraska. Once they were north of the Platte River, the band divided into two groups. One, led by Little Wolf, fled into the

DOI: 10.5876/9781607323273.c006

Pine Ridge area; the other, led by Dull Knife, headed for Fort Robinson in Nebraska, seeking Red Cloud's protection.[1]

Little Wolf and his group managed to hide out near Pine Ridge through the winter of 1878–79. In the early spring they set out again for the north. On the way, soldiers under the command of an officer Little Wolf had known and trusted prior to the Oklahoma exile found them and took them to Fort Keogh in Montana, at the confluence of the Tongue and Yellowstone Rivers.[2]

Dull Knife and his band fared less well. The army intercepted them on their way to Fort Robinson. The soldiers took them to the fort and warehoused them in an abandoned barracks without food or firewood. This only made them more determined to escape. In the dead of night, Dull Knife and 150 others broke out of the barracks and fled on foot into the bitterly cold, snow-clogged plains. The soldiers killed or captured most of them the next day. Only 38, including Dull Knife and his family, eluded the pursuers that day, but the soldiers tracked and killed all but 9 of them in succeeding days. Dull Knife made it to Pine Ridge but ended up imprisoned there. Eventually, the pathetic remnant of Dull Knife's group joined Little Wolf's band at Fort Keogh. Years later, in 1884, President Chester Alan Arthur established their reservation adjoining the eastern boundary of the Crow Reservation. So, in the end, the few surviving Northern Cheyennes did manage to remain in the land they called home.[3]

The terrain along the Warrior Trail, at least as far as the town of Broadus, was a pleasant surprise. I had never been in this part of Montana and expected it to resemble the plains of Colorado, Kansas, Nebraska, and Wyoming. Instead, the route passes through the northern edge of the Wolf Mountains, rising and falling over rolling hills and small mountains covered with pine forest. Only east of Broadus does the terrain flatten and turn to sagebrush plains

DEVILS TOWER

At the tiny town of Alzada, we turned south into Wyoming. The countryside changed again as we pushed south along the Belle Fourche River. The road rises and falls continuously, with lots of curves ranging from tight to sweeping. After the arrow-straight run across Montana, this part of the ride was just plain fun. We stopped for lunch in Hulett, a tiny hamlet that supports itself with a lumber mill and a few small shops. The Feed Bunk Café occupies the

FIGURE 6.1. Devils Tower is the object of a cultural struggle between Plains Indians and white society.

backroom of a gas station convenience store. After lunch, we rode south 9 miles to Devils Tower.

This stone monolith, the product of an intrusion of magma into surround-ing sandstone and exposed over eons by erosion, rises more than 1,200 feet from the Belle Fourche Valley. The 1977 film *Close Encounters of the Third Kind* made Devils Tower a modern cultural icon.[4] In the film, a visitation by space aliens is an irresistible invitation to a select few earthlings to venture off into a new frontier. As the alien ship departs from the tower, one wonders what far-flung cultures the explorers will encounter on their journey. Perhaps, like Lakota chiefs visiting Washington, DC, in 1870, the earthlings will learn that they have been conquered by a power they had not before comprehended.

The setting of Devils Tower is a verdant valley of farms, ranches, forests, and streams. But the tower, like the Little Bighorn and the nearby Black Hills, is a battlefield in the ongoing cultural war between Plains Indians and the dominant white society. Plains Indians, including Lakotas, Cheyennes, Arapahos, Crows, and Kiowas, claim it as a sacred place. The Cheyennes call the tower Bear's Lodge (or Tepee) and Bear Peak. There, according to their beliefs, their prophet and cultural hero, Sweet Medicine, died. Lakotas also call the tower Bear Lodge, among many other names. White Buffalo Calf Woman gave the Lakotas their most sacred object, the White Buffalo Calf Pipe, there. In addition, the Lakotas often held their Sun Dance at the tower.[5]

By the late 1990s, Indians were demanding that the tower be renamed Bear Lodge or some other traditional name. They also sought to ban rock climbing on the tower, especially during June, the time of the Sun Dance. That, in turn, provoked strong opposition from whites in the area who asserted, in effect, that their claim supersedes the Indians'. "My dad came here in 1913 in a covered wagon," said Hulett's mayor in 1997. "I've been here ever since I was a little girl, and I never saw any Indians here until two years ago. If the tower's sacred to them, it's sacred to us, too." A local rock-climbing guide dismissed Indian claims as based only on oral tradition, not written records. The "Euro-Americans were the great record keepers, the great cartographers," he noted.[6] Indeed, they were.

A US Army officer, Colonel Richard Irving Dodge, the namesake of Dodge City, Kansas, led an expedition into the Black Hills and northeast Wyoming in 1875 to follow up on Custer's previous explorations. It was Dodge who, through his published journals of the trip, popularized the name Devils Tower. However, Dodge was not the first white American to see the tower, and maps published in the early nineteenth century identify it as Grizzly Bear Lodge or Bear Lodge, suggesting that documentary evidence that long predates significant white occupation of the area does in fact exist for traditional Indian names.[7]

Located on the western edge of the Black Hills, Devils Tower is one of several historically important stone landmarks in the continuing struggle over the Black Hills.

STURGIS

From Devils Tower we headed south and east to Interstate 90, bound for our stop for the day: Sturgis, South Dakota. Yes, that Sturgis, South Dakota. Named for Colonel Samuel D. Sturgis, who had overall command of the Seventh Cavalry at the time of the Little Bighorn fight, this pleasant small town on the northern edge of the Black Hills is the site of one of the largest annual gatherings of humanity in the world, the Sturgis Motorcycle Rally.

Each August hundreds of thousands of motorcyclists descend on the region, occupying every hotel room, bed and breakfast, and camping spot within a radius of at least 100 miles of Sturgis. In 2000, the peak year of attendance, 633,000 people showed up. The town of Sturgis, with a permanent population of about 6,400, has a government department dedicated to the rally.[8]

The rally's story dates to 1936 when a Sturgis man, Clarence "Pappy" Hoel, opened a motorcycle store in the town. Hoel's store soon became the home of the Jackpine Gypsies Motorcycle Club, which in August 1938 hosted the first rally, calling it the Black Hills Classic. With the exception of the World War II years, the rally has met every year since then. Rally events include various track and off-road races, along with displays by motorcycle manufacturers and vendors selling clothing, equipment, and other paraphernalia. The rally is a significant part of the Sturgis area's economy, generating millions of dollars in sales and tax revenues.[9]

Beyond making money and generating tax revenue, the rally is a celebration—albeit contrived—of motorcycling and the cultural mystique surrounding it. The foundational image is an elemental male, the bearded, leather-clad, outlaw biker living on the edge of or beyond the restraints of mainstream society. Subtexts of the image include uninhibited personal freedom, contempt for conventional mores, and even violence and criminality. Women inhabit this subcultural image as sexual appendages.

Even though the rally is largely a bacchanal, with alcohol flowing and recreational drugs circulating freely, the social reality of the motorcycling subculture today is actually quite different from the edgy, outlaw mystique. The contemporary motorcyclist in America is, well, me: middle-aged (or older) with an upper-middle-class income. One reason for this is economic; the iconic big bikes, such as the Harley-Davidson and Honda touring machines, are expensive. Another reason is the very effective marketing strategies deployed by motorcycle manufacturers, who now link motorcycling less to the image of an outlaw culture than to much more traditional appeals to tourism. Television ads in the 1960s encouraged middle-class consumers to "see the USA in a Chevrolet." Substitute Harley or Honda, and the appeal is very much the same. On my journeys around the West, I have yet to encounter a motorcyclist more menacing than a dentist. Manufacturers today also actively court women as potential buyers, recognizing the changes in American society and culture that have propelled women into positions of professional authority and economic power. My dog's veterinarian—all 4 feet 11 inches of her—rides to Sturgis each year with her husband in tow. I, however, do not like crowds, and the idea of being surrounded and jostled by 600,000 people in a small area, collectively celebrating their individuality and personal freedom, does not appeal to me. I was perfectly happy to see Sturgis as a quiet small town.

We pulled into Sturgis about mid-afternoon. After showers, naps, and bike de-bugging, Phineas and I found a small steakhouse downtown. I ordered a New York strip, which turned out to be a sirloin. I wanted to complain but let it go because the waitress looked like she could, and would, hurt me. The next morning I set off to ride around the Black Hills. Phineas was saddle-weary and stayed in Sturgis to visit the town's motorcycle museum and other attractions.

Every square inch of the Black Hills is contested territory and has been since Custer led his cavalry into the hills in 1874. When the US Congress confiscated the Black Hills in 1877, it did so in violation of the Fort Laramie Treaty of 1868. That treaty, which created the Great Sioux Reservation, forbade any cession of the reservation's territory without the agreement of three-fourths of the adult male Indian population. As war raged on the Northern Plains in 1876, a commission visited the reservation to push a deal to buy the hills at bargain-basement rates. Using intimidation and trickery, the commission members secured the signatures of only about 10 percent of the adult men. Undeterred by the commission's failure, in 1877 Congress simply abrogated the 1868 treaty and confiscated the Black Hills without paying any compensation. Many years later, the government made the preposterous claim that the promise of a few additional years of rations amounted to payment for the land.[10]

The Lakotas have never accepted the loss of the Black Hills, but it is a legal and a political certainty that they will never get them back. A 57-year legal battle did net a victory of sorts for the Lakotas, but even that proved pyrrhic. In 1920 Congress established a Court of Claims to adjudicate Indian claims against the United States. The Lakotas filed suit in 1923, claiming that Congress had taken the hills without paying just compensation. The Court of Claims mulled the case over for 19 years before deciding that it had no authority to rule on the question of compensation. In 1946 Congress created a new Indian Claims Commission to hear tribal grievances against the

United States, and in 1950 the Lakotas took their case to that body. Twenty-four years later, in 1974, the commission ruled that the government had indeed taken the Black Hills without just compensation. The commission specifically rejected the government's claim that the delivery of additional rations amounted to payment for the hills and awarded the Lakotas $17.5 million plus interest. The ruling found that "a more ripe and rank case of dishonorable dealings will never, in all probability, be found in our history." A round of appeals dragged the case out for 6 more years. Finally, in 1980 the US Supreme Court settled the matter in a ruling that upheld the award of financial compensation and interest.[11]

In winning their legal case, however, the Lakotas once again lost the Black Hills. They did not want the money and have refused to take it (the money remains in a trust account and today totals more than $750 million); instead, they want the land back.[12] But the Supreme Court, as it awarded the Lakotas a huge financial judgment, ruled that Congress had acted within its power of eminent domain in confiscating the Black Hills. Congress had only failed to pay just compensation. The award of money was the Lakotas' legal remedy and the only one within the Court's power to grant. The Black Hills will remain under non-Indian private ownership, or under the control of the US Forest Service and mining and timber interests.

In the 1980s the Lakotas asserted a religious claim to gain control of at least a small piece of the Black Hills. In April 1981, less than a year after the defeat-in-victory in the Supreme Court, a group led by American Indian Movement (AIM) activists occupied a small valley in the Black Hills National Forest near Rapid City, South Dakota. They called their settlement Camp Yellow Thunder. Raymond Yellow Thunder was an Oglala from Pine Ridge. In February 1972 Yellow Thunder suffered a horrific night of harassment and beating at the hands of thugs in Gordon, Nebraska, a small town south of the reservation. Yellow Thunder's dead body turned up eight days later in an old pickup truck at a used car lot. He had died of brain injuries suffered during his beating. Three of his assailants eventually served prison time for manslaughter. In March 1972 AIM organized a massive demonstration in Gordon to call attention to the crime. The protest helped bring about prosecution of Yellow Thunder's assailants and also established AIM as a political force on the Pine Ridge Reservation. That, in turn, set the stage for conflict on the reservation in 1973 (discussed later).[13]

Despite US Forest Service and law enforcement harassment, Camp Yellow Thunder lasted until 1987. During those years the occupants applied for a Forest Service permit to establish a permanent 800-acre settlement where they would practice traditional Lakota religion and cultural ways. Historian Donald Worster notes that the Forest Service granted many special-use permits in the Black Hills, including some for religious groups. In fact, the agency had denied only four applications; three of those were for Indian groups. In this case the Forest Service demurred on the grounds that the Yellow Thunder application asked for more land and a longer tenure than regulations allowed. Years of legal wrangling followed. The Indians won their case in a federal district court, which ruled that denial of the permit violated their religious rights. An appeals court, however, reversed that decision, and the Supreme Court declined further review. Camp Yellow Thunder soon disbanded. At the same time, Christian groups' occupation of public land in the Black Hills continued unimpeded.[14]

Crazy Horse

As much as any place, the town of Deadwood symbolizes the transformation of the Black Hills from a "food pack" and sacred place for the Lakotas into a zone of white settlement and economic development. The town, located about 15 miles west of Sturgis, popped up in 1876, a product of the Black Hills gold rush. Deadwood's most famous mine, the Homestake, produced gold until 2002. Even more than Dodge City, Deadwood epitomized the rip-roaring frontier town. Saloons, gambling halls, and brothels lined the streets, ready to serve the miners' social and carnal needs and to empty their pockets. Even as the town settled down, gambling remained an economic mainstay well into the twentieth century, except for two hiatuses during the prohibition era of the 1920s and early 1930s and from 1947 to 1989. Prostitution was just as durable. The state shut down most of Deadwood's brothels in the 1950s, but one, Pam's Purple Door, stayed in business until 1980.[15]

Today, gambling and related tourism are the foundation of Deadwood's economy. Tax revenue from casinos, hotels, and restaurants has enabled Deadwood to preserve and renovate many of its Victorian-era buildings. Riding through Deadwood, however, left me with the sense of visiting a Wild West–themed amusement park, an image Deadwood promotes. In a local hotel's hyperbolic description, Deadwood "is an old mining town that's still as wild at heart as it was in the 1800s when the outlaws, gamblers and gunslingers ruled the streets."[16]

An hour's ride south from Deadwood took me to the Crazy Horse Memorial, located near the town of Custer. During the 1920s and 1930s a Lakota chief named Henry Standing Bear watched with growing frustration as the likenesses of four American presidents appeared, one after another, on the face of Mount Rushmore. In 1931 Standing Bear asked Gutzon Borglum, the artist in charge of the Mount Rushmore project, to include a likeness of the Oglala war chief Crazy Horse on the monument as "a most fitting tribute to pay to a great American." Borglum obviously rejected the request. Finally, in 1939 Standing Bear wrote a letter to another artist, Korczak Ziolkowski, an award-winning studio sculptor who had worked at Mount Rushmore for a few weeks. Standing Bear asked Ziolkowski to consider returning to South Dakota to carve a monument in honor of Crazy Horse. In one of his letters, Standing Bear told Ziolkowski, "My fellow chiefs and I would like the White Man to know the Red Man had great heroes, too."[17]

The idea intrigued Ziolkowski, but nothing came of it for several years. When the United States entered World War II, the sculptor enlisted in the army and served in Europe. After the war, he turned down offers to build war memorials in Europe in favor of the Crazy Horse project. Ziolkowski arrived in South Dakota in May 1947 and, accompanied by Standing Bear and other Lakotas, scouted sites for the monument. They finally chose Thunderhead Mountain near the town of Custer and acquired the property; Ziolkowski began blasting in June 1948. Five Lakota men who had been at the Battle of the Little Bighorn attended dedication ceremonies that month as honored guests.[18]

Ziolkowski worked on the project until his death in October 1982, and his wife (who died in 2014) and family have continued his work. The artist's vision for the monument was, and remains, stupendous. Unlike the faces on Mount Rushmore, the sculpture is to be a free-standing representation of Crazy Horse mounted on horseback, his long hair flowing behind him and his left arm extended, pointing into the *Paha Sapa*. Crazy Horse's head is more than 87 feet in height, dwarfing the Mount Rushmore heads, and his arm and hand extend 296 feet. A small house would fit inside one of the horse's nostrils. The statue's face was completed and dedicated in June

FIGURE 6.2. Carved by artist Korczak Ziolkowski and his family and conceived by Lakota chief Henry Standing Bear, who wanted white Americans to know that Indians also have heroes, the Crazy Horse Memorial emerges from Thunderhead Mountain, near Custer, South Dakota.

1998, 50 years after Ziolkowski fired the first dynamite shots on the mountain. Today, the extended arm and hand have begun to emerge from the rock.[19]

Even though the idea for the Crazy Horse Memorial originated with Henry Standing Bear, the project is not without Indian critics. One criticism is that the statue of Crazy Horse cannot possibly be accurate since the Oglala warrior never permitted himself to be photographed. Ziolkowski's answer was that, even though the statue is based on descriptions given to him by people who knew Crazy Horse, the monument was never intended to be "a lineal likeness but more . . . a memorial to the spirit of Crazy Horse—to his people."[20]

Perhaps more serious are complaints that the memorial is yet another unwanted spoliation of the Black Hills' natural environment, that it is just another white man's moneymaking scheme. John Yellow Bird, president of the Oglala Tribal Council in 1997, asked, "How can we tear up a mountain for a statue?" Similarly, Cheyenne River Sioux Tribal Council chairman Gregg Bourland said, "You don't need to carve up a whole mountain" to remember Crazy Horse and what he represented. "You can look at a beautiful sunset, watch a bird fly or look at a cloud drift by to remember the spirit of Crazy Horse."[21]

American Indian Movement leader Russell Means (who died in 2012) was an especially strident critic of the Crazy Horse project. In his view, the memorial had always been just a moneymaking scheme and a sacrilegious one at that. In a 2001 interview, Means recalled getting drunk with Ziolkowski at the artist's home in 1972. According to Means, Ziolkowski told him, "In the words of P. T. Barnum, there's a sucker born every minute." The monument, in Means's view, "is farce" and, he prophesied, "once it is completed, lightning is going to strike and destroy the whole thing."[22]

Asked if the memorial could not have a positive influence by inspiring people to learn more about Crazy Horse and Indians in general, Means answered that the opposite was more likely. In his view, the monument and the story of Crazy Horse essentialize Indians in an arcane image irrelevant to modern reality, relegating them "to the eighteenth and nineteenth centuries." Because of that, he argued, "Indian people are relics; we do not exist in the present. That makes it easy for non-Indians to say, 'Oh, lo, the poor Indian, and we love his romantic image, and we are sorry for what our ancestors did to him, but we can continue to do it to these Indian people today with impunity.'" That is why, he said, "responsible Indian people abhor carving up one of our sacred mountains in our holy land."[23]

Ziolkowski and his heirs have answered such criticism by pointing out that the idea for the memorial originated with the Lakotas in the person of Henry Standing Bear, who recruited the artist, chose the subject, and help select the site. To be sure, Ziolkowski may have approached the project with some paternalism. His wife, Ruth, recalled that "Korczak used to say, 'I will give the few remaining Indians a little pride.'"[24] But that paternalism, however great or slight, does not negate the Lakotas' role in founding the project; nor does it necessarily negate the Ziolkowski family's sincerity.

One of the most interesting justifications for the memorial is the claim that Crazy Horse himself prophesied it. Stone is a motif in the story of Crazy Horse. He was said to have worn a stone amulet in battle that protected him from harm. Black Elk, the Oglala holy man and a second cousin of Crazy Horse, told John G. Neihardt, "They used to say that he carried a sacred stone with him . . . and that when he was in danger, the stone always got very heavy and protected him somehow." The stone's weight, it was said, wore out his horses, explaining why "no horse he ever rode lasted very long." Black Elk, however, had his doubts about the story, saying "it was only the power of his great vision that made him great."[25]

Crazy Horse's alleged prophecy is linked to that protective stone. When asked about it, the story goes, Crazy Horse is said to have replied, "I will return to you in stone." I spent many hours searching library and Internet sources, trying to track down the source of the quote. I found no scholarly sources for it, and the Internet sources generally led back to unsourced quotes in a 1997 *New York Times* article on the Crazy Horse Memorial. Finally, though, I found the story's apparent source: Korczak Ziolkowski. In a self-published interview in 1982, the year of his death, the artist told the story of Crazy Horse's stone amulet and of his prophecy. Ziolkowski said in the interview that each of the five veterans of the Little Bighorn who attended the 1948 dedication ceremonies told him the story: "Each one said that the story was true. They saw him wear the stone, they heard him say, 'I will return to you in stone.'"[26]

In that light, the story of Crazy Horse's prophesizing the memorial seems more than a bit self-serving for Ziolkowski. That, however, does not mean that the five old Lakotas did not tell him the story or that they did not hear Crazy Horse say, "I will return to you in stone." And it certainly does not mean Ziolkowski made it up. But it does suggest that Ziolkowski himself is the best available documented source for the story.

The Crazy Horse Memorial is a piece, or another layer, of the long struggle over the Black Hills, dating from Custer's invasion in 1874 to later struggles over Devils Tower, motorcycles around Bear Butte (discussed later), and every event and place in between. An even more profound scene of that struggle is located several miles to the northeast, at Mount Rushmore. Between them is one of the most beautiful and challenging motorcycling roads in the country.

From Crazy Horse I backtracked a few miles north and turned into Custer State Park and the Peter Norbeck Scenic Byway. Peter Norbeck, who served as South Dakota's governor (1917–21) and US senator (1921–37), was a determined promoter of both conservation and tourism in his state. His influence was key in securing funding for construction of two key segments of the scenic route named for him, Needles Highway and Iron Mountain Road.

Needles Highway is named for the tall granite spires, some rising many stories into the air, found all along its 14-mile course through the Harney Range. When Norbeck proposed building the road, engineers declared that

FIGURE 6.3. Custer State Park's resident burros make their living mooching food from tourists.

it could not be done. Norbeck rejected the opinions of the "diploma boys," personally surveyed the road's route, and pushed it to completion in 1922.[27] As the narrow two-lane road rises into the mountains it passes by, and some- times between, the Needles. Tight turns and switchbacks are the rule, and some are posted with a 5-mile-per-hour maximum speed recommended. The road descends to Alternate US Highway 16, a less twisty stretch leading to Iron Mountain Road. Near the park's east entrance I came upon one of its mainstays, a small herd of friendly burros that make their living by being cute and mooching food from tourists.

The turns and switchbacks of Needles Highway proved but a tune-up for Iron Mountain Road, which runs north to Mount Rushmore from Alternate US 16. Where Needles Highway had the occasional short, straight stretch, the Iron Mountain Road is mile after mile of sharp corners and tight twists winding up the mountainside. Several pigtail bridges are particularly interest- ing. The bridges span narrow chasms on the mountain. As the road crosses a bridge, it turns quickly and passes directly under the structure's supports, completing a more than 360-degree turn in only a few hundred feet. At one such pigtail, the bridge connects to one of the road's one-lane tunnels. Coming out of the tunnel, I had the feeling of being propelled into midair as I crossed the bridge. I had barely come to grips with that sensation when I had to make a sharp downward turn and circle under the bridge. Other Iron Mountain Road tunnels frame views of Mount Rushmore.

At the top of Iron Mountain I pulled into the Norbeck Scenic Overview, which affords a grand view of Mount Rushmore just across the valley below. As I approached the viewing area, a very friendly man greeted me in a thick southern accent and asked, "Have yew ever hear'd of the Dragon?" Yes, I replied, I did know of the Dragon, or the Tail of the Dragon, a stretch of US 129 near the North Carolina–Tennessee border. Motorcyclists consider the Dragon, with more than 300 curves in 11 miles, one of the country's must-ride roads. Alas, I had to confess that I had not yet ridden the Dragon. "Way-ul," the man replied, "I have rid the Dragon, and this here road y'all just come up is a lot harder 'n twistier 'n sceerier than the Dragon!" My chest swelled with pride, and I thanked the gentleman very much for that information. As he walked away, he turned and shouted, "Y'all keep the rubber side down." I promised to do my best.

MOUNT RUSHMORE

Looking at Mount Rushmore through my telephoto lens, I could see from the Norbeck overlook that the memorial's parking lot was packed with visitors' cars and RVs. After a short ride down the rest of Iron Mountain Road and over to the memorial, I found a line of cars waiting to enter the parking area. More than 3 million people (more than 8,000 per day) toured Mount Rushmore in 2009, making it one of the most heavily visited sites in the country, if not the world.[28] With the all too vivid memory of the Old Faithful parking lot still fresh in my mind, I decided not to risk another such entrapment and contented myself with the very impressive views of Mount Rushmore's presidential figures available from the roadside.

If American Indians, especially Lakotas, harbor ambivalence toward the Crazy Horse Memorial, the same cannot be said of their opinions about Mount Rushmore. To them, the memorial is a thumb in the eye, a humiliating symbol of all they have lost. But to other Americans, Mount Rushmore is a shrine to the visions of American democracy, patriotism, egalitarianism, and nationalism embodied in the lives and legends of the four presidents whose likenesses are carved into the mountain. In short, Mount Rushmore is a contradiction in stone, a powerful symbol of both the triumphant conquest of the American West and its bitter legacies.

Why Mount Rushmore, I wondered? Why create a memorial to Washington, Jefferson, Lincoln, and Theodore Roosevelt in the heart of the Black Hills, an area that even today is remote from the main centers of American life and culture? Why not put it in Virginia's Shenandoah Mountains, in the state where Washington and Jefferson were born? Why not in the Adirondacks of Theodore Roosevelt's New York? Why not in Illinois, which calls itself the land of Lincoln (though finding a rock big enough there would be difficult)? The answer, I learned, was that the monument had to be in the West and it had to honor those four presidents to fulfill the vision of the artist who made it.

South Dakota state historian Doane Robinson first conceived of a monument in the Black Hills honoring heroic figures of America's westward movement. He did not have Mount Rushmore in mind as the site; nor did he intend to inflict more humiliation on South Dakota's Indian population. Instead, his major motivation was to lure tourists to the hills. In 1923 Robinson approached artist Lorado Taft with his idea. Taft was a renowned sculptor famous for monumental works, including his 126-foot-wide *Fountain of Time* at the University of Chicago. In his letter to Taft, Robinson described the Needles and suggested that some of them might "lend themselves to massive sculpture." Robinson also suggested that the Oglala chief Red Cloud would be a good subject. Taft had no interest in the project, so in August 1924 Robinson wrote to another artist gaining fame as a sculptor of monuments: Gutzon Borglum.[29]

Borglum was a westerner by birth. Born in 1867, he was the son of Danish Mormon immigrants. In his youth he lived in Idaho, Nebraska, Kansas, Missouri, and California. As a young man, Borglum left home to study art in San Francisco, where he became a protégé of Jesse Frémont, daughter of Thomas Hart Benton and wife of John C. Frémont, both of whom were apostles and agents of Manifest Destiny.

Borglum was an artist of monumental talent and energy, absorbed by his work and by himself. He was also an American patriot with a fierce and chauvinistic devotion to the country and to his conception of its ideals and culture. Having matured in the Gilded Age and the early twentieth century, Borglum identified very strongly with notions of American moral virtue and especially

FIGURE 6.4. South Dakota state historian Doane Robinson initially envisioned carving monumental sculptures from the Black Hills Needles.

of American power. But he rejected much of that era's art, especially the popular Greek Revival style of public art and architecture. He scorned the American taste for the "rotting trophies of Greece and Rome." "Art in America," he insisted, "should be drawn from American sources, memorializing American achievements." American artists, he believed, should "give, serve, and complete the spirit and concept of Columbus, of Washington, of Lincoln."[30]

When Doane Robinson wrote to him in August 1924, suggesting that "in the vicinity of Harney Peak, in the Black Hills of South Dakota are opportunities for heroic sculpture of unusual character," Borglum was already engaged in a large-scale project, one that revealed other aspects of his character and values.[31] In 1915 the United Daughters of the Confederacy had invited Borglum to visit Stone Mountain, near Atlanta, Georgia, where that year a new version of the Ku Klux Klan was founded. The women's group wanted Borglum to carve a relief sculpture of Confederate general Robert E. Lee's head on the side of the massive granite lump. Borglum told the ladies that "the head of Lee on the side of that mountain would look like a postage stamp on a barn door" and sold them instead on a much more ambitious scheme—a tableau depicting Lee, Jefferson Davis, and Thomas "Stonewall" Jackson at the head of a column of Confederate soldiers.[32]

Borglum began work on that monument to treason in 1923 but soon found himself embroiled in conflicts with the project's business directors. Much of the trouble stemmed from finances and Borglum's demands for control over the project's money. However, another source of tension came from the internal politics of the Ku Klux Klan. Borglum and the directors were members of that racist, anti-Semitic, and xenophobic organization but found themselves attached to contending leaders. The Stone Mountain directors gave their allegiance to the nominal national Klan chieftain, Hiram Wesley Evans, but Borglum became an associate of Indiana Klan leader David Stephenson, who challenged Evans's control of the organization in the early 1920s. By early 1925, tensions between Borglum and his employers had reached a breaking point, and the directors dismissed the artist from the project. Borglum destroyed his models for the Stone Mountain sculpture and fled Georgia with the police hot on his trail for allegedly vandalizing the project's property.[33]

Borglum quit the Ku Klux Klan in 1925, suggesting that his membership may have been a gratuitous, self-serving gesture, albeit one that backfired. However, a letter to David Stephenson, written before he left the Klan, makes it clear that he had no argument with the KKK's racist views but had come to see the group as ineffectual. "I am now thoroughly convinced," he wrote, "that the South will continue its bondage; that the nigger will continue to nominate the President of the United States; and that the Klan, as such, will not raise an intelligent, helpful, constructive finger to free the South and to free the nation from that damnable situation." In a previous screed, Borglum also railed against the "mongrel hoard that is fleeing from its own responsibilities in Europe and pouring over our National Border."[34]

So, in the mid-1920s Gutzon Borglum, a racist and the xenophobic son of immigrants, set out to carve a shrine to American democracy in the Black Hills of South Dakota. Borglum welcomed Doane Robinson's invitation, which came as the conflict in Georgia reached its breaking point. He was very interested in Robinson's "great scheme," which, he said, the "North will welcome." Borglum told Robinson that he could visit the Black Hills in September 1924.[35]

During his first visit to the Black Hills, Borglum rejected the concept of a monument honoring major figures in the history of the American West; it was too provincial, not grand enough. Instead, repeating his performance of a decade before in Georgia, he sold the locals on something much bigger. The Black Hills monument would be colossal, representing American democracy, expansion, and power. Over the next couple of years, as he looked for the right place for it (the Needles would not do—too small and the granite was too soft), the monument took shape in Borglum's mind. It would include the heads of four American presidents—Washington, Jefferson, Lincoln, and Theodore Roosevelt—flanked by a huge entablature commemorating the major milestones of US history. For Borglum, the four presidents symbolized "the founding, preservation, growth, and development of the nation," including the expansion of its territory and political power.[36] Inside the mountain, behind the monument, Borglum planned to carve out a huge Hall of Records, where the great documents of American history, along with records and artifacts of American culture, science, and industry, would be stored (assuming, evidently, that the archivists and museologists of the National Archives and the Smithsonian Institution would turn their precious collections over to him). The heads of the four presidents were the central element of the monument and the only part of the plan to be completed.

As he formulated his plan to memorialize America's founding, preservation, and expansion with gigantic images of Washington, Jefferson, Lincoln, and Roosevelt, Borglum continued his search for the right place to carve it. Finally, in August 1925 he saw the mountain the Lakotas call Six Grandfathers, Mount Rushmore (named for a New York attorney, Charles Rushmore, who visited the area in the 1880s), and is said to have declared, "America will march along that skyline."[37]

Borglum detonated the first dynamite charges in October 1927, and for the next fourteen years, until October 1941—assisted by his son, Lincoln, and a dedicated crew armed with explosives and pneumatic drills—blasted and scaled the likenesses of the four presidents out of the mountain's white granite. They dedicated the Washington bust in 1930, followed by Jefferson in 1936, Lincoln in 1937, and Theodore Roosevelt in 1939. Borglum died in March 1941 and Lincoln Borglum took charge of the project until funding ran out in October of that year.[38]

FIGURE 6.5. Mount Rushmore, viewed from the Norbeck Scenic Overview. Most Americans see the monument as a shrine to democracy. Many Indians see it as a symbol of all they have lost.

Mount Rushmore was wildly popular from its beginning. Today, most Americans who visit the monument see in the four colossal faces an expression of American success and power. But not all American visitors view Mount Rushmore that way. Indians, especially Lakotas on whose stolen mountain the monument is carved, see it quite differently. Indians' dislike of the memorial goes beyond the criticism leveled at the Crazy Horse Memorial, that it is an unnecessary, unwanted, and even sacrilegious destruction of the *Paha Sapa*'s natural environment. The massive faces of four presidents, carved from their sacred mountain, are a humiliating statement by the conqueror to the conquered. In the 1970s John Lame Deer, a Lakota medicine man from the Rosebud Reservation, stated the case clearly. The white man first made a treaty recognizing the Black Hills as Lakota land forever. Then he found gold in the hills and took them by force. Later, the white man made the Black Hills "into one vast Disneyland." Finally, said Lame Deer, speaking in the white man's voice, "after we did all this we carved up this mountain, the dwelling place of your spirits, and put our four gleaming white faces here. We are the conquerors." To Lame Deer, who died in 1976, the memorial said that the white man takes what he wants and nothing can stop him: "They could just as well have carved this mountain into a huge cavalry boot standing on a dead Indian."[39]

In the early 1970s Lame Deer participated in demonstrations at Mount Rushmore demanding the return of the Black Hills to Indian control. One group occupied the mountaintop for a week in August 1970. Another occupation, in 1978, lasted ten days. The demonstrations were, of course, about much more than Mount Rushmore, but the memorial's symbolic power for both mainstream American culture and Indians made it an important stage for the expression of mounting political and cultural militancy among American Indians. Indeed, the first Indian demonstrations at Mount Rushmore proved rather tame harbingers of things to come in South Dakota.

Indian activists stopped demonstrating at Mount Rushmore after the 1970s. Perhaps that is in part a result of the Supreme Court's 1980 decision that effectively settled in the negative the legal question of returning the Black Hills to the Lakotas. Nevertheless, feelings about the Black Hills remain strong among the Lakotas and other Indians, and rhetoric about the memorial reflects those strong feelings. Russell Means called Mount Rushmore "the Shrine of Hypocrisy." The leader of an Indian organization called Defenders of the Black Hills has said of the memorial that it is "like a slap in the face to us—salt in the wounds—as if a statue of Adolf Hitler was put up in the middle of Jerusalem."[40]

In 2004 the National Park Service, in the person of Superintendent Gerard Baker, began including an Indian presence at the memorial. Baker, a Mandan-Hidatsa Indian, had served previously as superintendent of the Little Bighorn Battlefield National Monument, where he took the lead in establishing the Indian Memorial there. Baker understood, and could articulate forcefully, the Indian view of Mount Rushmore. For Indians, he said, Mount Rushmore does not mean the "Success of America." Instead, "It means the desecration of the sacred Black Hills; it means the losing of the Black Hills to the United States government, to white people that came in and shoved everybody out of here and put us on a reservation."[41] But Baker also understood his professional obligation at Mount Rushmore. As he had at the Little Bighorn, he set out to make the memorial more inclusive of all Americans. He explained, "I want everybody to understand that this is a part of American history, and we need to show all sides of that story," including the history of the area's

Indian population. Mount Rushmore, he said, "should be a place for people to come and reflect on who you are as an American." At first, Baker simply talked with tourists who wanted to know about the larger context of the history of Mount Rushmore and the Black Hills. Eventually, he set up a Heritage Village, a cluster of three tepees staffed by Indian dancers and storytellers. Next to the presidential sculptures, Heritage Village quickly became the memorial's most popular feature.[42]

Though tourists like Heritage Village and the inclusion of American Indians as part of the story of American history at Mount Rushmore, some Black Hills–area residents do not approve of it. To them, the Indian presence there violates notions of ideological correctness that they associate with the memorial. Mildly stated objections included the complaint that Superintendent Baker's innovations did not fit the memorial's theme and that, as one man put it, he was more interested in "Native American cultural diversity rather than the Memorial's intended purpose: celebrating the lives and ideals of Washington, Jefferson, Roosevelt and Lincoln." Much more strident was the comment of a Rapid City man who, on learning that Baker was leaving Mount Rushmore for a promotion as the Park Service's assistant director for Indian relations, said "That's great! Now maybe we can keep Mount Rushmore safe from terrorist activities."[43]

American Indians are not the only people who have used Mount Rushmore as a stage for political protest. In October 1987 Greenpeace and Earth First activists draped over Washington's face a banner declaring "We the people say no to acid rain." Park rangers rounded up the group before they were able to deploy a large replica of a gas mask. On the day I visited the area, Greenpeace activists had scaled the mountain and hung next to Lincoln's head a banner reading "America honors leaders not politicians: stop global warming." The text was superimposed over an image of President Barack Obama.[44] The demonstrators later pled guilty to federal charges of trespassing and illegal climbing. Their sentences included fines, suspended jail time, and community service. One member of the group spent two days in jail. In addition, Greenpeace paid $30,000 in fines for the stunt.[45]

The Greenpeace demonstration, and what many considered meaninglessly light sentences for it, outraged some local guardians of Mount Rushmore's ideological meaning. An article on a right-wing website in South Dakota exclaimed "Environmental Extremists Hijack National Monument, Get Off

Light" and complained that the court "should have dealt with this matter firmly to send a message to anyone else—environmental extremists, potential vandals, or whoever—that such law-breaking insults to the American people will not be tolerated."[46]

Sitting in my motel room after a long day of riding around the Black Hills, I saw the news reports of the Greenpeace action. I thought the demonstration was pretty silly, but as a patriotic American I did not feel especially insulted by it. But I knew that the folks who like to compare President Obama to Adolf Hitler, or those who approve of violating the decorum of a State of the Union Address by yelling "liar," would go nuts over it. I was right. Just imagine the unpatriotic effrontery of those tree-huggers engaging in unauthorized free speech at the Shrine of Democracy!

Is Mount Rushmore, or any other monument to America and its heroes, some sort of church where one speaks, if at all, only in hushed tones and nods in prayerful agreement with the approved message? George Washington, Thomas Jefferson, Abraham Lincoln, and Theodore Roosevelt never shied away from a debate or a fight. Many of their contemporaries believed they were political extremists. They understood that debate—sometimes raucous, sometimes quiet—is the essence of democracy. Silence does them no honor. But the concern of some citizens for enforcing ideological correctness at Mount Rushmore is connected to another issue in the struggle over the Black Hills: the nature and meaning of the sacred in American culture.

BEAR BUTTE

As we rolled out of Sturgis the next morning we passed Bear Butte, the focal point of a genuine clash between the sacred and the profane in the Black Hills. This great igneous hump rises more than 1,200 feet above the surrounding plains. It has been sacred to Northern Plains Indians for hundreds of years. Bear Butte is the physical and symbolic focal point of Cheyenne cultural and historical identity. It was there that the creator gave to the Cheyennes' prophet, Sweet Medicine, the tribe's four sacred arrows and the cultural values of respect, honor, humility, and courage they symbolize. For Lakotas, the mountain is a place of prayer, where people seek connection with *Wakan Tanka*, the Great Holy, especially through the intense experience of the vision quest. There, Crazy Horse and Sitting Bull had visions that shaped their lives.

FIGURE 6.6. Bear Butte, near Sturgis, South Dakota, is one of the Northern Plains Indians' most sacred sites. Photographer: Dana Rae Echohawk.

Bear Butte is also a traditional gathering place for the Lakotas. In 1857, all of the Lakota bands met there for a great council to discuss how to meet the growing challenge of white penetration of the plains.[47]

Bear Butte continued to be a place of pilgrimage and prayer for Indian people, despite the catastrophes of the Northern Plains wars, the breakup of the Great Sioux Reservation, and the determined efforts of missionaries and the government to suppress Indian religion and culture. In recent times, the butte has acquired some measure of protection as both a state park and a national historic landmark. Thousands of people, Indian and non-Indian, visit each year and the mountain's trails are festooned with brightly colored prayer cloths and tobacco offerings. Jim Jandreau, a Brulé Sioux and the state park manager, described the mountain's power: "Everyone that comes off this mountain, it doesn't matter if they are Indian or non-Indian or what tribe they are from, when they come away from this mountain . . . none of them will ever be the same."[48]

Jay Allen is one of the people affected by the mountain, though not in the way Jim Jandreau describes the Bear Butte experience. Allen, the owner of the largest saloon in Sturgis, a rambunctious, barn-like place called the Broken Spoke, loved to watch the sunset behind the mountain. But he also saw Bear Butte as an irresistible backdrop for a commercial enterprise, a

600-acre campground and recreation center featuring an enormous bar to cater to the Sturgis Motorcycle Rally crowd.

Allen ran into vocal opposition when he proposed building his campground and bar just outside Bear Butte State Park's boundary. Indians and their supporters, including some motorcyclists, argued that the campground and especially the noise from hundreds of motorcycles would ruin the mountain's spiritual qualities. Alex White Plume, then president of the Oglala tribal government at Pine Ridge, noted, "We need integrity in our ceremonies here, and it requires a certain amount of quiet." Eugene Blue Arm, a Lakota elder, agreed, saying, "When you come here it's to gain a solitude that's necessary for prayer and deep thought." He added, "You need solitude. You need to be quiet. You need to look at the—and experience—the elements like the wind. You can hear messages in the wind." Motorcyclist Kenneth Robinson, a Sturgis rally attendee, likened Allen's enterprise to building a bar in the Vatican. (Robinson's analogy was not entirely apt. The Vatican, in the heart of densely populated Rome, is surrounded by bars, restaurants, boutiques, and noisy street vendors hawking papal bobble-head dolls to tourists.) More telling, perhaps, is Dickinson State University scholar Clay Jenkinson's observation that if someone opened "a porn shop next to the new Lutheran mega church on north Washington Street . . . all of Bismarck would rise up to force the shop's relocation. Build a wet T-shirt bar in the precinct of the Indian 'cathedral of the Northern Plains and most of the white community shrugs its shoulders and gets on with life."[49]

Allen denied that his enterprise would disturb Bear Butte and the worshippers who came there. "I know for a fact that this isn't a disruption," he declared while the facility was under construction. Allen also professed sympathy for the Indians' point of view. Referring to a proposal to establish a 5-mile quiet zone around the mountain, he said, "I don't blame them for wanting it. They love that mountain. Hell, if I was them I'd want a 25-mile buffer around it." But, he pointed out, in town "people have churches within 500 feet of a bar, and they haven't lost their religion." Allen did not like being made out as "the bad guy" in the controversy, especially since he believed he had "approached this whole project with love and compassion." Even though he had the right to do pretty much what he wanted with his property, he said, "what I wanted to do was in respect to them [the Indians] and was to share their culture and their belief system. It's just amazing how that got turned around." For example, he was distressed that Indians found offensive his plan, which he scrapped, to build an 80-foot-tall statue depicting an Indian in prayer. "Everyone loved it," he noted, "but the Native Americans."[50]

One measure of Allen's and his corporate partners' respect for Bear Butte's environment and spiritual character, and for Indian culture, is the enterprise's operations. The 45,000-square-foot saloon is painted bright red, standing out against the plains like an open flesh wound. Inside the saloon, waitresses work dressed only in underwear. Patrons, especially women, are invited to compete in wet T-shirt, bikini, and pole dancing contests. During the annual motorcycle rally, nightly outdoor rock concerts send the sounds of heavy metal reverberating across the plains.[51]

In addition to his reverence for Indian culture and for Bear Butte's spiritual character, Allen has also expressed a sense of personal proprietorship toward the mountain. In a 2006 interview he said, "I come out here all the time for sunsets, and to me this is sacred ground. Look at that mountain. No one has anything like it." In another interview, Allen promised to invite "open-minded and open-hearted" Indians to join him and "let them look at the mountain from the top of the deck."[52]

Allen and his partners, unsurprisingly, beat back efforts to block the Bear Butte saloon and campground. Any other outcome would have flown in the face of almost a century and a half of precedent in the Black Hills region. Indeed, other campgrounds and a shooting club have popped up around the state park. Despite what is going on at its base, however, Bear Butte park manager Jim Jandreau has a sanguine attitude about the mountain and its future. "You cannot take away the spirituality of the mountain, which is its true draw," he has said. "That is its true magnificence."[53]

The conflict over Bear Butte, over Devil's Tower, over all of the Black Hills is rooted in the vast disparity of political, economic, and cultural power between Indian people and the dominant, white American culture. The dominant culture is more powerful, so Indian people lose. An aspect of the dominant culture's power is manifested in its conception of the sacred. To most Americans, the Vatican, the Wailing Wall, and the little white church down the street are sacred places. So, too, are cemeteries, especially military cemeteries. So, too, are places like Ground Zero in New York City. And they are sacred. They are sacred because of what they are, because of what they represent, because of what has happened there, and because we believe them to be sacred.

While the Vatican, the Wailing Wall, and the little white church down the street are sacred to the dominant culture, natural places like Devils Tower and Bear Butte are not. They are instead primarily resources, or commodities, to be acquired and used. Thus Devils Tower becomes something to be climbed for personal enjoyment and, for the climbing guides who ply their trade there, a source of profit. The land around Bear Butte is an area for commercial development. So, while Indian people view commercial and recreational use of their sacred places as disrespectful of their religious practices, the dominant culture dismisses Indian claims for protection of those sites as illegitimate efforts to restrict commercial and recreational access. The dominant culture is stronger; Indian people lose.

I wonder if the people in America who so loudly denounced and worked to block the construction of an Islamic community center several blocks from Ground Zero in New York City would recognize the contradiction. They opposed the Islamic community center on the grounds that it is disrespectful to the memory of the victims of the 2001 terrorist attacks (including, I suppose, the memory of the scores of Muslims who died there on that terrible day) and because it would be insensitive to the feeling of the victims' survivors. I wonder if they would identify with the feelings of Indian people who find rock climbing at Devils Tower or 45,000-square-foot saloons at Bear Butte insensitive to their religious and cultural values.

It is impossible to truly comprehend another people's historical experience, but it must seem to Indian people that episodes such as the commercialization of Bear Butte are continual reminders of how much they have lost and continue to lose to the dominant culture. As Clay Jenkinson has noted, "Respect and cultural sensitivity are not legally enforceable. They are habits of the heart."[54] Slights that to many in American society might seem trivial, if slights at all, loom large in the minds and hearts of others.

An example occurred in Rapid City, just a few weeks before Phineas and I rolled through on our way to the Pine Ridge Reservation. Paraphrasing the humorist Dave Barry, you could not make this up. At a McDonald's restaurant in Rapid City, children—including Lakota kids—found included in their Happy Meals little plastic dolls of George Armstrong Custer, mounted on a tiny motorcycle. The dolls were part of McDonald's participation in the promotion of the motion picture comedy *Night at the Museum: Battle of the Smithsonian.*[55] The local Lakota community was not amused. One activist likened the promotion to distributing Adolf Hitler dolls in Israel. A local teacher pointed out, less hyperbolically, that the dolls were painful to Indian people. "Custer didn't kill Indians or Natives," she said, "he killed relatives." McDonald's did not apologize for distributing the toy in the heart of Indian country, and a corporate spokesperson insisted that "we value and respect people of all ethnicities, as well as their cultural history." With that, however, the Custer biker doll disappeared from Rapid City.[56]

WOUNDED KNEE

We had bad coffee and gassed up at a convenience store in Rapid City and then headed southeast. Near a ramshackle spot named Scenic, the remnant of a town where a bar and self-proclaimed museum seemed to be staying upright mostly out of habit, we entered a narrow neck of Badlands National Park. The barren-looking, brown sandstone parapets and canyons justified the area's name. A few more miles down the road, we crossed into the Pine Ridge Reservation, home of Red Cloud and Crazy Horse's people, the Oglala Lakotas.

Pine Ridge is a legacy of the catastrophe the United States and the American people inflicted on the Lakotas during and after the Northern Plains war. In 1889 the government tore up the tattered remains of the 1868 treaty, pushed the Lakotas onto five reservations, and opened most of the former Great Sioux Reservation to white settlement.[57] Conditions were desperate on all of the Lakota reservations. Corrupt and incompetent reservation agents stole or lost much of the little food that was delivered, and malnutrition left the Lakotas vulnerable to diseases such as influenza and measles, which swept through the reservations.[58] In addition to hunger and disease, the Lakotas also faced an all-out cultural assault. Their children were herded into mission-run schools, where they were forbidden to speak their language and subjected to physical punishment if they disobeyed. This violent cultural imperialism persisted long into the twentieth century. In the mid-1990s, Pine Ridge resident Dale Looks Twice recalled that teachers at a Catholic boarding school he attended whipped his hands with a leather belt if they caught him speaking Lakota. "Imagine that . . .We were beaten for speaking our own language."[59] Agents and missionaries also attacked Lakota religion, most notably by banning the Sun Dance.

The Lakotas were ripe for something—anything—that offered hope for relief from the privation and despair of reservation life. That hope came from far to the west, from Nevada, in the message of a Paiute prophet named Wovoka. In January 1889 Wovoka received a powerful vision in which the Great Holy revealed to him a renewed world where all Indian people who had lived before would live again alongside their descendants, practicing the old ways of life. It would be a world of peace and happiness, with abundant game. And it would be a world without white people. But for this renewed world to come about, Indian people had to prepare themselves. Wovoka instructed his followers that they must not quarrel or fight among themselves, they must work and be honest, and they must live in peace with the whites. Finally, they must perform the Spirit, or Ghost, Dance (in Lakota, *wanagi wacipi*), which he taught them.[60]

Lakotas at the Pine Ridge and Rosebud Reservations began performing the Ghost Dance in early 1890. Dancing spread during the summer to Cheyenne River and Standing Rock and peaked during the fall, when as many as one-quarter to one-third of the reservation populations participated.[61] After performing purification rituals, dancers formed a circle, joined hands, and moved in a simple rhythmic step around a sacred tree or pole. Dancing for hours, even days, on end, dancers often collapsed and, when revived, reported having visions of their dead relatives and of the renewed world to come.[62]

As the Ghost Dance spread across the West, it undermined efforts to liquidate Indian culture and thus also challenged government authority. Nevertheless, the government resorted to armed force to suppress it only among the Lakotas, resulting in the only serious episodes of violence during the Ghost Dance movement: the killing of Sitting Bull and the massacre at Wounded Knee. That, of course, begs the question of why the government resorted to violence only against the Lakotas. Two factors were key: a long-standing struggle for political and cultural power between Sitting Bull and the white administration of Standing Rock and a unique feature of the Lakota Ghost Dance: the Ghost Shirt.

Lakota dancers were wearing Ghost Shirts (*ogle wakan*) and Ghost Dresses (*cuwignaka wakan*) by the fall of 1890. The garments—usually made of cotton and painted with spirit symbols such as birds, animals, stars, and the moon—had two important functions, both rooted in Lakota religious culture. First and most important, they connected the dancers to the spiritual power and so helped them to experience visions. The Ghost Shirt's second purpose was to provide the wearer with a measure of personal protection. Ghost Dance leaders assured their followers that the shirts and dresses would protect them from harm, even from soldiers' bullets. This was not unique in Lakota culture, as sacred symbols and objects had always been used to invoke spiritual protective power. One example was the stone amulet Crazy Horse wore into battle to ward off his enemies' arrows and bullets.[63] Lakota Ghost Dancers did not wear Ghost Shirts and Dresses because they intended to turn to violence but because they expected the government to use force against them to suppress their religion. After all, the *wasicus* had already banned the sacred Sun Dance. Surely, they would act forcefully against a religion that envisioned their disappearance.

White authorities did see the Ghost Dance as a challenge to their authority, and the Ghost Shirts proved to some that the Lakotas were preparing for battle. Why else would they need such protection? By mid-November 1890, with eastern newspapers doing their best to drum up a war on the Northern Plains and the commander of the army's Department of the Missouri, the assiduously self-promoting General Nelson A. Miles, agitating for a military takeover of the reservations, the government dispatched the US Army to the Lakota reservations to suppress the Ghost Dance. To firm up the commitment to military intervention, Miles sent a report to Washington in late November asserting "there never has been a time when the Indians were as well armed and equipped as the present." War, the general implied, was imminent.[64]

The stunningly incompetent government agent at Pine Ridge, a political hack named Daniel Royer—who quickly earned the Oglala's contempt, expressed in their nickname for him, "Young Man Afraid of Indians"—welcomed the army's arrival. However, the agent at Standing Rock, James McLaughlin, was unhappy.[65] McLaughlin understood, correctly, that the army's presence would undermine his authority on the reservation. So McLaughlin set out to demonstrate that he was in control of his reservation by bringing to an end his long-standing battle with his most famous ward, Sitting Bull.[66]

Though Sitting Bull accepted the reality of his confinement to the reservation and even abandoned the tepee for a compound of log cabins, he steadfastly resisted acknowledging McLaughlin's authority over him and his immediate band of followers. Sitting Bull's ardent opposition to the 1889 land cession hardened the white authorities' attitudes, and those of some former followers, against him. However, the wily old man had succeeded in giving McLaughlin no cause to arrest and deport him—at least until the last weeks of 1890.[67]

The Ghost Dance "crisis" created the pretext McLaughlin needed to get rid of his nemesis. Sitting Bull was agnostic about the Ghost Dance. He did not participate in the dance, but he also refused to go along with McLaughlin's demands that he cooperate in stopping it. Sitting Bull's resistance gave McLaughlin license to brand him as "the high priest and leading apostle of this latest Indian absurdity" and "the chief mischief-maker" and to assert that "if he were not here, this craze, so general among the Sioux, would never have gotten a foothold at this agency." Unfortunately, McLaughlin soon over-played his hand, with tragic results for Sitting Bull and all the Lakotas.[68]

In mid-November McLaughlin wrote a long dispatch to the commissioner of Indian affairs suggesting a plan to defeat the Ghost Dance and Sitting Bull by ordering all the non-dancers at Standing Rock to come into the agency. The rest would be left alone but would be denied any rations. In short, he pro-posed to starve the dancers and Sitting Bull into submission. By then, however, the army was on its way to the reservations and, succumbing to the increas-ingly militant political environment, the commissioner ordered McLaughlin to prepare a list of names of dance leaders for possible arrest by the army. Many years later, McLaughlin wrote that he "feared military interference with the Indians" because he was "convinced that a military demonstration would precipitate a collision and bloodshed which might be avoided."[69]

McLaughlin's own actions soon set the stage for collisions and blood-shed, first at Standing Rock and then at Wounded Knee. In mid-December McLaughlin received reports that Sitting Bull was about to flee Standing Rock and take his followers to Pine Ridge. Leaving the reservation would in itself have been an act of defiance of the agent's authority, but going to Pine Ridge would have created the possibility of an alliance with Red Cloud. Even without the element of the Ghost Dance mixed into the equation, such an alliance would have been a formidable political or even military problem.[70]

His hand forced, McLaughlin ordered his agency police, staffed with many officers hostile to the old chief, to arrest Sitting Bull. In his order, McLaughlin

instructed his policemen that they "must not let him escape under any cir-
cumstances."[71] Before sunrise on the morning of December 15, 1890, a detail
of agency police officers, led by Lieutenant Henry Bull Head, one of Sitting
Bull's most bitter opponents on the reservation, burst into his cabin and
seized him. Sitting Bull cooperated initially with his captors but began to
resist as they escorted him from his cabin. Outside, in the gray light of dawn,
Sitting Bull's followers gathered and began to menace the officers and encour-
age their chief's resistance. The scene quickly turned lethal. Police accounts
claimed that one of Sitting Bull's loyalists drew a gun and shot Bull Head,
who had hold of Sitting Bull. Though mortally wounded, Bull Head fired a
shot point blank into Sitting Bull's head, killing him instantly. As Sitting Bull
fell, another police offer, Red Tomahawk, fired a second shot into his chest.
Witnesses among the slain chief's family and friends, however, maintained
that Bull Head fired first.[72]

With the shots that killed Sitting Bull, a lethal firefight erupted between
the police and the dead chief's followers, resulting in several casualties on
both sides. Several policemen retreated with the dying Bull Head into Sitting
Bull's cabin, where they gunned down the chief's son, Crow Foot, and waited
out the battle. The fighting lasted about ninety minutes, until a unit of the
Eighth Cavalry arrived to rescue them.[73] The army's arrival at Sitting Bull's
compound was a crucial moment. Agent McLaughlin's attempt to arrest
Sitting Bull resulted in the very outcomes he had hoped to prevent: military
intervention and armed clashes between the army and the Lakotas.

It is unclear whether Sitting Bull actually planned to flee Standing Rock
for Pine Ridge. Even if that had been his plan, it is unlikely that his presence there would have strengthened the Ghost Dancers. Only a minority of
Lakotas, substantial as that minority was, ever joined in the movement. In
addition, the army's deployment, especially to Pine Ridge, had caused serious polarization among the Lakotas. Non-dancers began to gather at Pine
Ridge, while the most militant dancers fled into the Badlands to a place
known as the Stronghold, an isolated plateau accessible only through a narrow, easily defended defile.[74] The army did not want to attack the Stronghold
if they could possibly avoid it. Doing so would result in heavy casualties. But
the army also did not want any more Lakotas to join the hundreds of dancers already holed up there. That aim was behind the decision to pursue the
Miniconjou chief Big Foot and his band.[75]

As tensions among the Lakotas grew, Red Cloud invited Big Foot to come to Pine Ridge. Red Cloud hoped that Big Foot, respected for his diplomatic skills, could mediate tensions between dancers and non-dancers. Sitting Bull's death and the now very real threat of violence at the hands of the US military convinced Big Foot to accept the invitation. Big Foot had good reason to be afraid of the army. Like Sitting Bull, he had opposed the 1889 land cession and resisted agency authority. During the Ghost Dance period he supported his people's right to participate if they wished, earning him the animus of both civilian and military authorities and gaining him a place on the list of troublemakers to be rounded up.[76]

On December 19, 1890, Big Foot and part of his band were on their way to the Cheyenne River agency in South Dakota, 60 miles downriver from their camp, when they came upon fleeing survivors of Sitting Bull's band who told them of their chief's death and the gun battle at Standing Rock. Fearing that if they continued to the agency they might be arrested or worse, Big Foot turned his group back toward their camp on Deep Creek. On their way home they encountered the rest of their band who, after learning that a force of the Eighth Cavalry led by Colonel Edwin V. Sumner Jr. was closing on them, had fled east. The Eighth Cavalry was operating as part of a military sweep of the area meant to round up dancers and their supporters who had not yet surrendered or were fleeing to the Stronghold. Big Foot met with Colonel Sumner the following day but agreed neither to surrender nor to go with him anywhere but back to his camp on Deep Creek. Sumner agreed, reluctantly, hoping he could calm Big Foot and his people and get them to go voluntarily to Fort Bennett, located near the Cheyenne River agency. Big Foot warned the colonel that there would be trouble if he tried to force him and his people away from their homes.[77] The Miniconjous and their Hunkpapa guests stayed in camp through the following day but, still fearing that Sumner meant to attack them, slipped away under cover of darkness and headed for Pine Ridge. Big Foot by this time had fallen deathly ill with pneumonia.

At his headquarters in Rapid City, General Miles was furious with Sumner for allowing Big Foot to get away. (Later, after Wounded Knee, Sumner explained that he could not bring himself to use armed force against peaceable people in their own homes.) Miles sent orders to his troops in the field to find, disarm, and detain the chief and his band. Assuming that Big Foot was headed for the Stronghold, for the next few days the soldiers concentrated their search in that direction.[78] Ironically, by that time most of the dancers at the Stronghold had left and were on their way to the reservations to turn themselves in.

On December 26 the army finally realized that Big Foot was headed to Pine Ridge, not the Stronghold. Orders went out to units of the Seventh Cavalry, stationed at Pine Ridge, to move out and intercept them. Once in custody, Big Foot and his people were to be disarmed and then exiled from the Dakotas. The following day Miles added to his orders the admonition that "if he [Big Foot] fights, destroy him."[79]

Two days later Major Samuel M. Whitside and a squad of Seventh Cavalry troopers met Big Foot and his followers at a spot about 5 miles north of Wounded Knee. Whitside decided against attempting to disarm the group right away. Instead, he shook hands with Big Foot and, seeing that the chief was gravely ill, had him moved into an army ambulance. The soldiers then escorted Big Foot and his band to a campsite along Wounded Knee Creek, where they put the chief in a heated tent at the foot of a small hill that rises just west of the road to Pine Ridge. The soldiers set up their camp just to the north, and the rest of Big Foot's band pitched their tepees a few yards to the west. At the top of the hill, Whitside deployed two Hotchkiss guns, light artillery pieces that could fire up to fifty exploding rounds per minute. At about 8:30 that evening, more Seventh Cavalry troops arrived with two more Hotchkiss guns. They also brought food for the captives. Colonel James W. Forsyth, leading the additional troops, assumed command at Wounded Knee. Forsyth deployed his troops so the Indian camp was surrounded. Once those dispositions were made, the officers tapped a keg of whiskey and toasted one another on capturing their prey. One wonders what else they may have talked about that night. Nineteen officers and soldiers at Wounded Knee had ridden with Custer to the Little Bighorn. Witnesses later reported that in the days before they rode out of Pine Ridge, some men talked of avenging Custer's defeat.[80]

Wounded Knee, like Sand Creek, is a pretty place. Approaching it from the north, the road winds down a long hill from Porcupine Creek until it spills out into the valley. It was early July when Phineas and I visited, but the native plains grasses were still green, and they swayed gently in the breeze. Trees mark the twisting course of Wounded Knee Creek as it runs east-west and then turns abruptly north around the area where Big Foot's band and the Seventh Cavalry made their camps. A deep, dry ravine opens into the creek a short distance to the southeast of the Indians' campsite.

As we rolled into the valley, I knew from photographs what I was looking for—a gateway of wrought iron supported by brick columns, perched atop a small hill. This was the hill where Major Whitside and Colonel Forsyth set up their Hotchkiss guns. It is also where some of those killed on December 29, 1890, are buried. At the foot of the hill, just across the road from the spot where Big Foot's tent was located, is a small parking area. On the day Phineas and I visited, a local family had set up a table and was selling bead-work and other arts and crafts items. Between their table and the road, a large sign, pale green with white lettering—weatherworn and defaced with graffiti—dominates the parking area. The text explains, mostly accurately, what happened there.

Phineas and I parked our motorcycles at the foot of the hill and walked up a path to the top. Just outside the gateway we stood where the Hotchkiss guns had been positioned and looked down into the valley. Even a poor artilleryman would have had difficulty missing targets just a few score yards below. Then we walked through the gateway into the small cemetery. In the middle a simple chain-link fence, festooned with colorful feathers and prayer cloths, surrounds a plot about 15 feet wide and 60 feet long. This is the mass grave of some of Wounded Knee's dead. Midway along one side of the grave stands a corniced granite monument, about 8 feet tall. On one face an inscription notes the date of the "Chief Big Foot Massacre" and says of him that he "was a great Chief of the Sioux Indians. He often said I will stand in peace till my last day comes. He did many good and brave deeds for the White Man and the Red Man. Many innocent women and children who knew no wrong died here." On the other sides are inscribed the names of some of those buried there.

As the sun rose on the morning of December 29, 1890, 500 heavily armed soldiers surrounded Big Foot's camp. Of the 400 Miniconjous and Hunkpapas, perhaps 120 to 150 were men and older boys of fighting age. The rest were women, children, and old people.[81] When the sun was fully up, Colonel Forsyth ordered the Indian men to assemble in the flat, open space between their camp and the soldiers' camp. Then, Forsyth ordered the men to sur-render their arms. Big Foot's brother, Frog, recalled later that the older men

FIGURE 6.7. The hilltop cemetery at Wounded Knee. The chain-link fence surrounds the mass grave of victims of the 1890 massacre. Seventh Cavalry artillery men placed their Hotchkiss guns near where the gateway stands.

"consented willingly, and began giving them up." Several yards away a medicine man began chanting and singing, urging the men to remember the power of the Ghost Shirts. A translator told Forsyth that the medicine man was bent on "making mischief," which had to have made a tense situation even more volatile.[82]

Big Foot's men surrendered a few weapons but not enough to satisfy Forsyth, who assumed, correctly, that his captives had concealed many more. The colonel ordered his soldiers to search the Indians and their camp. The troops moved into the camp and ransacked tents and travel packs, seizing anything resembling a weapon. They found several more rifles, some hidden under women's clothing, and also confiscated knives, clubs, and even household implements. As some soldiers searched the camp, others began to search the men. A young man named Black Coyote, who may not have fully understood what was going on because he was deaf, produced a rifle but resisted giving it up. While Black Coyote and some soldiers grappled over the weapon, a shot rang out. It is not clear whether that shot

FIGURE 6.8. View of Wounded Knee Valley and massacre site from the hilltop cemetery. Big Foot's band made their camp at the foot of the hill, where they were easy targets for the army's artillery.

came from Black Coyote's rifle or from somewhere else. It really does not matter.[83]

In an instant, the soldiers began firing from all sides. Big Foot and many of the men died in the first volleys. Several soldiers died in the first moments, too, most likely killed by friendly fire from their comrades whose positions surrounded the Indians. Up on the hill, the Hotchkiss guns began to rain shells into the Indians' camp where there were only women, children, and old people. Those men not killed right away picked up weapons, either from the pile of confiscated guns or from where they had concealed them, or seized them from soldiers and began to return fire. Their main concern was to provide covering fire for the women, children, and old people, who immediately began running away from the shooting. They fought bravely and well, taking heavy casualties, but they were too few and outgunned. The women and children and old people fled in all directions away from the soldiers. Many of them, along with some warriors, tried to take cover in the dry ravine. But as they ran across the open ground and down into the ravine, shells from the Hotchkiss guns and bullets from the soldiers' rifles tore through them. A witness, watching the carnage from the hilltop, said, "They fell on all sides like grain before the scythe."[84]

The initial, most ferocious fighting lasted only about ten minutes. However, the shooting went on for as long as four hours as soldiers hunted down and killed as many of the Indians as they could find. Searchers later found the bodies of 4 people—a woman, 2 young girls, and a boy—3 miles from Wounded Knee, all shot at very close range. In all, the soldiers of the Seventh Cavalry slaughtered as many as 300 members of Big Foot's band that day. Of that number, perhaps 200 were women and children. The troops delivered 33 wounded survivors to a temporary hospital set up in the Episcopal Church in Pine Ridge, where Dr. Charles Eastman—a Lakota—and his wife-to-be, Elaine Goodale, treated them as best they could. Two days later Dr. Eastman rode out with a party to the massacre site and found a few other survivors. The Seventh Cavalry suffered 25 dead.[85]

On January 1, as Dr. Eastman searched for survivors, reporters and a burial detail arrived at Wounded Knee. Photographers took pictures of Big Foot and the other dead, their bodies frozen in grotesque death poses in the wake of a blizzard that had blown through. The burial detail dug a trench atop the hill from which the Hotchkiss guns had blasted the camp below and, with no ceremony, tossed the bodies into the trench. A photo of the horrific scene shows workers and soldiers standing in and around the trench with the dead, some bodies already in the pit and others stacked beside it. One soldier stands with his rifle pointed at the dead. The contractor in charge of the burial billed the government for 168 bodies. More than 100 of Wounded Knee's other Lakota dead lay un-recovered but not un-mourned on the Dakota plains.[86]

The finger pointing began immediately, especially by the men ultimately the most responsible for Wounded Knee. Standing Rock agent James McLaughlin, whose vendetta against Sitting Bull triggered the sequence of violence that led to the massacre, blamed the army, saying "it was not a battle; just a killing." General Miles, who had told his officers in the field to destroy Big Foot and his people if they resisted disarming, now blamed his subordinates for the slaughter. Miles trained his bureaucratic guns on Colonel Forsyth, ordering two courts of inquiry to investigate his actions. Both investigations cleared the colonel of any serious wrongdoing. A report to the secretary of the army, written by the officer in charge of the inquiries, shows that the military was more interested in protecting itself than in assigning responsibility or hanging one officer out to dry. General J. M. Schofield wrote that the officers and enlisted men of the Seventh Cavalry had "taken great care" in trying "to avoid unnecessary killing of Indian women and children in the affair at Wounded Knee" and that throughout the engagement had displayed "excellent discipline and, in many cases, great forebearance" in their conduct. A sure measure of the army's embarrassment over Wounded Knee was its attempt to gild the event with a gloss of valor by awarding eighteen Medals of Honor to participants. By comparison, only 124 servicemen received the Medal of Honor in all of World War I.[87]

Historians sometimes say the Wounded Knee Massacre ended the era of warfare on the Great Plains. In the 1930s the Oglala holy man Black Elk described Wounded Knee even more starkly, as virtually the death of the Lakota nation. "A people's dream died there," he said. "There is no center any longer, and the sacred tree is dead."[88] But American Indians, including the Lakotas, never gave up their struggle—against the most daunting odds—for dignity, basic civil rights, and economic security and to preserve their culture and community. On one occasion the sound of gunfire again echoed across the Valley of Wounded Knee Creek.

Federal Indian policy through much of the twentieth century remained paternalistic, bent on pushing Indian people toward some vision of cultural and economic assimilation, to make them individually, if not collectively, self-sufficient. So much the better if, coincidentally, assimilation and self-sufficiency resulted in lower costs to US taxpayers and opened reservation lands and resources to commercial development by business interests. Nevertheless, determined efforts by Indian people, their leaders, lawyers, and friends, produced important changes that led in the direction not of assimilation but of cultural and legal self-determination.

Beginning with the Indian Reorganization Act of 1934, which permitted Indian people to begin forming tribal governments, changes in federal policy—along with major court decisions affirming treaty rights over natural resources, protecting reservations from state taxation, expanding tribal lawmaking and enforcement powers, and recognizing cultural and religious freedom—have made tribes more self-governing. In the process, the courts have also established the legal principle that Indian tribes have at least limited sovereignty. Nevertheless, the paternalistic and heavy-handed authority of the government, especially of the Bureau of Indian Affairs (BIA), working in alliance with supporters within the tribes, proved remarkably durable. Pine Ridge was a case study.[89]

In the early 1970s the Oglala tribal government at Pine Ridge came under the control of Chairman Dick Wilson, who ruled the reservation with an iron fist, relying on intimidation and force to stay in power. Wilson was also a reliable ally of the BIA. However, in 1973 an alliance of anti-Wilson Oglalas and American Indian Movement (AIM) activists, who had won a following on the reservation because of their protests over the Raymond Yellow Thunder killing and other incidents, challenged Wilson's power by organizing an impeachment campaign against him. When that effort failed, they decided to escalate the confrontation with a more militant protest. One idea was to occupy tribal and BIA offices. Anticipating such a move, Wilson garrisoned the facilities with police and private gunmen. Oglala holy man Frank Fools Crow advised the militants to "go to Wounded Knee and make your stand there."[90]

During the night of February 27, 1973, 200 AIM and Oglala activists occupied the church, store, and several other buildings in the village of Wounded Knee. Armed with rifles, pistols, and shotguns, they held the village for seventy-one days. Within hours of the takeover, a heavily armed force of tribal, state, and federal police, including the FBI, backed up by the US Army, surrounded them. The government forces fired thousands of rounds into the village, killing 2 of the occupiers. One of the dead, Buddy Lamont, is buried next to the mass grave of the 1890 massacre victims. One federal agent was wounded during the siege.[91]

After the militants surrendered, little changed politically in the short term. Dick Wilson remained in power until 1976, and the federal government spent years and millions of dollars prosecuting AIM's leaders. In the mid-1970s an FBI official could still say of the Oglalas and of Indian people in general, "They're a conquered nation, and when you're conquered the people you're conquered by dictate your future." The same official likened the FBI to "a colonial police force."[92] But the siege at Wounded Knee did focus national attention on Pine Ridge, and things there gradually began to change as the Oglalas grew more insistent about taking control of their lives. As a result, their tribal government has become more democratic and autonomous; and their language, culture, and religion have been regenerated. Schoolchildren are no longer beaten for speaking the Lakota language.

This hardly means that Pine Ridge is a success story. There is no real economy there, and unemployment is typically in the range of 80 percent or more. Ninety-seven percent of the reservation's 40,000 residents live below the federal poverty line. Infant mortality is 300 percent above the national average. The privation and despair are obvious. Phineas and I stopped for gas in the town of Pine Ridge and were panhandled three times in the few minutes it took to fill our tanks. Even worse was the scene we witnessed in the neighboring town of Whiteclay, Nebraska, which sits on the reservation's southern boundary, right next to the town of Pine Ridge. Whiteclay hardly qualifies as a town. It has 14 residents who operate four liquor stores. They sell more than 4 million cans of beer per year, almost all of it to the residents of legally dry (until 2013) Pine Ridge. As we rolled by, we saw dozens of people standing, sitting, and lying on the sidewalks, some obviously passed out.[93]

Later, I thought about that FBI official's idea that the Oglalas were a conquered people and that, as such, their conquerors would dictate their future. After the United States conquered Japan and Germany, our nation poured billions of dollars into rebuilding those defeated enemy powers and within a couple of decades transformed them into allies and economic powerhouses. One hundred and twenty-five years after the Wounded Knee Massacre denoted the final military conquest of the Lakotas, it seems that the best the United States can do for that conquered people is sell them 100 cans of beer per capita each year.

We rode south out of Pine Ridge and Whiteclay for about 20 miles and then turned west. It seemed as if we had entered another world, one of prosperous and orderly farms and towns. Within an hour we rolled into Chadron, Nebraska, where we stopped for lunch. A town festival celebrating Chadron's roots in the early-nineteenth-century fur trade was a cheerful and stark contrast to the despair of Pine Ridge. South of Chadron we rolled across the forested escarpment of the Pine Ridge, the geological formation from which the Oglala reservation takes its name, and then descended into the alternating rolling hills and flat plains of western Nebraska. We crossed the North Platte River at Bridgeport and pushed on to Sterling, in northeastern Colorado. As we raced toward Denver on Interstate 76, we kept a close eye on a massive thunderstorm just to the north. It had the shape and lurid colors of a thermonuclear explosion. Fortunately, we caught only some peripheral winds and rain. No wind-driven bugs pelted my back, as had happened a couple of years before in Kansas.

Finally, as the sun slipped below the crest of the mountains, I pulled into my garage and parked Old Blue in its familiar spot. We had covered well over 500 miles since leaving Sturgis that morning. I was bone tired and wanted only to hug my wife and daughter, then a hot shower, dinner, and the comfortable familiarity of my own bed. Haywood the Wonder Cat, who had taken over my side of the bed while I was away, made room for me, grudgingly at first, and then happily jumped on my shoulder and drooled in my ear. It was nice to be home.

NOTES

1. Dee Brown, *Bury My Heart at Wounded Knee: An Indian History of the American West* (New York: Henry Holt, 1970), 340–43; Robert M. Utley, *The Indian Frontier of the American West, 1846–1890* (Albuquerque: University of New Mexico Press, 1984), 208.

2. Brown, *Bury My Heart at Wounded Knee*, 348–49; Utley, *Indian Frontier*, 208.

3. On the Northern Cheyenne's odyssey, see Brown, *Bury My Heart at Wounded Knee*, 331–49.

4. *Close Encounters of the Third Kind*, directed by Steven Spielberg, Columbia Pictures Corporation, 1977.

5. National Park Service, Devils Tower National Monument, George L. San Miguel, "How Is Devils Tower a Sacred Site to American Indians?" at http://www.nps.gov/deto/historyculture/sacredsite.htm, accessed February 3, 2010.

6. James Brooke, "What's in a Name? At Wyoming Butte, a Culture and a History," *New York Times*, July 8, 1997, at http://www.nytimes.com/1997/07/08/us/what-s-in-a-name-at-wyoming-butte-a-culture-and-a-history.html?pagewanted=1, accessed February 4, 2010.

7. Arlington National Cemetery Website, "Richard Irving Dodge, Colonel, United States Army," at http://www.arlingtoncemetery.net/ridodge.htm, accessed February 4, 2010; Brooke, "What's in a Name."

8. http://www.sturgis.com/2kstats.html, accessed February 3, 2010; "Sturgis Area Statistics," http://www.sturgismotorcyclerally.com/info-guide/faq.php, accessed February 3, 2010.

9. http://www.sturgismotorcyclerally.com/info-guide/faq.php, accessed February 3, 2010; http://www.sturgis.com/2kstats.html, accessed February 3, 2010.

10. United States Supreme Court, *United States v. Sioux Nation of Indians*, 448 US 371 (1980); James Donovan, *A Terrible Glory: Custer and the Little Bighorn—the Last Great Battle of the American West* (New York: Little, Brown, 2008), 327; Bray, *Crazy*

Horse: A Lakota Life (Norman: University of Oklahoma Press, 2006), 246; North Dakota Studies, "The History and Culture of the Standing Rock Oyate: The Taking of the Black Hills," at http://www.ndstudies.org/resources/IndianStudies/standingrock/historical_blackhills.html, accessed August 9, 2014; *An Act to Ratify an Agreement with Certain Bands of the Sioux Nation and Also with the Northern Arapaho and Cheyenne Indians*, Fortieth Congress, Second Session (1877), 19 Stat. 254, at http://www.littlebighorn.info/Articles/agree76.htm, accessed August 9, 2014.

11. *United States v. Sioux Nation of Indians*; Donovan, *Terrible Glory*, 327; Bray, *Crazy Horse*, 246; North Dakota Studies, "History and Culture of the Standing Rock Oyate."

12. Tim Giago, "The Black Hills: A Case of Dishonest Dealings," *Huffington Post*, June 3, 2007, at http://www.huffingtonpost.com/tim-giago/the-black-hills-a-case-of_b_50480.html, accessed March 3, 2010.

13. Kerri Remp, "Journalist Explores History of Reservation's Border Town," *Chadron* [NE] *News*, September 2, 2008, at http://rapidcityjournal.com/thechadronnews/news/journalist-explores-history-of-reservation-s-border-towns/article_79761b2a-8e62-5c46-942e-6990be6550ca.html, accessed February 28, 2010; Chadron State College, "Author Recounts 1972 Murder Case," http://www.csc.edu/modules/news/public_news/view/4947, accessed August 13, 2014; Philip D. Roos, Dowell H. Smith, Stephen Langley, and James McDonald, "The Impact of the American Indian Movement on the Pine Ridge Indian Reservation," *Phylon* 40, no. 1 (1st quarter, 1980): 90.

14. Donald Worster, *Under Western Skies: Nature and History in the American West* (New York: Oxford University Press, 1992), 108–9.

15. City of Deadwood, "Deadwood: An Entire American City Named a National Historic Landmark," at http://www.cityofdeadwood.com/index.asp?SEC=269A8C80-9F36-4D72-A17D-DF18E23E10FF&Type=B_BASOC, accessed August 13, 2014.

16. Holiday Inn, Rushmore Plaza Hotel, "Deadwood," at http://www.rushmoreplaza.com/ap-deadwood-1303427814.php, accessed August 13, 2014.

17. Robb DeWall, *Crazy Horse and Korczak: The Story of an Epic Mountain Carving* (Crazy Horse, SD: Korczak's Heritage, 1982), 50.

18. James Brooke, "Crazy Horse Is Rising in the Black Hills Again," *New York Times*, June 29, 1997, at http://www.nytimes.com/1997/06/29/us/crazy-horse-is-rising-in-the-black-hillsagain.html?pagewanted=all, accessed March 24, 2010; Crazy Horse Memorial, "About Us: The Story of Crazy Horse Memorial," at http://crazyhorsememorial.org/about-us/, accessed August 13, 2014; Crazy Horse Memorial, "Korczak—Storyteller in Stone," at http://crazyhorsememorial.org/about-us/korczak-storyteller-in-stone/, accessed August 12, 2014.

19. Albert Boime, "Patriarchy Fixed in Stone: Gutzon Borglum's 'Mount Rushmore,'" *American Art* 5, no. 1-2 (Winter-Spring 1991): 161; Crazy Horse Memorial, "Korczak—Storyteller in Stone"; Brooke, "Crazy Horse Is Rising in the Black Hills Again"; Crazy Horse Memorial, "About Us"; "Crazy Horse" (brochure) (Crazy Horse, SD: Crazy Horse Memorial Foundation, 2008).

20. Brooke, "Crazy Horse Is Rising in the Black Hills Again"; Crazy Horse Memorial, "Frequently Asked Questions," at http://www.crazyhorsememorial.org /frequently-asked-questions/, accessed August 13, 2014.

21. Brooke, "Crazy Horse Is Rising in the Black Hills Again."

22. Chris Roberts, "Russell Means," *The Progressive* 65, no. 9 (September 2001): 38.

23. Ibid.

24. Brooke, "Crazy Horse Is Rising in the Black Hills Again."

25. John G. Neihardt, *Black Elk Speaks: Being the Life Story of a Holy Man of the Oglala Sioux Tribe,* premier edition (Albany: State University of New York Press, 2008), 67–68.

26. Brooke, "Crazy Horse Is Rising in the Black Hills Again"; DeWall, *Crazy Horse and Korczak,* 140.

27. South Dakota Department of Game, Fish, and Parks, *Tatanka: The 2010 Guide to Custer State Park,* 27, at http://gfp.sd.gov/state-parks/directory/custer/docs /tatanka.pdf, accessed May 10, 2010.

28. National Park Service, Mount Rushmore National Memorial, "Park Statistics," at http://www.nps.gov/moru/parkmgmt/statistics.htm, accessed May 20, 2010.

29. Rex Alan Smith, *The Carving of Mount Rushmore* (New York: Abbeville, 1985), 25–27; Northern Illinois University, "Lorado Taft Biographical Sketch, 1860–1936," at http://www.niu.edu/taft/aboutus/loradotaft.shtml, accessed June 20, 2010.

30. Gilbert C. Fite, "Gutzon Borglum: Mercurial Master of Colossal Art," *Montana: The Magazine of Western History* 25, no. 2 (Spring 1975): 6.

31. Doane Robinson to Gutzon Borglum, August 20, 1924, copy at National Park Service, Mount Rushmore National Memorial, at http://www.nps.gov/moru /historyculture/upload/Doane%20letter2.pdf, accessed August 13, 2014.

32. National Park Service, Mount Rushmore National Memorial, "Sculptor Gutzon Borglum," at www.nps.gov/moru/historyculture/upload/Sculptor%20 Gutzon%20Borglum%20A.pdf, accessed April 10, 2010.

33. See Jesse Larner, *Mount Rushmore: An Icon Reconsidered* (New York: Thunder's Mouth/Nation Books, 2002), 187–238, for a detailed study of Borglum's connection to, and activities with, the Ku Klux Klan.

34. Letter cited in ibid., 222–23.

35. Gutzon Borglum to Doane Robinson, August 28, 1924, at National Park Service, Mount Rushmore National Memorial, at www.nps.gov/moru/historyculture /upload/Borglum%20letter2.pdf, accessed April 10, 2010.

36. Lincoln Borglum, *Mount Rushmore: The Story Behind the Scenery* (Las Vegas: KC Publications, 1977), 13, quoted in Boime, "Patriarchy Fixed in Stone," 150; Gutzon Borglum, "The Political Importance and the Art Character of the National Memorial at Mount Rushmore," *Black Hills Engineer* 18 (November 1930): 285, quoted in Boime, "Patriarchy Fixed in Stone," 150.

37. Larner, *Mount Rushmore,* 89; National Park Service, Mount Rushmore National Memorial, "Carving History," at http://www.nps.gov/moru/historyculture/carving-history.htm, accessed August 12, 2014.

38. National Park Service, Mount Rushmore National Memorial, "Carving History"; Smith, *Carving of Mount Rushmore,* 211–14, 311–15, 330–35, 369–72, 386.

39. John (Fire) Lame Deer and Richard Erdoes, *Lame Deer: Seeker of Visions* (New York: Washington Square, 1972), 82.

40. Tim Giago, "Mt. Rushmore Seen through Native Eyes," *Huffington Post,* July 7, 2010, at http://www.huffingtonpost.com/tim-giago/mt-rushmore-seen-through_b_105931.html?view=point, accessed July 7, 2010; Indian leader quoted in Tony Perrottet, "Mt. Rushmore," *Smithsonian Magazine,* May 2006, at http://www.smithsonianmag.com/travel/mt-rushmore-116396890/?page=3, accessed August 12, 2014.

41. Public Broadcasting System, "The National Parks: America's Best Idea, Untold Stories Discussion Guide: Mount Rushmore National Memorial and National Park Superintendent Gerard Barker," at http://www-tc.pbs.org/national-parks/media/pdfs/untold_stories_mount_rushmore.pdf, accessed August 13, 2014.

42. First Baker quote in Babette Hermann, "Mt. Rushmore Continues to Become More Native Friendly," *Indian Country Today,* April 5, 2009, at http://indiancountrytodaymedianetwork.com/2009/04/05/mt-rushmore-continues-become-more-native-friendly-84563, accessed August 12, 2014; second Baker quote in Associated Press, Barbara Soderlin, "Heritage Village at Rushmore Sparks Comments," *Indian Country Today,* January 12, 2010, at http://www.indiancountrynews.com/casinos tourism-sections-menu-75/4499-heritage-village-at-rushmore-sparks-comments, accessed August 12, 2104.

43. First quotation in Soderlin, "Heritage Village at Rushmore Sparks Comments"; second quotation in Tim Giago, "A Man of Great Vision Departs Mount Rushmore," *Native Sun Times,* April 19, 2010, at http://www.huffingtonpost.com/tim-giago/a-man-of-great-vision-dep_b_542023.html, accessed August 12, 2014.

44. "Greenpeace Members Charged in Mount Rushmore G-8 Protest," CNN, July 9, 2009, at http://edition.cnn.com/2009/US/07/08/south.dakota.protest/index.htm, accessed July 6, 2010; Matthew Glass, "Producing Patriotic Inspiration at Mount Rushmore," *Journal of the American Academy of Religion* 62, no. 2 (Summer 1994): 279.

45. "Greenpeace Activists Sentenced for Climbing Mount Rushmore, Hanging Anti–Global Warming Banner," *Huffington Post*, January 4, 2010, at http://www .huffingtonpost.com/2010/01/04/greenpeace-activists-sent_n_411096.html, accessed July 14, 2010.

46. Bob Ellis, "Environmental Extremists Hijack National Monument, Get Off Light," *Dakota Voice*, January 5, 2010, at http://www.dakotavoice.com/2010/01 /environmental-extremists-hijack-national-monument-get-off-light, accessed July 6, 2010.

47. *Tribal Report of the Northern Cheyenne Nation* 1, no. 9 (August-September 2006): 12, at http://www.cheyennenation.com/tribalreport/August_Sept/The%20 People%20page%2012, accessed August 13, 2014; Elliott West, *The Contested Plains: Indians, Goldseekers, and the Rush to Colorado* (Lawrence: University of Kansas Press, 1998), 75–76; Kari Forbes-Boyte, "Respecting Sacred Perceptions: The Lakotas, Bear Butte, and Land-Management Strategies," *Public Historian* 18, no. 4 (Autumn 1996): 104–7.

48. Vincent Schilling, "Bear Butte Mountain: A Beautiful, Sacred Site in South Dakota," *Indian Country Today*, April 7, 2009, at http://indiancountrytodaymedia network.com/2009/04/07/bear-butte-mountain-beautiful-sacred-site-south-dakota -84128, accessed August 13, 2014.

49. White Plume and Robinson quoted in Jim Robbins, "For Sacred Indian Site, New Neighbors Are Far from Welcome," *New York Times*, August 4, 2006, at http://www.nytimes.com/2006/08/04/us/04sacred.html?pagewanted=all&_r=0, accessed August 12, 2014; Blue Arm quoted in https://groups.yahoo.com/neo /groups/ancient-native-heritage/conversations/topics/11892, accessed August 12, 2014; Clay Jenkinson, "An Elegy for Historic Bear Butte," *Bismarck Tribune*, December 2, 2006, at http://bismarcktribune.com/news/opinion/columnists/clay_ jenkinson/an-elegy-for-historic-bear-butte/article_56baca83-e389-5b06-a8cf-0fc9e21 95de1.html, accessed August 14, 2014.

50. First and last Allen quotes in Robbins, "Sacred Indian Site"; remaining Allen quotes in Public Broadcasting Service, Religion and Ethics, "Bear Butte," at https:// groups.yahoo.com/neo/groups/ancient-native-heritage/conversations/top- ics/11892, accessed August 12, 2014.

51. Broken Spoke Campground, http://www.brokenspokecampground.com /facilities.php, accessed September 21, 2010; Broken Spoke Campground, http:// www.brokenspokecampground.com/girls.php, accessed September 21, 2010; http://www.brokenspokecampground.com/contests.php, accessed September 21, 2010.

52. Robbins, "For Sacred Indian Site, New Neighbors Are Far from Welcome."

53. Schilling, "Bear Butte Mountain."

54. Jenkinson, "Elegy for Historic Bear Butte."

55. *Night at the Museum: Battle of the Smithsonian*, dir. Shawn Levy, Twentieth Century Fox Film Corp., Los Angeles, 2009.

56. Jeremy Fugleberg and Andrea Cook, "Custer Toy Makes for Not-So-Happy Meals," *Rapid City Journal*, June 15, 2009, at http://www.rapidcityjournal.com/news/local/article_b7c282e5-b1a9-5ffd-8186-45b23e4a3e5a.html, accessed September 25, 2010.

57. Jeffrey Ostler, *The Plains Sioux and U.S. Colonialism from Lewis and Clark to Wounded Knee* (London: Cambridge University Press, 2004), 229–39; Utley, *Indian Frontier*, 246–51. The five Lakota reservations were Pine Ridge; Rosebud, adjoining the latter, where the Sicongu Oyate, or Brulés, settled; Standing Rock, straddling the North Dakota–South Dakota border, home to the Hunkpapas and Blackfoot bands; Cheyenne River, directly south of Standing Rock, where Miniconjou, Two Kettle, Sans Arc, and Blackfoot settled; and the Lower Brulé. Directly east of the Missouri River from the Lower Brulé is the Crow Creek Reservation, home of the Dakota-speaking Santee and Yankton bands.

58. Utley, *Indian Frontier*, 251.

59. Conger Beasley Jr., *We Are a People in This World: The Lakota Sioux and the Massacre at Wounded Knee* (Fayetteville: University of Arkansas Press, 1995), 24–25.

60. Ostler, *Plains Sioux*, 244; Raymond J. DeMallie, "The Lakota Ghost Dance: An Ethnohistorical Account," *Pacific Historical Review* 51, no. 4 (November 1982): 385, 399.

61. Ostler, *Plains Sioux*, 273–74. The estimate of 5,500 to 7,500 Ghost Dancers is based on data in US Department of the Interior, Census Office, "Report on Indians Taxed and Indians Not Taxed in the United States (Except Alaska)" (Washington, DC: Government Printing Office, 1894), at http://www.census.gov/prod2/decennial/documents/1890a_v10-26.pdf, accessed October 8, 2010.

62. Ostler, *Plains Sioux*, 244–47, 256–60; William S.E. Coleman, *Voices of Wounded Knee* (Lincoln: University of Nebraska Press, 2000), 9. Both Ostler and DeMallie, "The Lakota Ghost Dance," argue convincingly that despite Christian features, the Ghost Dance religion was most strongly rooted in Lakota religious traditions.

63. Ostler, *Plains Sioux*, 279–82; Coleman, *Voices of Wounded Knee*, 40–41; Brown, *Bury My Heart at Wounded Knee*, 434, 436.

64. Coleman, *Voices of Wounded Knee*, 56; Miles quoted in Ostler, *Plains Sioux*, 302–3.

65. Coleman, *Voices of Wounded Knee*, 61.

66. Ibid., 125–26; Ostler, *Plains Sioux*, 314–15.

67. Ostler, *Plains Sioux*, 213–16, 221–23, 292.

68. Ibid., 278; McLaughlin quoted in Coleman, *Voices of Wounded Knee*, 78.

69. Coleman, *Voices of Wounded Knee*, 79, 83–84.

70. Ostler, *Plains Sioux*, 321–23.

71. Coleman, *Voices of Wounded Knee*, 185–86.

72. Ostler, *Plains Sioux*, 324–25; Coleman, *Voices of Wounded Knee*, 198–206.

73. Ostler, *Plains Sioux*, 207–12, 326.

74. Ibid., 319, 321–24; Coleman, *Voices of Wounded Knee*, 180, 310–11.

75. Ostler, *Plains Sioux*, 316–17, 326; Coleman, *Voices of Wounded Knee*, 115, 174–75, 237–38.

76. Ostler, *Plains Sioux*, 327; Coleman, *Voices of Wounded Knee*, 242–43.

77. Ostler, *Plains Sioux*, 329.

78. Ibid., 329, 332–33.

79. Miles quoted in ibid., 334; Coleman, *Voices of Wounded Knee*, 271.

80. Ostler, *Plains Sioux*, 335–36. Both Indian and white witnesses claimed that officers and soldiers drank heavily during the night of December 28–29; Coleman, *Voices of Wounded Knee*, 268, 273–74, 277–78.

81. Ostler, *Plains Sioux*, 338; Coleman, *Voices of Wounded Knee*, 268.

82. Coleman, *Voices of Wounded Knee*, 282 (Frog quotation), 290–91, 296; Ostler, *Plains Sioux*, 342.

83. Ostler, *Plains Sioux*, 338–48; Coleman, *Voices of Wounded Knee*, 282–97.

84. Coleman, *Voices of Wounded Knee*, 296, 301–2, 305 (witness quotation); Ostler, *Plains Sioux*, 343–45.

85. Ostler, *Plains Sioux*, 345; Coleman, *Voices of Wounded Knee*, 340, 350, 355. In *Bury My Heart at Wounded Knee,* Dee Brown says 51 wounded survivors were taken to Pine Ridge.

86. Coleman, *Voices of Wounded Knee*, 352.

87. Ibid., 310 (McLaughlin quote), 364 (Schofield quote); United States Army, Center of Military History, "Medal of Honor Recipients: Indian Wars Period," at http://www.history.army.mil/html/moh/indianwars.html, accessed October 18, 2010; United States Army, Center of Military History, "Medal of Honor Statistics," at http://www.history.army.mil/html/moh/mohstats.html, accessed October 11, 2010.

88. See, for example, George Brown Tindall, *America: A Narrative History*, 4th ed. (New York: W. W. Norton, 1996), 823; Utley, *Indian Frontier,* 257. Utley also argues more broadly that Wounded Knee marked the closing of the frontier phase of American history. Quotation from Neihardt, *Black Elk Speaks*, 218.

89. Richard White, *It's Your Misfortune and None of My Own: A New History of the American West* (Norman: University of Oklahoma Press, 1991), 492–93; Charles Wilkinson, *Blood Struggle: The Rise of the Modern Indian Nations* (New York: W. W. Norton, 2005), 9–12, 21–22, 60, 62; James O. Gump, "Civil Wars in South Dakota and

South Africa: The Role of the 'Third Force,'" *Western Historical Quarterly* 34, no. 4 (Winter 2003): 431.

90. Wilkinson, *Blood Struggle*, 145.

91. Ibid., 145–49; White, *It's Your Misfortune and None of My Own*, 587–88; Tim Giago, "Whatever Happened to the So-Called Goons?" *Huffington Post*, September 16, 2007, at http://www.huffingtonpost.com/tim-giago/whatever-happened-to-the-_2_b_64611.html, accessed October 26, 2010.

92. Steve Hendricks, *The Unquiet Grave: The FBI and the Struggle for the Soul of Indian Country* (New York: Thunder's Mouth, 2006), 8.

93. American Indian Humanitarian Foundation, "Pine Ridge Statistics," at http://aihf4.tripod.com/id40.html, accessed October 26, 2010; Red Cloud Indian School, "The Reservation," at http://redcloudschool.org/reservation, accessed August 14, 2014; *Lincoln Star Journal*, April 12, 2010, at http://journalstar.com/news/state-and-regional/govt-and-politics/article_c9fde3cc-4656-11df-8b22-001cc4c002e0.html, accessed October 27, 2010. In 2013 Pine Ridge residents voted to end prohibition and allow liquor sales at reservation government-operated stores. Profits are to be used to finance alcohol education and treatment programs. Carson Walker, "Oglala Sioux Tribe Votes to End Alcohol Ban on Pine Ridge Reservation," at http://talkingpointsmemo.com/news/oglala-sioux-tribe-votes-to-end-alcohol-ban-on-pine-ridge-reservation?ref-fpb=, accessed August 14, 2014.

Don't Fence Me In

"I want to ride to the ridge where the West commences."[1]

I happen to know where that ridge is.

Ride or drive westbound on Interstate 70 from Topeka, Kansas, for 10 miles or so. You ascend a long, steady rise. The landscape changes as you top the ridge. Look around you. You have left the Missouri River Valley and rolled onto the Great Plains. The change is subtle at first, as the tree-filled valley gives way to the plains, undulating for a few miles and then becoming flatter as the road speeds you westward.

"Don't fence me in."[2]

I also happen to know many other places where the West commences. One is the 100th meridian. For geographers and many historians, this line on the map, which runs through Dodge City, Kansas, denotes the beginning of the arid West. Other boundaries are the Mississippi and Missouri Rivers. Saint Louis, with its Gateway Arch near the confluence of the two rivers, claims to

DOI: 10.5876/9781607323273.c007

FIGURE 7.1. On the ridge where the West commences: Kenosha Pass, overlooking South Park, Colorado.

be the jumping-off point to the West. For overland traders and migrants, other towns—Franklin, Missouri, where the Santa Fe Trail began, or Independence, Missouri, where the Oregon Trail originated, or Omaha, Nebraska, where the Mormon Trail started—marked the beginning of the West.

Asking where the West commences invites the question of where it ends. Perhaps it is the crest of the Sierra Nevada and Cascade Mountains. Or is its western boundary the Pacific Ocean? For Frederick Jackson Turner and other imperialists of the late nineteenth and early twentieth centuries, America's western frontier extended all the way across the Pacific Ocean and into Asia. We might also ask where the West begins, or ends, to the north and to the south.

The West is a hard place to pin down. There are the plains West, the arid Southwest, and the rainy Pacific Northwest. The mountain West (Rockies, Sierras, and Cascades) rims the Great Basin West. Then there are the urban West, the agrarian West, the natural resources West, and the scenic and recreational West.

And there are the human, cultural, and idealized Wests. These are polyglot Wests, filled with conflict, nostalgia, and contradiction. Long before

Europeans appeared, native peoples traded and fought with one another. They struggled with the western environment, sometimes winning, sometimes losing. Some, especially the Ancestral Puebloans, built complex and sophisticated agrarian societies. Most of the others developed as semi-nomadic societies. When Spanish, French, English, and American traders, migrants, and armies entered the scene, they conquered the native inhabitants and transformed the West economically, politically, and environmentally. Santa Fe and its environs—its population composed of descendants of the Ancestral Puebloans, Spanish conquistadors, Mexican migrants, and American traders and soldiers—represents a five-century history of the meeting, conflict, and mixing of ethnicities, cultures, and empires in the West.

Historian Clyde A. Milner II has written, "The American West is an idea that became a place."[3] I think the reverse is equally true, that the West is a place that became an idea, or a collection of ideals and values—individualism, freedom and democracy, opportunity—all deeply imbedded in Americans' notions of who they are as persons and as a society. Iconic characters associated with the American conquest of the West—the explorer, trapper, cowboy, prospector, and farmer—seem to embody those American virtues. The cowboy was, and is, an especially powerful figure. More than any other cultural icon, at least until the Beatles came along, the cowboy defined the identity and aspirations of American boys in the post–World War II era. His image was powerful enough to induce a four-year-old to insist to his preschool teacher that he was the Lone Ranger. And it was powerful enough to conjure in the imagination of a fifty-five-year-old images of free roaming independence.

The reality of the cowboy's life, work, and place in society was quite different from this image. The same can be said of the trapper, the prospector, and the farmer. Despite the hazards and isolation they undoubtedly endured, the real human beings behind these western icons did not live and work as totally independent actors. The seemingly most autonomous and enterprising of them, the early-nineteenth-century trappers, relied on complex economic systems. Even if they did not work directly for fur companies, they sold their pelts to them. Their most important business and social event, the annual rendezvous, brought them together to sell their pelts, buy supplies and equipment, and, of course, raise hell. The cowboys and farmers of the Great Plains all labored in an economic system dominated by the railroads, eastern financiers, and the government. Prospectors needed loans from merchants and bankers to finance their expeditions. Even when they hit pay dirt, few could muster the capital to turn their diggings into working mines, and so they sold out to finance capitalists.

The fur trappers' rendezvous illustrates another reality of the West that challenges the image of individualism—community. As powerful and tenacious as the images of the itinerant cowboy and the plains farmer living in remote isolation are in the cultural memory of the American West, most people in the region lived in communities. This was as true of Ancestral Puebloans, Plains Indians, and nineteenth-century American settlers as it is of twenty-first-century occupants. Their communities may have been as transient as a Rocky Mountain mining camp (or later Jeffrey City, Wyoming) or a roadside community created by travelers stuck at a construction stop in Yellowstone, or they may have been as fixed as Taos Pueblo or the West's great cities; but the reality of community as the backbone of human life in the West is as powerful as the legends of self-reliant individualism.

Add to that the equally powerful historical fact that government policy and government money underwrote the American conquest and settlement of the West. In the second half of the nineteenth century especially, Americans moved west on a tide of federal money. Railroad land grants gave financiers the capital to lay tracks across the continent, and homesteading laws opened public land to settlement. Later, government dollars built dams and irrigation systems to make dry lands fertile. And the national government deployed its military power to advance conquest and protect American settlement.

Violence is a core part of the cultural memory of the West. Children of my generation grew up watching cattle town sheriffs besting desperadoes in weekly Front Street duels, while wagon train guides led migrants in fending off Indian raids as they crossed the Plains. But that kind of violence was rare in the historical West. Instead, communal violence, the violence of the strong against the weak, the conqueror against the conquered, was much more the norm. The Lakotas pushed the Crows out of the Northern Plains. The American army subjugated the Plains Indians and drove them onto reservations, usually to places for which white Americans had no use. Industrialists, backed by the government and determined to keep laborers powerless, resorted to armed force at Coeur d'Alene and Ludlow. Sometimes the weak pushed back, as at the Little Bighorn and in the labor war in southern Colorado after Ludlow. Resistance almost always failed. More often, the weak simply endured, as at Pine Ridge, in Colorado's coal camps, and at Amache. And sometimes, in enduring, the weak triumphed, as the Navajos did at Bosque Redondo.

The most significant American conquest in the West has been the transformation of nature itself. Wheat and cornfields replaced the thick Plains sod, and cows and sheep displaced native fauna. Hunters slaughtered some animal species, especially bison and beaver, nearly to the point of extinction. Miners extracted gold, silver, copper and coal, oil, natural gas, molybdenum, and other valuable resources, driving the region's and the nation's financial and industrial growth. But they left behind mounds of yellow, gray, and black tailings, scarring the mountains and plains and poisoning groundwater. In addition, Americans built a vast network of dams and irrigation canals to capture the West's most precious commodity, water, to irrigate their fields and light their towns and cities.

It was a privilege to see all of these Wests and to think about their history on Old Blue's road. The road reconnected me to history in a very personal way. Out there I saw the past, touched it, and sometimes even felt it emotionally. Out there I sensed more clearly than I ever had in books and archives how the past and the present rub up against one another. I heard and saw that friction at the Little Bighorn in the debate over the Indian Memorial; at Devils Tower and Bear Butte, where Indian religion and resurgent Indian cultural identity run into the economic demands of the tourism industry. I saw it at Pine Ridge, where the historical horror of Wounded Knee is bookended by the contemporary horror of the liquor store–cum-town called Whiteclay. In northern New Mexico, Pueblo, Hispanic, and modern American cultures vie with one another over the region's cultural soul. At Blue Mesa Reservoir (and at Hoover, Glen Canyon, and a hundred more dams), the West's economic and demographic dream of endless growth, floating on inland seas of captured snow and rain, runs into the long-term reality of aridity. In northern Idaho, discomfort, even rage, at the drift of modern society and culture—especially quickly changing values about gender, race, and sexuality—prompt some self-styled traditionalists to defend human slavery in the name of a loving God and to fabricate a nostalgic memory of an American past that never existed. People who fictionalize history in an effort to feel more comfortable with their religious and political peculiarities probably get more attention than they merit. They certainly do not typify the West or the westerners I met on the road.

Most of the folks I met on the road were kind and almost relentlessly optimistic. They were the Yellowstone motor home family (from Massachusetts), whose simple act of kindness was the foundation of a temporary roadside community; the Tonasket Character, who, driven from his home by a wildfire, was more interested in my journey than in his own predicament; the farmers in British Columbia, who left their produce and their money unguarded by the roadside; Robert, the man in Hope who let me take over his parking spot and then invited me to lunch; the farmers in Tribune, Kansas, who insisted on visiting with Phineas and trading observations about the Plains wind; the people of Holly, Colorado, who, after a tornado wrecked their town, told the world "we're okay, we're Holly"; and the sheep ranchers in Tres Piedras, New Mexico, who, with their different ethnic backgrounds, shared a deep bond of experience and friendship.

That determined optimism sustained Susan Magoffin on her arduous trek west on the Santa Fe Trail. It put Daniel Blue on the Smoky Hill Trail in 1859, where a powerful sense of decency and generosity motivated the Arapaho man who saved him from a cruel death by starvation and thirst. Courage, decency, and a powerful sense of community inspired striking Colorado coal miners in 1913 to race over Raton Pass to try to join the effort to rescue fellow miners buried in an exploded mine at Dawson, New Mexico. If you look at it hard enough and in just the right light, a kind of optimism can even be seen in the Lakotas' ill-fated Ghost Dance, a desperate longing for something better.

> On my cayuse
> Let me wander over yonder till I see the mountains rise.[4]

A sense that something different, perhaps even better, awaited me out there along the West's highways drew me, a discontented and restless professor, out of my office and put me on the saddle of a motorcycle. And every adventure on Old Blue's road brought me closer to home, closer to my roots as a son of the American West and a historian.

The Warrior Trail journey was my final adventure with Old Blue. That long final day proved to me that, despite all I had invested in making it more suitable for touring, it really was not a touring bike. The weekend before I retired from the university (or semi-retired, as I decided to continue terrorizing graduate students and teachers-in-training for a while), I visited a Harley-Davidson dealer, intending only to buy a new tire gauge. I made my purchase and headed for the door, but the sight of a big Electra Glide stopped me dead in my tracks. It had a two-tone paint job, glossy black over a shining metallic finish that faded back and forth from deep blue to purple, depending on how the light hit it. A stereo system, heated handgrips, three big luggage containers, and a deep, wide saddle, the kind you can sit on all day without getting sore, made the bike a two-wheeled land yacht. I felt guilty about trading Old Blue, but my old friend covered almost half the cost of the new bike.

I miss Old Blue. But Old Blue's road is still out there. Free of vice-chancellors and their schemes and still a historian and a teacher, I look forward, and westward, to new sights and smells and sensations waiting for me out there, along with more of the West's history rubbing up against the western present.

NOTES

1. Cole Porter and Robert Fletcher, "Don't Fence Me In" (Los Angeles: WB Music Corp., 1944).
2. Ibid.
3. Clyde A. Milner II, "America Only More So," in *The Oxford History of the American West,* ed. Clyde A. Milner II, Carol A. O'Connor, and Martha A. Sandweiss (New York: Oxford University Press, 1994), 3.
4. Porter and Fletcher, "Don't Fence Me In."

Index

Page numbers in bold indicate illustrations.

Pullman Palace Cars, 182
Pullman Strike (1894), 25, 174
Purgatoire River (CO), 103, 104
Purple Heart (medal), 98

Quillen, Ed, 161
Quivira (legend), 113

Rapid City, SD, 219, 238–39
Raton, NM, 105
Raton Pass (CO, NM), 104, 105, 107
Rawhide (TV series), 94
Rawlins, WY, 13, 184
Red Cloud, 194, 195, 214, 227, 239, 242, 244
Redden, James, 57
Red Mountain Pass (CO), 150
Red Tomahawk, 243
Redstone, CO, 173–75
religious paintings. *See retablos*
Religious Right, 49–50
religious sculptures. *See bustos*
religious statues. *See santos*
Reno, Marcus, 199–200, 204
Republican River (KS), 80
retablos (religious paintings), 117, 118
Ridgway, CO, 150
Righter, Robert W., 186, 188
Rio Grande, 78, 115, 124, 125, 129, 131
Rio Grande Valley (NM), 113–15, 122, 124, 125, 159
Riverton, WY, 15
Roaring Mountain (Yellowstone), 28
Robinson, Doane, 227–29
Robinson, Kenneth, 236
Rockefeller, John D. Jr., 174, 186–87
Rockefeller family, 104
Rocky Flats nuclear weapons plant (CO), 46–47
Rocky Mountain News, 81, 86
Rocky Mountains, 2, 10, 53, 70, 79, 103, 141, 148, 262
Rohn, Arthur H., 157, 158
"Roll On Columbia, Roll On," (song, 1941), 32
Romeo, CO, 126
Roosevelt, Franklin D., 97, 187–89
Roosevelt, Theodore, 26, 185, 188
Roosevelt, UT, 64, 65
Roosevelt Gate (Yellowstone), 28, 191
Roosevelt Lake (WA), 30, 32
Rosebud Creek (MT), 197–98

Rosebud Reservation (MT), 240
Royer, Daniel, 241
Rushmore, Charles, 230
Russell, William Green, 80
Ryan, Susan, 157, 158

Sacagawea, 15, 41n4, 48
St. James Hotel (Cimarron, NM), **109**–10
St. Vrain, Ceran, 100
Sakura Square (Denver, CO), 98
Salish Indians, 30–31
Salmon, 30; Snake River dams endanger, 56–57
Salt Lake City, UT, 52, 61
Salt Lake Valley (UT), 60, 61, 63
Sand Creek (river, CO), 81, 82, 85–88, 90, 98
Sand Creek Massacre (1864), 82–90, 95, 97, 99, 103, 115, 131–33, 194, 196, 245
Sandia Mountains (NM), 3
Sanford, CO, 126
Sanford, Elliot F., 62
San Francisco Peaks (AZ), 163–64
San Gabriel, NM, 115, 122
San Geronimo Church (Taos Pueblo, NM), 103
Sangre de Cristo Land Grant (1843), 126, 128
Sangre de Cristo Mountains (CO, NM), 78, 113, 115, 126, 127
San Ildefonso Pueblo, NM, 119
San Jose de Garcia Church (Las Trampas, NM), 118
San Juan, NM, 115, 122
San Juan Basin, 159
San Juan Mountains (CO), 65, 126, 128, 129, 149, 150, 172, 173
San Juan River, 171, 172
San Luis, CO, 126
San Luis Valley (CO), 78, 124, 126–31
San Miguel River (CO), 173
Sans Arc (Lakota) Indians, 197, 198
Santa Fe, NM, 3, 77, 78, 95, 115–21, 131, 133, 263; architecture, 118; art, 119–21; Flea Market, 121; founded, 115; Hispanic culture, 119–21; opera, 121; surrendered to US, 116; tourism, 119–20
Santa Fe Railway (Atchison, Topeka, and Santa Fe), 93, 99, 105, 112, 119
Santa Fe Ring, 109
Santa Fe Trail, 77, 78, 80, 85, 95–115, 131, 133, 262, 266; Cimarron Cutoff/Desert Route, 95–96; Mountain Route, 95–96